ESSENTIALS

of Online Payment Security and Fraud Prevention

ESSENTIALS SERIES

The Essentials Series was created for busy business advisory and corporate professionals. The books in this series were designed so that these busy professionals can quickly acquire knowledge and skills in core business areas.

Each book provides need-to-have fundamentals for professionals who must:

- Get up to speed quickly because they have been promoted to a new position or have broadened their responsibility scope
- Manage a new functional area
- Brush up on new developments in their area of responsibility
- Add more value to their company or clients

Other books in this series include:

Essentials of Accounts Payable, Mary S. Schaeffer

Essentials of Balanced Scorecard, Mohan Nair

Essentials of Business Ethics, Denis Collins

Essentials of Business Process Outsourcing, Thomas N. Duening and Rick L. Click

Essentials of Capacity Management, Reginald Tomas Yu-Lee

Essentials of Cash Flow, H. A. Schaeffer, Jr.

Essentials of Corporate and Capital Formation, David H. Fater

Essentials of Corporate Fraud, Tracy L. Coenen

Essentials of Corporate Governance, Sanjay Anand

Essentials of Corporate Performance Measurement, George T. Friedlob, Lydia L. F. Schleifer, and Franklin J. Plewa, Jr.

Essentials of Cost Management, Joe and Catherine Stenzel

Essentials of Credit, Collections, and Accounts Receivable, Mary S. Schaeffer

Essentials of CRM: A Guide to Customer Relationship Management, Bryan Bergeron

Essentials of Enterprise Compliance, Susan D. Conway and Mara E. Conway

Essentials of Financial Analysis, George T. Friedlob and Lydia L. F. Schleifer

Essentials of Financial Risk Management, Karen A. Horcher

Essentials of Foreign Exchange Trading, James Chen

Essentials of Licensing Intellectual Property, Paul J. Lerner and Alexander I. Poltorak

Essentials of Knowledge Management, Bryan Bergeron

Essentials of Managing Corporate Cash, Michele Allman-Ward and James Sagner

Essentials of Managing Treasury, Karen A. Horcher

Essentials of Patents, Andy Gibbs and Bob DeMatteis

Essentials of Payroll Management and Accounting, Steven M. Bragg

Essentials of Sarbanes-Oxley, Sanjay Anand

Essentials of Shared Services, Bryan Bergeron

Essentials of Supply Chain Management, Michael Hugos

Essentials of Technical Analysis for Financial Markets, James Chen

Essentials of Trademarks and Unfair Competition, Dana Shilling

Essentials of Venture Capital, Alexander Haislip

Essentials of XBRL, Bryan Bergeron

For more information on any of the above titles, please visit www.wiley.com.

ESSENTIALS
of Online Payment Security and Fraud Prevention

David Montague

WILEY

John Wiley & Sons, Inc.

For general information on our other products and services or for technical support, please contact our Customer Care Department within the United States at (800) 762-2974, outside the United States at (317) 572-3993 or fax (317) 572-4002.

Wiley also publishes its books in a variety of electronic formats. Some content that appears in print may not be available in electronic books. For more information about Wiley products, visit our web site at www.wiley.com.

Library of Congress Cataloging-in-Publication Data:
Montague, David A., 1967–
   Essentials of online payment security and fraud prevention/David A. Montague.
     p. cm. – (Essentials series; 54)
   Includes index.
   ISBN 978-0-470-63879-8 (pbk.); ISBN 978-0-470-91512-7 (ebk);
   ISBN 978-0-470-91513-4 (ebk); ISBN 978-0-470-91514-1 (ebk)
   1. Electronic funds transfers–Security measures.   2. Electronic commerce–Security measures.   I. Title.
  HG1710.M67 2010
  332.1'78–dc22   2010021354

Printed in the United States of America

10 9 8 7 6 5 4 3 2 1

Contents

Acknowledgments   vii

Introduction   ix

1   **Understanding Online Payment Options**   **1**

2   **Key Concepts for E-Commerce Credit Card Payments**   **27**

3   **Fraud Basics for Companies Doing Business Online**   **56**

4   **Fraud Management Key Concepts**   **101**

5   **Fraud Prevention Techniques: Identity Proofing**   **127**

6   **Fraud Prevention Techniques: Guaranteed Payments**   **175**

7   **Fraud Prevention Techniques: Fraud Scoring**   **183**

8   **Fraud Prevention Techniques: Operational Management (Enterprise)**   **190**

9   **Fraud Prevention Techniques: Analytics**   **231**

10   **Fraud Prevention Techniques: Data Quality**   **238**

11   **Fraud Prevention Techniques: Technology**   **247**

12   **Fraud Prevention Techniques: Data Sharing**   **272**

Appendix A: Protecting Yourself from Identity Theft   277

Appendix B: Sample Strategy   281

About the Author   283

Index   285

Acknowledgments

This book is the culmination of more than 13 years of learning, consulting, and teaching. During that time, my peers, clients, friends, and prospects have helped me develop into who I am. I owe thanks to all of them for their support and could not have written this book without them.

Most importantly I would like thank my family—Carrie, Andy, Sara, Izzy, and Hunter—for their support and patience as I spent so much of our "quality" time writing this book.

Introduction

Doing business online is no longer an oddity, but the norm, and companies desiring to remain competitive have to maintain some form of online presence. Doing business online means a company has to be able to efficiently, reliably, and securely take payments from consumers and other merchants. This book is written to provide the essential information companies need to find, assess, and select the right fraud management options they will need for their electronic commerce (*e-commerce*) channels.

As an essentials guide, the depth of coverage is intended to provide an introduction and working knowledge of e-commerce payments and fraud. This book provides the basic concepts around payment flow and management as well as the ways fraud is perpetrated, along with write-ups that define and provide best practices on the most commonly used fraud-prevention techniques. This book will not go into any detailed strategy design because strategies are proprietary and, once made public, are rendered obsolete.

Payments and fraud go hand and hand. Fraud is nothing new to the merchant. Since the beginning of time, man has always looked for the opportunity to defraud others—to gain goods or services without making payment. For the e-commerce channels, fraud is a part of doing business, and is something that is always a challenge. The merchants that are the best at preventing fraud are the ones that can adapt to change quickly.

Consumer-Present versus Consumer-Not-Present

Consumer-present (CP) and consumer–not–present (CNP) are a spin on the credit–card industries' definition of payment transactions. The credit card industry describes purchases as being either "card-present" or "card-not-present." The difference between the two is the presence of the physical card. If a merchant processes a transaction in which the consumer physically gives the card to process the order, the transaction is considered card-present. If the merchant doesn't take physical possession of the card to process the order, such as in the case of a telephone order, it is considered a card-not-present transaction. This book will be talking about a number of payment types beyond credit cards, but the concepts of card-present and card-not-present still hold true; thus the reason for the generalization of the concept to CP and CNP. Fundamentally "card-present" and "consumer-present" mean the same thing; it really doesn't matter what form of payment is being used, it is the physical presence of the consumer and payment medium that matter. These terms can be used interchangeably.

So who pays when a fraudster steals goods and services? It may surprise you to find out the merchant is left with the bill in most of the cases. For CNP purchases, the merchant is typically liable, while in CP purchases, the card association protects the merchants.

CNP includes all transactions in which the goods and services are sold to a consumer and the physical card is not given to the merchant. CNP includes three groups of transactions: phone-in orders (telephone order), catalogue orders (mail order), and e-commerce orders. Mail order and telephone orders are typically lumped together in a category we call MOTO. E-commerce typically refers to the sale of goods and services online.

This book focuses on the prevention of fraud for the CNP transaction. The payment process, fraud schemes, and fraud techniques will all focus on these types of transactions. In some cases, comparative views of

CP to CNP are made, but for the most part, I only speak to the CNP transaction.

It is important to understand the fraud-prevention techniques used in the CP world do not translate to the CNP world. There are a number of books and references available for preventing fraud in the CP space, but very few resources for the CNP space. The specific payment options and fraud-prevention techniques discussed in this book are designed specifically for the CNP space and will provide far better results for merchants.

In terms of orders processed, far more orders are processed in the CP space than the CNP space. While the CNP space represents less than one-third of the total credit card purchases annually, the e-commerce space is showing significant year-over-year growth. Today, e-commerce orders represent a very small percentage of the total CNP transactions occurring annually, but as you explore and expand into this channel, it is important that you have the processes and tools to prevent fraud losses.

In terms of fraud, the incidence of fraud in the CNP channel is far greater than the CP channel. Orders given in the CNP channel are far riskier for a merchant because the fraudster is anonymous to you.

Your Background with Fraud

If you are new to the fraud space, you are probably feeling a little overwhelmed. But don't despair—with the right tools, you can quickly make a difference for your company. Everyone assumes the other guy has a great fraud-prevention process in place, but in reality, everyone could use some help.

This book was written with the concept of a *fraud practitioner* in mind. A fraud practitioner is a person who is actively engaged in defining, managing, and monitoring fraud-prevention practices for a business. These individuals may or may not have a background in preventing fraud, security, or criminology, but they do have a responsibility to stop fraud.

From my experience working with merchants all over the world, I have seen many different departments in an organization that are responsible for the set-up and management of fraud prevention for the business. Likewise, the individuals tasked with setting up and supporting a fraud-prevention strategy come from a variety of backgrounds, including customer service, finance and accounting, and information technology. Only some come from actual fraud, criminal, or security backgrounds.

It is important to understand that you will need input and assistance from multiple departments to build an effective fraud-prevention strategy. Customer service, sales, information technology, finance, operations, and legal departments all have a role to play. You have to integrate these departments into your plans to ensure that the impact of your new business processes and fraud-prevention techniques are well understood and can be interwoven with their goals.

Regardless of the department you report to, and your background with fraud, I have taken a lot of effort in this book to keep the concepts and explanations easy to understand. I have also provided many examples to illustrate fraud schemes and to help visualize how fraud techniques are used.

How to Use This Book

If you are new to e-commerce payments and fraud, start from the beginning of this book and work your way through it, and you will find that each chapter will build on what you learned before. When you are done, you will have a good foundation on payments and preventing fraud. For the more advanced fraud practitioner, you may use this book more as a reference tool to look up certain techniques or schemes.

Before you can successfully build an effective strategy to combat fraud, you have to understand the business processes and techniques that are available to you. In this book, I focus on the payment process, the anatomy of fraud, and the most common fraud techniques in the industry. Beyond understanding the techniques, I discuss how you can use them and provide some best-practice advice so you can implement them.

Once you read this book, you will find yourself coming back to it as a reference to brush up on fraud-prevention techniques and how to use them.

CHAPTER 1

Understanding Online Payment Options

After reading this chapter, you will be able to:

- Discuss the payment options merchants have to do business online through mail order and telephone order.
- Describe the primary factors a company should use to evaluate and select payment options for its business.
- Describe the role and importance of credit cards and alternative payments in the e-commerce channel.

How do you begin to understand consumer-not-present (CNP) payments and fraud, and the mechanics behind it? You start with the CNP payment process. This gives you a basic understanding of the touch points and the order, people, and organizations that facilitate those touch points. Starting with a good understanding of e-commerce payments will help you see how the fraudster can manipulate these people and business processes to their advantage.

Don't shortchange yourself on understanding this process. Too often I see that fraudsters understand the business processes around payment better than the merchant does—and you can't afford that. You don't have to be an expert in e-commerce payments, but you had better understand the basics, or you will struggle in developing an effective strategy. How will you know where the best points are to implement fraud-prevention techniques if you don't understand the payment processes? How will you know how to balance your fraud-prevention goals with the sales and administration goals if you don't understand the impact of your strategies on the payment processes?

You will also find the need to understand the payment process because you and your staff will naturally gravitate to what you know best. If you are like most merchants, you probably don't come from a law enforcement background. Depending on your background and the background of your team, you will find certain topics in developing your new fraud-prevention strategy more difficult than others.

Think about your background and others' on your team. If they came from the web site development or content teams, they will understand the buy page and shopping cart. If they came from the credit or finance side, they will understand the money flow, but not how the order is placed or filled. If they came from the call center, they will understand the order page, but not where it goes from there. You, as the fraud practitioner, are responsible for making sure everyone on the team understands how fraud touches all these points. You are also the one who has to create a seamless fraud-prevention business process that spans all these departments.

Remember, although your primary goal is fraud prevention and reduction, that is not every department's goal. Envision three major goals in a business:

1. Increase revenue.

2. Lower costs.

3. Reduce losses.

These goals can be in direct conflict, and your job is really to balance these goals to ensure maximum profitability to the company.

A good way to understand this is to look at it from a sales, finance, and operations perspective. Your finance department will focus on profitability, and profitability means looking at how much the business is losing, how much it is spending to manage the processes today, and how revenue is impacted. In working with your finance department, you have to be prepared to explain the impact of any changes in terms of profitability.

Your operations and customer service departments will focus on managing administration costs. In working with them, you can expect to get questions about associated head counts. Does your new strategy reduce the need for people? Does it increase the head count? Does it add any costs to completing sales, such as transaction costs?

Your sales department will be focused on sales conversion, making sure it can get every possible sale it can. Those fraudulent orders still represent sales to these employees, so they are very leery of anything that might kill a potential sale. You will have to show the sales force that your efforts are not barriers to sales and are not insulting good customers.

For all of these departments, fraud is not the primary goal, so you have to be the champion to get them to feel the pain and to help in finding the right solution to stop fraud.

In Chapter 1, we discuss the payments landscape to lay the groundwork, so to speak, for fraud management.

The Payments Landscape

When most people think of online payments, they immediately think of credit card payments. While it is true that credit cards represent the majority of online payments today, there are a number of other payment options available. In all, eight categories of payment solutions exist with hundreds of service providers offering their services globally:

1. Credit card payments
2. Automated Clearing House (ACH) and bank payments
3. Payment aggregators
4. Credit-term providers

5. Cash–alternative providers

6. Advertising/promotional providers

7. Mobile payment providers

8. Invoicing payment providers

Payment methods other than credit card payments are called *alternative payments.*

Alternative payment solutions offer merchants payment methods they can offer to their consumers that don't require the use of one of the major credit card associations. Merchants and consumers look into alternative payment types for a number of reasons. Fundamentally, the market drivers are cost, security/trust, and ease of use.

The best-known alternative payment type is PayPal, which has grown exponentially and is becoming very much a mainstream payment method. If you research the market, a lot of providers out there are competing for mind share and market share. The risk for any merchant is adopting a payment type that will eventually die on the vine due to lack of adoption.

Most merchants view the alternative payment market as a limited competitive field with few real differentiators between the players. More often than not, merchants investigating alternative payments are limiting their discussion to ACH, PayPal, Amazon, and Google Checkout. In fact, there are a number of payment options and a rapidly growing number of service providers offering them.

TIPS AND TECHNIQUES

Not all alternative payment options will produce the same results; determining the right alternative payment options for your company means evaluating payment options based on regional support, consumer preference, customer base, and return on investment (ROI).

Regional Support: No one payment option is equally effective in all regions worldwide. Credit cards are accepted worldwide, but while they have dominated the U.S. and Western European e-commerce markets, they have not shown the same dominance in emerging markets such as Africa, South America, Asia, and Eastern Europe. In these markets, merchants need to support other payment options; otherwise, they will be limiting their potential customer base to only a small fraction of the overall population.

Consumer Preference: It is not enough to simply find an alternative payment method supported in the region you are doing business in; the payment method needs to be one that consumers in the region recognize, trust, and want to use. In Germany, credit cards are present and used, but they are not the preferred payment method. The preferred payment method is direct debit, *Elektronisches Lastschriftverfahren*.

Customer Base: The best alternative payment option has little value if the supported customer base isn't large enough to warrant the effort to integrate and support it. Evaluating a customer base should be done on two levels, potential and current. Consider China: 93 percent of the population of 1.3 billion people have access to direct debit, while according to *China Daily*, there were just over 100 million credit cards in circulation in China as of June 2008. In contrast, there were more than 596 million mobile phone subscribers as of June 2008. In terms of potential use, the ranking would be direct debit, mobile phones, and then credit cards. In terms of current use, the ranking would be direct debit, credit cards, and then mobile phones. Mobile payments offer excellent potential in China, but it is not the current preferred choice for paying for services in China. Does this mean you should not be looking at mobile payments? Not at all; in some regions, mobile payments are the dominant payment method, and three out of the top five alternative payment providers are working on plans to support mobile payments.

Return on Investment (ROI): The reasons why a merchant may implement alternative payments vary, from access to markets to cost reduction or easier supportability to consumer preference.

> ### TIPS AND TECHNIQUES (CONTINUED)
>
> In a majority of cases, merchants are able to show a favorable ROI on integrating alternative payments in a time frame that is more tactical than strategic. This is primarily attributed to increased sales from new consumer populations, lower costs than traditional credit cards, and better fraud protection.

Online customers and merchants have begun to turn to alternative payment methods for a variety of reasons ranging from lower costs, improved technology, and increased availability to security reasons. The debate is ongoing as to whether alternative payments are taking away market share from credit cards or are adding to it, but the fact remains that online credit card sales have been rising right along with alternative payment types.

According to *E-Commerce Times*, by 2012 online payments will gross USD $355 billion in value with alternative payments holding a 30 percent market share.[1] Javelin Strategy and Research predicts that overall growth for online payments is expected to reach $268 billion by 2013. Alternative payments will likely grow at a faster pace than credit cards with certain brands experiencing significant growth. More established brands are best poised to increase market share in this time of growth.

> ### IN THE REAL WORLD
>
> Alternative payments represent only a fraction of e-commerce total sales today, but according to Javelin Strategy and Research, about one-third of all online retail transactions ($268 billion) are predicted to be alternative payments by 2013.[a]
>
> The probability of alternative payments growing to one-third of all sales by 2013 may be questionable, but it demonstrates the prevailing opinion that there is huge growth potential for alternative

payments. The explosive growth of alternative payments can be attributed to consumer and regional preferences. As every sale counts in these economic times, it is now more critical than ever that e-merchants understand and offer payment choices based on consumer and regional preferences.

[a] www.javelinstrategy.com/2008/11/10/new-javelin-study-forecasts-cash-based -alternative-payment-methods-growing-in-popularity-with-consumers-shopping-online/ #more-1384.

Remember, not all alternative payment solutions work the same or produce the same results. To compare solutions against each other and to compare vendors, we need to group the solutions into categories of like services. In general, when you look at the competitive landscape, start by bundling alternative payment providers into a couple of categories, and then use those categories as methods to determine the payment positioning in general. From there, compare the detailed positioning of one vendor in relation to the other dominant players in each category.

Credit Card Payments

A credit card is part of a system of payments that enables the holder to buy goods and services based on the holder's promise to pay for these goods and services. The issuer of the card grants a line of credit to the consumer from which the user can borrow money for payment to a merchant. The major credit card brands—American Express, MasterCard, Visa, and Discover—have been the online payment option of choice since e-commerce was born. According to Entrepreneur.com, it's been repeatedly proven that if you don't accept credit cards on your site, you'll only capture about 15 percent of your potential sales.[2]

Credit cards are the alternative payment method to cash, and they are the dominant players in e-commerce transactions. Credit card associations charge *interchange fees* that range in value and differ from country

to country. In the United States, the fee average is approximately 2 percent of the transaction value.

Customers and merchants have accepted credit cards as the dominant form of payment because they're ubiquitous and easy to use. Merchants are motivated to credit cards because they remain the dominant
form of payment and are relatively secure from fraudulent chargebacks
(given they have proof). Merchants have begun to include other forms
of payment alternatives because they are cheaper and convenient, and
can increase their customer base. Bill Me Later and others can competi-
tively undercut the interchange fees charged by the credit cards and
financial institutions.

Examples of Credit Card Associations

- American Express
- Discover
- Gratis Card
- Japan Credit Bureau (JCB)
- MasterCard
- Revolution Card
- Universal Air Travel Plan (UATP)
- Visa

Credit cards dominate the mind share in e-commerce business.
They control the vast majority of transactions, and if you're not utilizing
credit cards, then you're not capturing your true market potential. It is
absolutely necessary to take these cards as forms of payment.

Credit card companies have poured billions of dollars, time, and
lobbying efforts to establish themselves as the premiere payment alternative. The economic, business, and political clout of these companies
is not to be underestimated and must be incorporated into every
e-commerce payment system. However, they do not have as exclusive a
hold on mind share as they once had. The card associates still dominate
market share, but the nimbler and smaller firms with differentiated and
multifaceted payment systems are expanding mind share.

Credit cards have very high market penetration and dominate the majority of e-commerce solutions. Visa, MasterCard, American Express, and other traditional credit and debit cards were still the only payment option at 76 percent of the web sites. According to Javelin Strategy and Research, credit card purchases will continue to grow and command the majority of e-commerce transactions, which amounted to $81 billion in 2008.[3] While credit card purchases may grow, the overall market share they hold today will start to decline as alternative payments become more widespread and adopted.

Direct Debit and Bank Services

Includes ACH, direct debit, electronic checks, Elektronisches Lastschriftverfahren, and bank transfer services.

Automated Clearing House (ACH) is an electronic network for financial transactions that processes large volumes of both credit and debit transactions, which are originated in batches. Businesses are increasingly using ACH to collect from customers online rather than accepting credit or debit card. ACH payments can take a plethora of different directions, from accepting direct deposits to processing debit card transactions; business-to-business payments; e-commerce payments; federal, state, and local tax payments; and direct debit payments.

ACH payment providers can use either a push or a pull method to allow consumers the ability to pay for their goods or services. With the push method, consumers "push" their funds to an online account at a payment provider. The payment provider then transmits these funds to the merchant through a secure channel. The benefit of this method is twofold in that the merchant never receives the consumer's bank account or credit card information, and the consumer doesn't have to provide it. The pull method is utilized by the majority of ACH payment providers. In essence, the payment provider stores the consumer's bank account information online; then, when the consumer makes a purchase, the funds are "pulled" from their bank account and transmitted to the merchant.

The major advantage to utilizing these services is decreased costs. If you sell anything online, whether physical goods or services, you're aware of the 2 to 3 percent (plus $0.30) spent on transaction fees every time someone makes a purchase with his or her credit card. These fees are incurred whether you use PayPal, Google Checkout, or Amazon Flexible Payments because those companies are just passing on the fees imposed on them by credit card companies. The ACH bank service providers incur a fraction of the cost but have chargeback limitations. As previously noted, ACH services have the ability to limit fraud and identity theft, which may persuade identity-theft–wary individuals to become customers. With the growth in ACH alternative payments expected to continue, there will be several new competitors entering the landscape. Success of these new entrants will be in their respective ability to differentiate themselves through value-added services.

Examples of ACH Providers

- Acculynk
- Billing Revolution
- BPay
- CashEdge
- Debit Asia
- Debit Card (via IPS)
- Discover's Current
- eBillme
- EFTPOS
- elayaway
- Elektronisches Lastschriftverfahren
- Faster Payments
- The Fraud Practice
- Giropay
- GoEmerchant
- GoPay
- GreenZap
- HomeATM
- iDeal
- ING Home Pay
- Inpay
- Mazooma
- Moneta
- NCMS
- Net Pay

- NOCA
- Pago
- Payfast
- Payment Asia
- Poli
- Safetypay
- Secure Vault Payments
- Sofort

- Stored Value Solutions
- Telecheck
- TreasureCom
- Todito.com
- White Hall
- WorldPay
- Yodlee

EXECUTIVE INSIGHT

Leveraging the Online Banking Payment Rails for ACH

SHEILA H. JAMES, VICE PRESIDENT OF OPERATIONS, eBILLME

There are many benefits of leveraging the online banking payment rails for e-commerce transactions—foremost among them is that users are authenticated and authorized by the banks themselves. This practice eliminates the need for customers to provide bank and routing numbers to any merchant or third-party processor. Moreover, online bank payments further reduce the amount of people who have access to a client's personal information since the payment card industry (PCI) is not involved in the transaction. Although this may sound like the perfect payments network, it is not without risk.

The challenge with online bill payments is that it offers a mix of guaranteed and non-guaranteed transactions, resulting in inconsistent levels of security. While this may be sufficient for a network designed to handle recurring monthly bill payments, it's simply not good enough for e-commerce transactions when physical goods and perishable services are involved.

ACH and bank service providers have no clear mind-share domination over other payment types, but they are well identified and understood in the marketplace. Several alternative payment providers have developed systems that utilize the ACH network while delivering cost savings through lower fees.

However, the lower fees come at a cost of no guarantee for fraudulent chargebacks and potential bad debt to the merchant. Some players in this segment have been able to deliver customers a feeling of safety because they limit the amount of information needed to complete a transaction. For example, as privacy concerns continue to rise, more and more have developed push-based ACH services to restrict the amount of information a customer must provide (i.e., no credit card information, no credit check). This in turn allows security-concerned consumers to purchase online safely and merchants to gain sales and reduce cost.

Entrants have flooded this segment due to the low cost and convenient nature of the ACH network. The real benefits delivered to merchants and customers will be the ways the providers innovate and drive value in this growing payment method. In terms of differentiated services, the more interesting alternative ACH providers are eBillme, Yodlee, Moneta, Worldpay, Debit Asia, and Stored Value Solutions.

While the growth in alternative payments is expected to continue, several new competitors will enter the landscape. There is talk already on the blogosphere that many alternative payment methods are already looking too similar. For example, the explosion of ACH providers has meant several new entrants look and function exactly the same.

Alternative payment providers must remember how to differentiate themselves and their products and services to best serve the merchants and ultimately the consumers.

ACH payments (such as debit cards) are expected to grow and continue to capture market share away from credit cards. ACH payments add real value to the merchant through lower costs and customer security. According to the National Automated Clearing House Association (NACHA), the ACH network grew by 4.5 percent in the fourth quarter of 2008 compared to 2007. Many nonfinancial institutions are now utilizing the banking industry's ACH infrastructure to capture interchange-like revenues.

The summary report of the 2007 Federal Reserve payments study revealed that 2.6 billion consumer checks were converted and cleared as ACH payments rather than check payments in 2006, an eightfold increase over 2003. Financial institutions will watch market share and transactional revenue with a close eye.

Payment Aggregators

Merchant aggregators, a type of payment aggregator, or *master merchants,* are service providers through which other e-commerce merchants process their transactions. In some instances, master merchants may hold the merchant account with the processors and banks. The relationship is called master merchant if the service provider will be collecting monies on behalf of the others, the submerchants. The collections are for the receipt of payments made for items sold online. These are the most popular forms of alternative payment behind credit cards. These companies may hold credit card information to allow for faster purchases or hold money in an account to allow for future purchases.

This payment alternative is attractive to merchants who have difficulties in opening a merchant account with a bank. The merchant account belongs to the master merchant, who is responsible for upholding the agreement with the acquiring bank. The submerchant will sign a separate agreement with the master merchant to authorize the latter to collect on their behalf and to ensure that the master merchant will reimburse the submerchant in return. Among the alternative payment services, these are the leaders and most widely accepted alternative payment methods among e-commerce merchants.

Examples of Payment Aggregators

- AlertPay
- Amazon Payments
- Click and Buy
- eWay
- eWise
- Global Collect
- Google Checkout
- MercadoLibre
- Neteller
- PayDotCom
- Paymate
- PayPal
- Rupay
- Webfarm
- Wirecard
- Valista
- 2Checkout.com

Payment aggregators are the top competitors in the payment landscape and have seen the most widespread adoption. When merchants are talking about alternative payments, they are typically referring to PayPal, Amazon, Bill Me Later, and Google Checkout. Three out of four of these are payment aggregators. The mind share of these companies is also seen by the recent surge in acquisitions as well as the launching of new products.

The most popular alternative payment method among the 100 leading retailers surveyed was Bill Me Later, PayPal, and Google Checkout. Only 7 percent of all retailers surveyed offered all three alternative payment options. Collectively, these credit card alternative payment services are the dominant competitors.

Credit Terms Providers

Credit term alternatives are services that extend credit to individuals to make purchases online. These services are valuable to both merchants and customers. These services allow customers to purchase items online without giving their credit card information, and it provides the merchant with guarantees on chargebacks. This alternative has become popular with consumers because they can receive credit to purchase items without giving their sensitive credit card information. Merchants can also benefit through the conversion of sales where consumers are credit dry. Examples of credit terms providers include Bill Me Later, Cred-Ex, and PayPal's PayLater.

Bill Me Later is the dominant player controlling both mind share and market share. It can provide merchants with guarantees on chargebacks and lower interchange fees while creating a feeling of safety for security-wary shoppers. Bill Me Later can, in seconds, ask the credit bureaus if the person attempting to purchase has a good enough credit score to be trusted. Bill Me Later is aimed at the large pool of individuals with good credit who don't want to purchase online because of identity-theft concerns.

This company has seen tremendous growth during its short existence while pitted against giants like PayPal, Google, and Amazon. In November 2008, Bill Me Later was acquired by eBay and was number six on the 2007 Inc 500 List of fastest-growing private companies in America. Bill Me Later is the credit alternative payment solution provider of choice in the U.S. market and will likely capture more mind share as this industry matures.

PayPal has developed an alternative to Bill Me Later called PayLater in hope of capturing further market share. However, as the credit crisis further unfolds, this segment could be at risk for an increase in delinquent payments. It should be noted that CIT Bank, a Utah state bank, has backed Bill Me Later, and it is in relatively good financial standing with Better Business Bureau (BBB) debt ratings.

The market share of credit alternative payment providers is relatively small compared with other options but has been growing. The leader of the pack, Bill Me Later, has driven merchants, financial institutions, and customers to notice and recognize them as a viable alternative. Bill Me Later's payment solutions are available when shopping online, via phone, and in-store. At current growth trends, Bill Me Later is likely to be an even bigger player in the alternative payment landscape.

Cash Alternative Payments

Cash alternative payment methods are not a new concept. The basic forms of cash alternative payments (i.e. escrow, paper checks, stored value accounts, and money order) have been around for years but in the e-commerce world they have limited success. These payment options have relatively low adoption rates among the merchant community. However, in developing countries like China and elsewhere these payment options are typically the dominant and preferred payment method.

According to Forrester's Asia Pacific 2007 Consumer Survey, online financial security is a major concern for Chinese and Japanese consumers, while a lack of credit cards is the top barrier for many affluent Indian consumers. Merchants seeking to sell their goods and services in Asia Pacific need to address consumers' payment concerns and barriers.

Examples of Cash Alternative Payment Providers

- 3V
- Alipay
- American Express
- Easecard
- EFICash
- Escrow
- Ficha Rap
- Forex Express

- GreenDot
- Hyperwallet
- "icash"
- Ixaris
- Liberty Reserve
- MOLePoints
- MoneyBookers
- MyCitadel Wallet
- NoChex
- Paper Checks
- PayGNN
- PayByCash
- PayPal
- PayPoint

- ProPay
- PaySafecard
- Pecunix
- Snap
- th!s
- toditoCash
- UAH iMoney
- UDpay
- Ukash
- Wallie
- WebMoney
- Western Union
- Wirecard
- Yandex

The mind share of these traditional service providers are on a downward trend as compared to the other methods of alternative payment. The mind share of new entrants such as Ukash and other similar alternative cash payments has generated a lot of interest in the gaming industry and shows potential for future growth in that vertical market.

Asia's promise can be demonstrated through its adolescents, who have been shown to be fanatical gamers, technologically savvy, and mobile payment users. Cash alternatives can keep the gamers' credit card number and identity safe while the merchant receives a lower cost than accepting credit cards. None of these providers controls a dominant piece of mind share or market share. However, the vertical market of gaming is looking promising in Asia, and some of the preferred cash alternative payment methods for Asia are Alipay, PayByCash, UDcard, and Easecard.

The relative global market for these services is low compared to other groups. However, special niche markets such as gaming, adult, and gambling may benefit tremendously from this payment type. These high-risk segments provide the merchant with the motivation to implement safe and secure payment solutions. These forms of digital cash can keep consumers' identities safe while allowing them to participate in this market.

Advertising Alternative Payments

Advertising has always been a source of revenue for companies, but alternative payments are pushing this to a new level. Who said you can't get something for nothing? Two specific methods have caught the blogosphere and business community's attention. The first new method, called transactional advertising, has allowed TrialPay to emerge as a promising new form of alternative payment. TrialPay has since launched into the top five for alternative payment providers and doesn't plan on looking back.

The second payment provider, Offerpal Media, has created a managed offer network for social applications and online merchants. Offerpal Media is built on the science of delivering highly relevant consumer offers and precisely targets millions of social network users based on their user profiles and the social graph. With an increasing percentage of people utilizing social networking sites, this service could prove to be a major competitor in the future of alternative payments. The differentiating qualities that these two encompass will help propel them to becoming major contenders and stand-outs among the crowd.

Examples of Advertising Alternative Providers

- Appsavvy
- Jambool
- Offerpal Media
- Super Rewards
- TrialPay
- Webloyalty.com

TrialPay has created its entire mind share through its unique transactional advertising model. There is chatter on the blogosphere about unwanted services and quoting free services above their true value. Despite these opinions, TrialPay dominates the field in this new area and looks to satisfy three important entities' desires: (1) The customer is able to purchase the product and receive a free trial service; (2) the advertiser receives name recognition; and (3) the merchant completes the sale and gets a customer.

Unlike traditional advertising and affiliate networks, Offerpal Media provides a turnkey, full-service Managed Offer Platform, which presents engineered offers and customized offer displays on the merchant's social application or e-commerce site. Offerpal works through a system in which once the user tries or buys one of Offerpal's offers, the user gets the web site's virtual points and Offerpal pays the user. TrialPay and Offerpal have successfully differentiated themselves from the mainstream payment services and dominate this segment, but watch for fast-approaching newcomers.

The market share of this segment is rapidly growing. TrialPay currently has more than 4.5 million registered users and adds 15,000 new users every day. However, Offerpal Media currently has more than 2,000 advertisers in the system and adds as many as 100 new offers to the system every week. Webloyalty is another long-standing competitor embedded in the international payment landscape. Watch for entrants to try to copy their unique platforms. There have already begun to be entrants into this competitive landscape with SuperRewards, AppSavvy, and Jambool, and I'm sure there will likely be more in the not too distant future.

Mobile Payments

The opportunities in mobile commerce have already begun to transform the industry and competitors are racing to gain a foothold and market share. The sophistication of their methods varies dramatically, but the speed, efficiency, and convenience to the customer is substantial. Mobile phones have improved over the years to include user-friendly browsers, and updated broadband networks have also helped drive this technology.

EXECUTIVE INSIGHT

According to Juniper Research, mobile payments are expected to reach more than $600 billion globally by 2013, while mobile payment markets for goods and services, excluding contactless National Finance Center (NFC) transactions and money transfers, is expected to exceed $300 billion globally by 2013.[4] The top three regions for mobile payments (Far East and China, Western Europe, and North America) will represent more than 70 percent of the global mobile money transfer gross transaction value by 2013.

These growth rates are unprecedented and require the attention of merchants, financial institutions, and payment providers. Parts of the world that lack sufficient infrastructure to allow online computer commerce have the chance to purchase online through mobile phones.

In addition to online purchases, individuals can also send remittances or transfer money to another network member. Budde-Comm estimates revenue from mobile content and services (excluding Short Message Service [SMS]), accounts for around 7 to 10 percent of total mobile revenues worldwide. SMS remains popular and accounts for a further 10 percent of total mobile data revenues.[5]

IN THE REAL WORLD

iPhone users can purchase and download TV shows and movies and play them right on their phones instantly. This would have been impossible if it had not been for deep 3G broadband network capability and improved mobile devices.

An article in *BusinessWeek* by Deborah Stead describes how there has been a push by businesses to go wireless only on the belief that wireless is the future. A study by Gartner suggests that by 2012 about 23 percent of North American businesses will be doing without desk phones—up from 4 percent in 2008. This data illustrates the fundamental movement toward increasing mobile phone use that has the potential to benefit mobile payments in the future.

Banks are also extending their reach into mobile payments and want to utilize their online banking capabilities to the fullest potential. Even Bill Gates has pledged $12.5 million to extend mobile phone payments to the "unbanked." Gates said, "Technology like mobile phones is making it possible to bring low-cost, high-quality financial services to millions of people in the developing world so they can manage life's risks and build financial security."[6]

Additionally, three of the top five alternative payment providers (PayPal, Amazon, and Google) have extended their payment services with a mobile payment option. Mobile phone providers are starting to integrate alternative payment options as well. Paymo recently signed a contract with three large mobile phone service providers (AT&T, T-Mobile, and Virgin Mobile) to allow the payment option to appear on the customer's invoice. The synergy of all these factors has placed mobile phone payments at the forefront of an industry poised for future growth and development.

Examples of Mobile Payment Providers

- Amazon TextBuyIt
- Banksys
- Bill2phone
- Billing Revolution
- Danal
- Dialogue
- EPay
- Fundamo
- Gemalto
- Google Checkout for Mobile
- Javien
- Luup

- Mblox
- Mobilians
- M-PESA
- Mx telecom
- Onebip
- Openmarket
- Paybox
- PayPal Mobile
- Paymate
- Paymo
- PayPay
- Sybase
- Self Bank Mobile
- UMPay
- Valista
- Zamano
- Zong

The mind share of any one mobile service varies dramatically. The simple and antiquated methods like billing your utilities to your mobile phone represent little presence. Historically, this kind of service lacks long-term success and massive adoption. However, the real value added benefits of mobile-commerce (m-commerce) will allow users a quick, safe, and convenient form of shopping.

There is no clear leader in the mobile payments industry, but PayPal Mobile seems to have the consumer's trust, a large customer base, seamless information, and brand recognition. The top five mobile payment providers are Sybase, PayPal Mobile, Paymo, Luup, and UMPay.

The market penetration of m-commerce payment providers is low, and they remain to be seen as contenders in the global alternative payment landscape. This can be attributed to the mobile payment providers having to forge strategic partnerships with mobile phone service providers. The mobile phone providers in different parts of the world (i.e., China) are majority controlled by the government. M-commerce is highly regional in nature, and many regions may prefer a homegrown m-commerce provider. Merchants should look toward m-commerce providers that have established strategic relationships with banks, governments, and financial institutions in that region. Other m-commerce services include financial applications such as m-banking. This service enables users to check their bank account details and pay bills. Such services have been especially popular in the Philippines, where the conventional banking system is arguably not as well developed as other regions of the world.

Invoice Services

The smallest group of the alternative payment methods is invoicing. This service is not new and has been around for a long time. This method may prove beneficial to merchants who want to accept payment but would rather a consumer send a check. Invoicing may also allow a merchant to access underbanked consumers who lack a credit card but possess a checking account. Instead of utilizing their own software to print and mail an invoice, they may want to contract a third party to send the bill through a secure channel. Overall, this method is not a real contender in options, and most payment providers already encompass this service into what they offer.

Examples of Invoice Service Providers

- AceFlex
- BillMyClients
- Citrus Online billing
- freshbooks
- Intuit Billing Manager
- Striata
- telepro
- Zuora
- 2ndSite

Everyone knows what invoicing is, but few would connect invoicing and e-commerce. Invoicing customers for goods and services has become incorporated into most complex payment systems. These sole invoicing agents will not dominate mind share as the alternative landscape changes. Invoicing is still very much a requirement for business-to-business e-commerce players.

The market share that corresponds to the invoicing service provider is minimal. Merchants could just as easily use QuickBooks or other software to produce invoices.

Internationalization: Cross-Border Transactions

Do alternative payments ease globalization and cross-border transactions? The vast majority of alternative payments are regional solutions. For example, if you wanted to create an e-commerce business in China but only wanted to use Visa or MasterCard, you would be unlikely to take your business very far. What works in the U.S. market does not work in all markets. One of the greatest value propositions for alternative payments is their ability to provide access to new international markets. In China, if you introduced Alipay along with credit cards (Alipay has higher brand awareness than credit cards in China), then you would have access to a far larger pool of consumers.

In today's market, credit cards still dominate the international e-commerce marketplace, and this is unlikely to change over the next three years. This being said, for merchants doing cross-border business, the decision to implement alternative payments is a must-do to stay competitive and grow.

There are also two important factors to consider when analyzing how globalization has affected alternative payment methods. The expansion of the Internet and mobile communication technology has greatly increased the capacity for global purchases and cross-border transactions.

Merchants, payment providers, gateways, and banks all will be affected by the introduction and adoption rates of alternative payment forms. The need for all players to evaluate and integrate key alternative payment methods has become a more immediate requirement to stay competitive. In the next five years, $1 trillion worldwide will be purchased online or influenced by information found about products and services online, according to Forrester Research.[7] Companies looking to take advantage of this opportunity in cross-border transactions need to focus on the specific needs of the regions, countries, and verticals in which they want to operate.

For example, in the United States, credit and debit cards are commonly utilized for online transactions, but bank transfers and cash on delivery are more common in parts of Europe and Asia.[8] Going for mass is not the only thing that matters. The infrastructure capabilities for the top three largest regions for Internet penetration—Asia, Europe, and North America—are vastly different, and payment options may be limited based on their capabilities.

Chapter Summary

Taking payments online isn't just about accepting credit cards. While credit cards are important, it is more important to understand the consumer and regional preferences in terms of potential market size and ROI.

Alternative payment options provide a means for merchants to gain new customers who may not have access to, or feel comfortable with, credit card payments. The decision to offer alternative payments is not an either/or decision; merchants must offer credit cards, but alternative payments must be considered for the value and opportunity they can bring. The solution is not about integrating the most possible payment options; it is about offering the right payment options.

Notes

1. www.ecommercetimes.com/story/Alternative-Payments-More
   -Ways-to-Close-the-Sale-65954.html?wlc=1235049585.
2. www.entrepreneur.com/ebusiness/networksolutions/
   article159682.html.
3. www.javelinstrategy.com/2009/02/05/alternative-payments-the
   -economy-and-fis-payment-strategy.

4. www.intomobile.com/2008/09/09/juniper-research-total-mobile
   -payments-to-grow-nearly-ten-fold-by-2013.html.
5. www.pr-inside.com/global-digital-economy-m-commerce-r1032699
   .htm.
6. www.itpro.co.uk/609895/mwc-09-gates-cash-means-mobile
   -payments-for-all.
7. www.oscworks.com.au/231-Australian-Ecommerce-Statistics.html.
8. www.idrc.ca/openebooks/179-5.

CHAPTER 2

Key Concepts for E-Commerce Credit Card Payments

After reading this chapter, you will be able to:

- Describe and define the key players for credit card payments.
- Define the core credit card payment processes.
- Describe the money flow for credit card transactions.
- Discuss credit card fraud and chargeback liability from a merchant perspective.

When it comes to e-commerce credit card payments and fraud, there are just some things everyone should know. Everyone should have a basic understanding of who the players are; how money is moved; globalization; and, of course, credit card chargebacks and fraud liability.

Consumer Perspective on E-Commerce Payments and Fraud

Let's start with two terms with which everyone is familiar: *consumer* and *merchant*. Consumers are individuals or organizations that have the intent of making a purchase. They have money or credit, and they desire goods and services. The merchant is the one with the goods and services and is looking to sell them to consumers.

Now the consumer can be motivated to select a particular merchant based on several things: price, service, selection, or preference. But the merchant's main motivation is to make money. Merchants are in business to make money, and they do so by selling the goods or services for more money than they bought them. This money between what they bought it for and what they sold it for is called their margin.

There are a lot of different ways to exchange money for services: bartering, cash, checks, debit cards, installment payments, or credit cards.

In short, when merchants increase the number of payment methods other than credit cards, they not only allow customers greater latitude and choice for payment of goods/services, but also increase the potential number of consumers who can make purchases online.

IN THE REAL WORLD

According to CyberSource, web sites that provide four or more payment methods other than credit cards have a sales conversion that's 12 percent higher than offering just one payment option in addition to credit cards.[a] Jupiter Research found that alternative payment solutions increase average order size by 13.3 percent.[b]

[a] www.entrepreneur.com/ebusiness/networksolutions/article159682.html.
[b] www.prweb.com/releases/2009/01/prweb1855264.htm.

Consumers buying items online overwhelmingly prefer to pay by credit card today, but segments of consumers do prefer to pay using something other than their credit card. Why?

- Some consumers still don't feel comfortable using their credit card to make a purchase online. Or, in some cases, they may not feel comfortable giving their credit card information to a particular merchant.

- More and more consumers are becoming power-buyers on the web, and for these consumers, any new tool that speeds up the checkout process is considered very cool. Some alternative payment types will allow the merchant to streamline the checkout process, in some cases making it as simple as a logon for the consumer, increasing the stickiness of the site and the satisfaction of the consumer.

- The rise of online banking and purchasing via online bank accounts has brought about serious concerns for security. Most banks fully protect the customers against fraudulent transactions, but the fact remains that customers don't want to go through the hassle of fixing their credit once it's been damaged.

- Communications technologies, mainly the Internet and mobile phones, have significantly changed the ways in which individuals interact with merchants. Merchants have adapted by creating multichannel payment methods, and banks are following suit by providing customers a new means to interact with their finances through tools such as online banking and mobile banking.

- The bad economy of 2008 to 2010 may be a driving factor for customers and merchants to search for payment alternatives as well. For example, the economy may drive consumers to find alternatives when they are denied credit or don't have a credit card anymore.

- Some specific consumer niches are not served by the current payment systems. These consumers include credit-wary consumers and the underserved who are searching for alternatives to the traditional payment methods. Alternative payments can help reach these potential niche market consumers (i.e., gamers) and convert their sales.

Merchants pay a lot to accept credit cards online, and when you add in the additional burden of fraud protection, these costs can be very significant. So when a merchant is looking at a potential new payment type that is cheaper than credit cards, or that provides fraud protection, the financial savings can really change the bottom line.

One of the greatest threats to a merchant's bottom line is the growing fear and insecurity consumers are feeling about shopping and paying for goods and services online. Studies from the Ponemon Institute and New York Cash Exchange (NYCE) have shown an ever-increasing concern by consumers about the safety and security of interacting and shopping online. A 2008 Ponemon survey discovered that 77 percent of respondents claimed to be concerned or very concerned about loss or theft of personal information, and 72 percent of respondents believed that their chances of becoming a victim of identity theft was greater than 20 percent. The NYCE 2008–2009 Internet Purchase Study of 2,500 respondents found that 43.5 percent of respondents who don't shop online and 26 percent of respondents who don't often shop online cited security concerns as the primary reason they didn't.

Are consumers scared? Why shouldn't they be? They constantly hear about viruses, identity theft, fraud rings, breaches, and stolen credit cards in the news. The effect of online fraud and security lapses on the market psyche has been profound. Consumers today are more likely to hear about online fraud and security lapses than they would have in 2000. The number of news articles released annually related to online fraud and security has increased 300 percent over the past nine years.[1] This increased awareness combined with personal experience with spam, phishing attacks, valid merchant security changes, and industry education has created an atmosphere of fear that is affecting the natural growth of Internet commerce.

Consumer fear impacts not only the consumers themselves but also the merchants, financial institutions, and other consumers in the marketplace. At the consumer level, the impact of consumer fear can be seen as the choice by some consumers not to go online at all or to limit their business only to the largest and most trusted brands.

At the merchant and financial institution level, it can be seen as the ever-increasing implementation of company-specific point solutions to try to convey a safer and more secure environment for these concerned consumers.

For those consumers not fearful of transacting online, it can be seen as frustration with the ever-increasing invasiveness of merchant and financial institution security protocols. These consumers are frustrated with the escalating security arms race effect of the marketplace. No two companies do it the same; solutions are fragmented, and consumers have to repeat security procedures for paying online over and over. For them they only see the inconvenience in the need to change passwords all the time, suffer through waiting periods, not be able to reuse old passwords, put in secret questions, or provide additional private information to complete a transaction.

Fear creates the need for all parties to resolve the fear that to date has meant an increase in the complexity of interacting and transacting on-line. As previously discussed, fear has produced an increased number of merchant-based point solutions, but it has also increased consumer use of third-party security software packages. When you begin to combine merchant–point solution requirements and consumer security solution requirements, it is clear that there will ultimately be gaps that still remain, with no complete solution.

Consumers don't want complexity; they just want to feel they are secure. Not only do they not want complexity, they are not typically in a position to understand and correctly respond to notifications from security programs, fake web sites, and breach notifications. Robert Kamerschen, vice president of Choicepoint, said that fewer than 10 percent of the 163,000 consumers affected by their data breach actually took advantage of the free credit-watch services offered.[2] Microsoft reported in May 2009 that 88 percent of users chose to ignore warnings about BearShare, 68 percent ignored a warning about adware Zango-Search, and 23 percent ignored warnings about a Trojan downloader.[3]

Consumers want simplicity, and when a fraud or security solution surpasses their comfort level, they will either stop using it or ignore it. In either case, all parties involved suffer.

Beyond the number of choices, the complexity, the likelihood of being victimized, and the difficulty in changing behavior is the overall lack of support for consumers. Resources for consumers to learn how to protect themselves can be difficult to understand and find. Noncomprehensive or easy-to-understand resources that exist offer only a partial view of the problem, and nobody is standing up to say "call me." More concerning is the general lack of support when a consumer does become a victim—who do they call, where do they turn? Merchants don't have the time or resources to help them, and law enforcement provides little more than lip service to any single incident focusing more on the aggregation of evidence to build larger cases. Consumers are isolated and left to figure it out.

Merchant Perspective on E-Commerce Payments and Fraud

The Internet has had a profound effect on how merchants and financial institutions interact with consumers and consumer data. The Internet has made it easier for merchants to gain access to new customers, expanding their markets. But it has also increased their vulnerability to third-party attacks and fraud. Fraudsters don't need to walk into a store with a gun to steal from a merchant or financial institution; they can use someone else's identity or hack in and steal the identity information from the merchant. The overall transparency of the Internet has increased the ease and speed in which fraudsters can attack companies.

The security and fraud problem for merchants is far more complicated than simply securing the checkout process. Merchants have to be concerned with the security of connecting with, securing the transfer of, and the ongoing safeguarding of sensitive consumer data. Past data breaches of PCI-compliant merchants, such as Hannaford, have shown that it is not enough to secure consumer data when it is at rest within a company. Merchants and financial institutions have to be concerned about security when data is in transit. In addition, initiatives such as PCI don't protect consumers or merchants from fraudsters attempting to exploit their customers with phishing attacks and lookalike pharming sites.

Security and fraud have implications beyond direct monetary loss for merchants and financial institutions. These events can cause significant short-term brand value erosion. When merchants or financial institutions suffer a data breach, they will most likely suffer a temporary drop in their sales and stock price, if they are public.[4]

Obviously merchants don't want to lose money to direct fraud, but online merchants are far more incented to care about it. Credit card fraud for merchants is very different in terms of consumer-present and consumer-not-present (CNP) transactions. For CNP transactions, merchants are not generally protected from credit card fraud, meaning they eat the loss and pay a fine on top of it. There are some exceptions to fraud protection for programs like Visa's Verified by Visa program, but these programs suffer from low adoption and the Verified by Visa program has already had multiple successful hacks. This means merchants who are experts in their products and markets have to also become experts in security, PCI compliance, consumer authentication, and fraud detection, which is not their core competency.

In the early days of the Internet, merchants and financial institutions were happy to process an order if a consumer could fill in all the blanks on the checkout page, and they could get a valid authorization on the credit card. Business was good, and there were plenty of good transactions to counterbalance the losses. Today, this is not the case, and for some merchants, the losses have resulted in reserves, heavy fines from the card associations, and, in some cases, the loss of their merchant account.

Here is the core challenge for merchants and financial institutions to answer: Is this consumer really who he says he is? The Internet makes it easy for fraudsters to look and feel like they are legitimate when they aren't. For some merchants and financial institutions, answering this question is not just a matter of fraud prevention, it is a legal requirement. Massachusetts and Minnesota have state laws on the books that set standards for safeguarding personal information. The FTC and National Credit Union Association (NCUA) have issued regulations known as the *red flags rules* requiring financial institutions and creditors to implement certain minimal security measures. These measures include establishing a baseline for knowing who your customer is.

Merchants understand having sufficient brand trust is critical to sales conversion. They know consumers are scared of sharing personal data online, and if consumers do not trust them, they will not transact with them. Consumers are, in general, concerned with sharing private information online, which means some consumers will limit their transactions to larger trusted brands. Small and medium businesses have to work harder to build brand trust to try to convert orders from risk-adverse consumers. These merchants will implement third-party alternative payment methods and will seek third-party ratings for their site to try to ease consumer concern. All merchants are looking for new methods and tools to try to convert sales from consumers who may not be comfortable sharing their sensitive data with them.

Issuing Bank

The consumer got his credit card from a bank or credit union called the *issuing bank*. Sometimes you may hear an issuing bank being called an *issuer*, which means the same thing. The issuing bank is not just associated with major credit card brands such as American Express, MasterCard, and Visa, but also with credit cards called *private label credit cards*. These are the ones that department stores or shops offer, such as Sears and Target cards.

Issuing banks are lending institutions that work behind these credit cards to grant and manage the extended credit. Some examples of these are Bank of America, Citibank, Household Financial, GE, and Wells Fargo.

The purpose of the issuing bank is to grant credit directly to a consumer. Consumers fill out an application, and then the issuing bank checks their credit history and maintains their accounts. The issuing bank decides what a consumer's credit limit is, based on credit history and current debt load. There are literally thousands of issuing banks in the United States—any bank or credit union you see on the corner could be an issuer. In Canada and the United Kingdom there are far fewer banks, so the number of issuing banks is much smaller.

What motivates the issuing bank? They are in it for the money as well. They make money on the interest the consumer pays on outstanding balances from previous purchases, and they get a part of every purchase a consumer makes with the card from a merchant.

Acquiring Bank

Acquiring banks (also known as *acquirers* or *merchant acquirers*) represent the merchant. They process all of the merchant's credit card payments with the associations (American Express, MasterCard, Visa) and provide the merchant with reconciliation tools. The acquiring bank makes money on every transaction a merchant processes.

There are numerous acquiring banks in the United States and abroad, and merchants are free to move from one acquirer to another. Merchants typically select their acquiring bank based on the amount of money, called *basis points*, they charge per transaction.

Payment Processors and Gateway Services

There is nothing stopping a merchant from directly connecting to their acquiring bank, but there are a number of reasons they may not want or be able to. There are technical and business requirements in conducting the payment process for credit cards, and most merchants don't want to have to worry about these requirements. Instead they choose to use a third party between them and their acquiring banks. These third parties are called *payment processors* and *gateway services.*

Payment processors offer the physical infrastructure for the merchant to communicate with the acquiring banks and the associations. They are the ones that connect everyone together. This allows some very small banks to offer merchant services that they could not provide on their own. Payment processors make their money by charging a flat transaction fee or by charging basis points to the merchant. Some payment processors also provide acquiring bank services directly.

Gateway services offer merchants physical infrastructure as well. They typically offer technology and integration services that are faster, easier, and less expensive to get started. They also give the merchant the freedom to move between acquiring banks so they can negotiate better rates without having to make changes to their production systems. The gateway service provider will charge a transaction fee or basis points for their services. These fees are on top of the payment processor fees the merchant is already paying.

If a merchant decides to use a gateway service provider, it will still have to set up accounts with an acquirer. The acquirer could be an acquiring bank or a payment processor that offers acquiring.

Card Associations

Finally there are card associations, such as Visa, MasterCard International, American Express, and Discover, to name a few, that are responsible for setting up the guidelines on how transactions, services, and disputes are to be handled. They interface with national banking laws and provide the money that covers some of the fraud that occurs within the membership. Each association runs a little differently, so one size does not fit all.

Visa has regions that operate pretty much autonomously. There is Visa U.S.A., Visa Europe, Visa Asia, and so on. Each of these regions may have slightly different rules, tools, and services it offers. Visa does not actually issue credit cards to consumers; they use issuing banks to issue credit cards that are branded as *Visa*.

MasterCard International is a little different from Visa in that it is one association for the entire globe—all regions go into the same structure. This has some benefits when it comes to regulations and tools. MasterCard International also uses issuing banks to issue credit cards to consumers that are branded as *MasterCard*.

American Express differs even more by acting as the issuer for all American Express–branded credit cards. American Express is one global organization with regional coverage. American Express also differs from Visa and MasterCard in allowing merchants to set up direct connections for performing the acquiring functions.

One of the side notes that should be understood is the concept of *cobranding*. Today consumers have credit cards sponsored by airlines, car companies, local clubs, and so on. These organizations get a percentage for each purchase. In some cases, it may be that the organization is actually the issuer, but in a lot of cases, it is an actual issuing bank that is offering a number of cobranded credit cards for consumers to choose from. The card is still an American Express, Visa, or MasterCard.

Each of these credit card associations has its own network of systems, policies for use, and payment processing. Each of these associations develops new fraud-prevention tools and tries to get merchants to adopt them. These fraud-prevention practices are only good for that type of card. Usually if good market adoption occurs, the other cards will adopt a similar technology.

The actual fraud programs and services an association offers changes often, and you should check out their web sites often to learn more about the types of fraud-prevention services and solutions they are endorsing.

Money Flow

What do money flow and credit cards have to do with fraud prevention? In a cash society, a merchant never cared about who the consumer was. With the introduction of credit cards, the merchant took on new responsibilities for authenticating consumers, showing proof of sales, and providing service and support after the sale. For most merchants, having to authenticate the consumer before taking their cash or having to worry about a bank coming back after the sale and taking the money back was a foreign concept. The concept of fraud went from just physically securing their shops to having to spot fraud in the money flow.

To understand the money flow, you need an understanding of the business processes and steps an order goes through for money and goods to exchange hands. With cash, the consumer hands a merchant cash and the merchant performs checks to make sure it is not counterfeit and calculates the change. With that done, the consumer is on his or her way. If a consumer returns the goods, the merchant simply has to pay the consumer back in cash. There are no third parties in the process—everything occurs between a merchant and consumer.

With credit cards, we introduce new complexities into processing an order:

- *Do you accept the card?* With a cash transaction, the merchant can immediately see if the currency the consumer is trying to use is an accepted currency. In the United States, if consumers try to make a purchase with euros, merchants will tell them they don't accept euros. With credit cards, there are also different credit card types, and as a merchant, you need to know which ones you can process. Your acquiring bank will support only a certain group of these cards, and you need to make sure you can process the card prior to accepting it from the consumer.

- *Is the card real?* Most people are very familiar with how cash looks and feels. There are a number of things a merchant can do to see if the cash is counterfeit, but, in general, everyone knows what a one-dollar bill is. Credit cards have different brands, different logos, colors, and names on them. To make it even more difficult, banks and associations change these looks often. Likewise, the credit card only has a set of numbers across the front of it—how do you know these numbers aren't just gibberish?

- *Does the consumer have money available on the card?* When you take cash, you know immediately if the consumer has enough money to pay for the purchase. With credit cards, there is no "value remaining" indicator on the card. With credit cards, a merchant has to go out and ask if the consumer has money remaining.

- *Is this consumer authorized to use this particular credit card?* When a credit card is used, there is no magic check occurring on the names authorized to use the credit card. If the credit card says John Smith, how do you know this is really John Smith?

- *Have you delivered the goods or services?* If not, you cannot ask for your money. With credit cards, there are rules about when you can request to have funds paid to you and how you have to handle customer service complaints. With cash, you can have consumers prepay for special orders, split shipments, and delay shipments, but you cannot do these things with credit cards.

Now instead of a transaction occurring between a merchant and consumer, there can be up to seven entities (merchants, consumers, issuing banks, acquiring banks, payment processors, gateway services, card associations) involved in a transaction. As a merchant, you have to rely on third parties to make sure the consumer can pay for the transaction and to authenticate that the consumer is authorized to make the purchase.

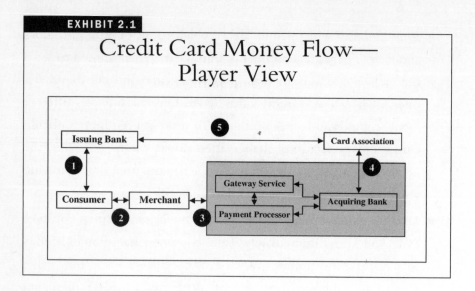

EXHIBIT 2.1

Credit Card Money Flow— Player View

Having so many more entities involved in a transaction means there are more steps a merchant has to go through to collect money on a transaction, as shown in Exhibit 2.1.

1. The consumer contacts an issuing bank, opens a credit card account, and is issued a credit card with a unique account number and a credit line (which is how much he or she is allowed to spend on the account).

2. A consumer goes to a merchant and selects goods or services to be purchased. He or she provides the credit card information to pay for the transaction.

3. The merchant takes the credit card information provided by the consumer and attempts to validate it through tests and checks and sends it to the acquiring bank to find out if the consumer has money available on the credit card to make the purchase. How the information is routed to the acquiring bank depends on the merchant's decision to use a gateway service or payment processor. Remember a gateway service and payment processor operates as a middleman in the transaction, giving value-added services to the

merchant. The merchant could be using any of the following methods to get credit card orders out to the acquiring bank:

a. Directly connecting to the acquiring bank

b. Connecting to a payment processor that connects out to an acquiring bank

c. Connecting to a gateway service that connects out to an acquiring bank

d. Connecting to a gateway service that connects out to a payment processor that connects to an acquiring bank

e. Connecting to a payment processor that offers acquiring bank services directly

4. The acquiring bank routes a request through the card association physical network to the issuing bank to see if funds are available on the consumer's credit card.

5. The issuing bank checks the consumer's credit line, and if funds are available, it will set aside the amount of money that the order requires for payment. This money is reserved only—it has not changed hands and is not the merchant's money yet. At this point, a reply is sent back through the card association network to the acquiring bank and then back to the merchant to let them know the status of the request for funds.

All of this has gone on, and all we have done is determine that the card is a valid credit card and that the consumer has enough money available on the credit card to make the purchase. There are seven major steps associated with processing a CNP credit card purchase. Exhibit 2.1 and the example depict only the first two steps in that process. The merchant still hasn't gotten paid for the goods or services. Additionally the merchant has to worry about the reserve on funds expiring, credits, and potential bad transactions, called *chargebacks*.

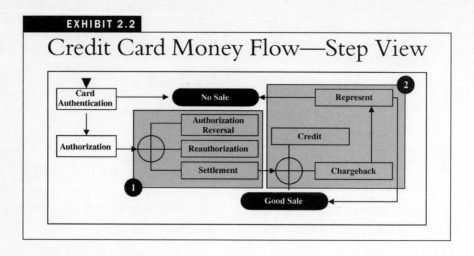

EXHIBIT 2.2

Credit Card Money Flow—Step View

The remainder of this chapter will discuss each of these seven steps in more detail, but let's take a brief look at the seven steps in processing a credit card transaction to get you familiar with the big picture as shown in Exhibit 2.2.

In Exhibit 2.2, the two major areas highlighted in gray represent two conceptual phases in the credit card process: prepayment (1) and postpayment (2). The prepayment phase shows all of the steps that can happen on a consumer's order before the merchant receives money from their credit card. The postpayment phase shows all of the steps that can happen on a consumer's order after the merchant has received money.

- *Card Authentication:* Validate the credit card number the consumer gave you to verify that it's actually a real credit card number and not just a bunch of random numbers. If the consumer fails this test, no sale. If the consumer passes this test, the order moves to authorization.

- *Authorization:* Check for and reserve funds on the consumer's credit card for the order.

- *Authorization reversal:* Contact the issuing bank to "un-reserve" funds on a credit card if a consumer decides not to make the purchase.

- *Settlement:* Request physical payment of funds from the consumer's credit card.

- *Credit:* Return physical payment of funds back to the consumer's credit card.

- *Chargeback:* This is a request from the issuing bank to provide additional documentation on a consumer's order to prove the consumer made the purchase. These requests can be based on customer service issues or suspected fraud.

- *Represent:* This is the presentation of additional documentation to the issuing bank to prove the consumer made the actual purchase.

Remember not every step will occur with every transaction. Exhibit 2.2 provided a quick overview of the seven steps and the major objective of each step. Even with the data you will receive in the remainder of this chapter, make sure you work with your acquiring bank to get more detailed information on the policies and procedures they have in place for these steps.

Card Authentication

Before you can check to see if the consumer has money available, you need to make sure the card number you were given is valid, and you do this by doing a *card authentication.* This means checking to make sure the card number given by a consumer could even possibly be a credit card number and is not just a random set of numbers. The card authentication check is not trying to see if the account is real or what money is available on it—it is just making sure the numbers the consumer gave you fit the normal credit card pattern and range.

Card authentication is typically accomplished by using a test called *MOD 10 check.* This check is built into many payment systems and is typically found on the buy page of a web site. This will catch things like too few or too many digits or an incorrect arrangement of the digits.

If you have made a purchase online, you may have added an extra digit and had an error message asking you to check your credit card number. This is most likely the MOD 10 check. The MOD 10 check is discussed in detail in Chapter 10.

If you think about it, the need to authenticate a credit card number is not unique to the CNP space. It is a more pronounced issue for the CNP space, but the card-present world also has to do the same check. For example, when a consumer comes to a store and hands the merchant a credit card, the merchant really has no idea if it is a valid credit card. Counterfeit cards are a serious problem in the industry, and credit card associations and issuers are constantly looking for new ways to prevent counterfeiting.

The difference between the card-present and the CNP world is that in a store the consumer gives the merchant a credit card to swipe through a card reader to perform the card authentication. Assuming the card is not damaged, the machine can then check to make sure it is a real card and start the payment process. If it is damaged, or fake in some cases, it may not swipe and the merchant will have to key it in to get the process started.

But think about the CNP credit card transaction. You can ask for all kinds of information from the consumer, but you cannot swipe a card for them. They give you a number and say "this is my credit card number." But how do you know this is a valid credit card number? Valid means it potentially could be a credit card number, not just a random set of made-up numbers. Credit cards today have between 13 and 16 numbers, with 16 being the most used standard. Would your staff still try to process an order if the credit card number received was 20 digits?

Authorization

Assuming the card number passed the card authentication check, now you need to find out from the card issuer if the consumer has enough money available to make the purchase. You do this by requesting an *authorization*. When you do this your request goes through the acquiring bank to the issuing bank, where they are responsible for checking the consumer's credit card number for authorization.

In the CNP transaction when you request an authorization, the request goes back to the issuing bank, who will see if the credit card account is an active account. If sufficient funds are available and you provide the address information, the issuing bank will perform an *address verification*. The address verification check provided in this process compares the billing address provided by the consumer with the billing address on record with the issuing bank.

Here are some things to keep in mind about authorizations:

- *Authorizations commit funds only; no money exchanges hands.* With an authorization, no money has exchanged hands; it has only been committed. For example, when you check into a hotel and your card is swiped when you arrive, the hotel is trying to get an authorization for the estimated total bill. This will commit that amount of money on the consumer's credit card to pay the merchant when the merchant processes a settlement transaction. The settlement transaction cannot be processed until the goods or services have been shipped to the consumer.

- *Authorizations are cumulative.* Every authorization on a card uses some of the consumer's credit line. If you make mistakes in your order process and rerun an authorization, you are committing more of the consumer's credit line. Likewise, if you process an authorization for a consumer who cancels the order before a settlement is processed or goods are shipped, the authorization you processed does not go away unless you reverse it or it expires. Even though no payment will ever be made on these authorizations, the consumer's credit line can be gobbled up with these commitments, and the consumer will not be able to make any purchases until the authorizations expire or are reversed by the requesting merchant.

Merchants who don't try to clean up these authorizations or who process multiple authorizations on a consumer can cause another merchant to get a decline on an order when money is really available. For example, a consumer with a credit line of $5,000 expecting to purchase a new computer finds one and starts the checkout process. The clerk runs the authorization for $3,000 and gets an approval. Later that same day the consumer finds an even better deal with the same computer and a flat-screen monitor from another merchant. The consumer wants a new flat-screen monitor to go with this new computer. So the consumer calls and cancels the original order and places a new order with the second merchant for $3,000. The original merchant hadn't shipped any goods yet and simply canceled the order in the system, but didn't process authorization reversals. When the issuing bank gets this request from the second merchant, there is still the other pending authorization for $3,000, and with the new request for $3,000, the consumer is now at $6,000. It looks as if the consumer is $1,000 over the credit limit, and the issuing bank will decline the authorization.

- *Authorizations expire on their own.* Authorizations don't last forever—they expire. The amount of time you have on an authorization may be different from card type to card type. Typically they last a week. If an authorization expires before you process a settlement, you may have to process a reauthorization. A reauthorization takes an expired authorization and reprocesses it to recommit the funds.

- *The authorization must be the amount you expect to settle on.* When you request an authorization, by rule from the card associations you are supposed to be requesting an authorization of the amount you expect to settle on. If you get an authorization for $100, you cannot process a settlement of $500 against it. The amounts don't have to be exact—the association has built-in variances to account for industries like food service in which tips are added after an authorization is requested. These variances are percentage amounts over or under an authorization amount on which the bank will still process a settlement.

Authorization Reversal

As you can see, you can get in trouble with authorizations under certain conditions, so a good tool to use is the *authorization reversal*. The authorization reversal is what you would process when you are not going to process an order to settlement, in order to free up a consumer's credit line. Sounds great, right? Well, the fact is most merchants don't use this process, as it can be complicated to integrate into their systems, and the number of times a consumer's credit line is tapped out by authorizations is generally rare because the authorizations do expire.

If you do implement authorization reversals, be aware that not all payment processing solutions, providers, and/or issuers support this process. In short, you could have this set up in your system and your payment processor could support this, but the consumer's issuing bank may not support it. In this case, you are out of luck—the only way to get rid of this authorization is to let it expire or call the issuing bank directly.

More than likely, you will never have to deal with this, but if you sell high-dollar goods or services, you should be prepared for it.

Settlement

So the card is good, and the consumer has money—how do you ask for your money? You do this by processing a settlement request. A settlement is where money actually changes hands. You request a settlement through your acquiring bank, which pulls it from the issuing bank.

You typically cannot submit a settlement request for payment until you have shipped the goods or services to the consumer. So for orders that have split shipments, delayed shipments, or backorders in play, you have to wait to settle until you have shipped each of the goods.

Generally, if you deliver your goods or services electronically, such as software downloads, subscriptions, or content viewing, you can immediately request a settlement when you request the authorization. If you have physical products, then you have to wait until the product is shipped to the consumer. In some cases, if your inventory is back-ordered or you are awaiting the products yourself, the authorization may expire before you can process the settlement. In these cases, you will have to reauthorize the transactions prior to processing a settlement.

Credit

So what happens when the consumer returns the goods to you? You had processed an authorization and a settlement and the money has been handed over, and now you have to refund money back to the consumer. This is done by processing a credit. When you do this, your acquiring bank will pass money back to the consumer's credit card.

When a consumer requests a refund, only refund back to the same method of payment he or she originally used to pay you. This is an easy scam from fraudsters to purchase goods with credit cards and request credits in cash.

Chargebacks and Representment

The final part of the money flow is not a merchant's favorite, and it has to do with what are called *chargebacks*. Chargebacks occur when consumers go back through their issuing bank to say that they didn't place an order or they didn't get what they were supposed to get.

There are two general categories of chargebacks. The first is fraudulent chargebacks, in which consumers say they did not place an order and did not receive goods or services. The other type is customer service chargebacks, in which consumers admit they placed an order, but dispute the charges for any number of reasons, such as they didn't receive the goods or services, or they returned them to the merchant, or they didn't get what they ordered.

Chargebacks are coded by type, and each card association and acquiring bank is a little different on how they present them to a merchant. But the process is basically the same: They will present the chargebacks to the merchant with a request to "represent" the order with supporting documentation to prove the order was valid.

As previously mentioned, when it comes to who pays for fraud, the merchant does in the CNP space. Part of what makes catching fraud so difficult is that chargebacks can take up to 90 days to be processed and sent back to a merchant. By that time, a fraudster could have already maxed out a credit card at your site, if you are not doing anything to stop it.

The chargeback is coming from an issuing bank, and the *represent* request will be coming from a merchant going through the acquiring bank back to the issuing bank. When you represent an order, you are trying to prove that the order was from the consumer who is disputing it and was completed in accordance with the association policies and procedures. In the card-present world, a merchant would send a copy of a signed register receipt. In the CNP world, there is no signed receipt. Here you are relying on the billing and shipping information provided and the signed delivery receipt, if you have one.

Chargebacks are nasty little buggers, as they have fees associated with processing them. In other words, every time merchants get a chargeback request from an issuing bank, they are charged a chargeback fee. As you can see, no one is really excited about chargebacks. They were intended to provide a means for merchants, banks, and consumers to resolve cases of abuse or fraud. They have been pretty good at doing this, but they have also created a lot of finger pointing and higher costs for everyone involved.

Let's refresh our memory when it comes to who is liable to pay for fraud. For fraud that occurs in the card-present world, the card association typically picks up the costs for fraud. However, the merchant will still have some associated costs that are not covered by this. These include the costs to process an order and to handle the chargeback, the shipping costs, and so on. The merchant will also have to pay a charge-back fee.

In the CNP world, the merchant is typically the one paying for the fraud. They already paid and lost the goods, as well as all of the overhead costs they spent on the order, and they will still have to pay a chargeback fee.

For customer service chargebacks, merchants pay a chargeback fee, and unless they can resolve the customer service issue, they may have physical loss of goods and services and associated overhead costs.

Some merchants will go out of their way to resolve customer service complaints up front to prevent a chargeback fee. They create policies of refunds on disputes, they encourage customers to call the business if they aren't happy, and they allow for refunds without returns. Why would a merchant do this? Consider what is at stake. Merchants risk the sum of the chargeback fees; the goods themselves, either lost or not returned; and the potential for increased basis points on their sales if their fraud losses get too high.

Chargeback Liability Example:

$$\textbf{Total Sale} = \$100.00$$

$$\textbf{Margin (22\%)} = \$22.00$$

$$\textbf{Credit Card Issuer Interchange \& Acquirer MDR (3.5\%)} = \$3.50$$

$$\textbf{Net Profit} = \text{Margin} - \text{Credit Card Issuer Interchange \& Acquirer MDR}$$

The merchant will make $18.50 from this one sale; if it ends up as a chargeback, it will cost them:

$$\textbf{Net Profit} = \$18.50$$

$$\textbf{Consumer Refund} = \$100.00$$

Chargeback Fee $= \$25.00$

Net Loss to Merchant $=$ Net Profit $-$ (Consumer Refund
$+$ Chargeback Fee)

The merchant will have lost $106.50 on this order. That means 4.8 more orders must be sold at this same amount just to make up this one loss. This example does not even take into account all of the merchant's costs, such as overhead and processing fees. It also assumes a very low chargeback fee—if they are doing e-commerce and are considered high risk, the chargeback fee could be $100 or more.

Chargeback fees are not fixed; they are different from bank to bank, and they also grow in cost depending on the number of chargebacks you have. If you have a significant problem with fraud, you could find yourself paying higher chargeback fees than the actual cost of the goods sold.

How did this happen? As merchants tried to prevent abuse by consumers, they pushed disputes to the bank. The banks retaliated by increasing their fees. The card associations reacted to the increase in chargebacks by setting thresholds for the total percentage of orders that are chargebacks, along with the total percentage of dollars processed. If your chargebacks go above these thresholds, you get hit with higher fines, and they keep going up until you get below the threshold. We call this the "going out of business plan" for the merchant. At the time of writing this book, these thresholds were around 1 percent of total monthly transactions or 2.5 percent of total dollar volume. Beyond the chargeback fees, the number of chargebacks you have can affect the basis points you pay on each order. Merchants that exceed these limits are considered high risk. If they were considered high risk, they would have lost $181.50 on that same order and would now have to sell 8.25 orders of the same size to make up that one loss.

As you can see, it is a scary proposition—one that has high stakes for the merchant. Merchants are very focused and motivated to control their losses to ensure that they don't get compounded by escalating chargeback fees.

Be forewarned: For Internet casinos, the U.S. card associations and issuing banks follow a policy that accepting a wager by a U.S. individual is in violation of federal law and, upon receiving a dispute from the cardholder, will immediately issue a chargeback.

IN THE REAL WORLD

ABC Electronics is evaluating the impact of chargebacks on their net profit. ABC Electronics is a $25 million a year business with margins of 14 percent. The company is experiencing 5 percent chargebacks, and the CEO has asked the CFO to explain the impact of chargebacks on the business, showing what the impact would be if they lowered it to 3 percent and what would happen if it increased further to 8 percent.

Assumptions			
Average Order Amount	$25	$25	$25
Orders	1,000,000	1,000,000	1,000,000
Chargeback Rate	3%	5%	8%
Impact on Operations			
Revenue	$25,000,000	$25,000,000	$25,000,000
Lost Goods	−645,000	−1,075,000	−1,720,000
Bank Refund to Cardholder	−750,000	−1,250,000	−2,000,000
Per Item Visa Fee (54% @ $100 per item)	−1,620,000	−2,700,000	−4,320,000
Per Item MC Fee (22% @ $100 per item)	−660,000	−1,100,000	−1,760,000
6-Month Visa High-Risk Fee ($20K/month)	−120,000	−120,000	−120,000
6-Month MC High-Risk Fee ($50K/month)	−300,000	−300,000	−300,000

Total Chargeback Impact	−4,095,000	−6,545,000	−10,220,000
Revenue Net Chargeback Fees	$20,905,000	$18,445,000	$14,780,000
Impact on Revenue	−16.4%	−26.2%	−40.0%
Operating Expense per Order	$14.94	$14.94	$14.94
Fraud Expenses per Order	$4.09	$6.56	$10.22
Margin	24%	14%	−0.6%

Chapter Summary

Consumer purchases drive the online payment economy. Aside from the consumers, the different players we have discussed in this chapter are all motivated to ensure consumers can make online purchases; because they make their money each time the consumer makes a purchase. For each consumer purchase the merchant is trying to make profit from a percentage of money called margin, which represents the difference between what it cost them to buy and sell the goods and what they sold it for to the consumer.

In that margin, the merchant has to pay for all of its overhead, staff, utilities, property, loss, insurance, and so on. Profit comes from the margin, and the merchant needs that margin to go a long way before actually making a profit, so every penny of it counts.

There is no denying that a merchant makes less profit on an order paid by credit card than by cash. But all merchants understand that having the ability to take credit cards means there are a lot more potential sales that would have never been possible as strictly cash deals. The merchant's additional costs for credit card transactions come from interchange rates and basis points.

The issuing banks, acquiring banks, associations, and sometimes the payment processors all get their money from the merchant in terms of basis points paid by the merchant. Basis points are percentage points of a sale a merchant pays on every purchase made with a credit card to the acquiring bank. Merchants negotiate with their acquiring banks, and sometimes the associations, to get the best possible interchange rates and basis points. The key point to understand is all of the players, aside from the consumer, have a vested interest in each consumer purchase.

Another key take-away from this chapter is to really understand that fraud is not defined or felt the same by all players in the payment process. Consumers worry about identity theft and having to rebuild their credit, while merchants worry about losing goods and having to pay fines. Acquiring banks worry about collusive merchants working with fraudsters to defraud the banks. Issuers worry about fraudulent applications, counterfeit cards, and stolen cards. Associations worry about how fraud will impact their brand name for consumers, merchants, and banks. So when talking, reading, or evaluating fraud-prevention techniques, remember to check whose perspective you are getting.

	Represents	Paid By
Consumer		
Merchant		Consumer
Issuing Bank	Consumer	Consumer, Merchant
Acquiring Bank	Merchant	Merchant
Payment Processor	Merchant, Acquiring Banks	Merchant
Gateway Service	Payment Processors, Acquiring Banks, Merchants	Merchant
Card Association	Issuers, Acquirers, Merchants	Issuers, Acquirers, Merchants

Notes

1. The Fraud Practice, Media Mindshare White Paper, 2009.
2. http://weis2008.econinfosec.org/papers/Romanosky.pdf (Section 6.1).
3. According to FAB 2009: Kevin Mitnick Presentation, slide 27.
4. http://weis2008.econinfosec.org/papers/Romanosky.pdf.

CHAPTER 3

Fraud Basics for Companies Doing Business Online

After reading this chapter, you will be able to:

- Categorize the types of fraud schemes in e-commerce.
- Discuss the history of e-commerce fraud and the lessons learned from it.
- Discuss the common fraud schemes used today.
- Discuss the methods for reporting fraud.
- Describe the role and working relationship of law enforcement with e-commerce fraud.

How Fraudsters Steal

Why do fraudsters steal? To make money. So when fraudsters steal from a merchant, it is their intent to make money. They may do this by directly reselling the goods or services they got from a merchant or by tricking a merchant into refunding cash or other monetary devices (gift cards) for goods or services that were theirs to begin with.

Fraudsters are going to make themselves look and seem like they are someone else, and they are good at it!

In this section of the book, we are going to dive deeper into understanding the fraudster. We are going to look at the history of fraudulent activity, the types of schemes they use, and ways to describe specific fraudster personalities. To begin our discussion, I want to segment fraudulent activity into four categories:

1. Identity theft

2. Social engineering

3. Convenience (ease of use)

4. Internal fraud

These four categories give us a generic way to describe a fraudster's trick or scam by describing the activities and characteristics of the order the fraudster is presenting. (See Exhibit 3.1.)

EXHIBIT 3.1	
Types of Fraudulent Activities	
Category	**Order Characteristics**
Identity Theft (Third Party)	Large purchases; bust-out activity (maxing out of cards in short time periods); many purchases; perfect identities; address, phone and credit card data look clean.
Social Engineering (Third Party)	Attempting to find out information by asking questions, or to change information through social interaction. Hijack orders by changing shipping information or changing billing data on an existing credit card account.
Convenience (Ease of Use) (Third Party)	Testing cards to see if they work by making small purchases at safe locations like gas stations, electronic download services, or fee-for-service locations.
Internal Fraud	Organized fraudulent activity by person or persons working in a company, sharing information on how to perpetrate fraud to conducting actual theft.
Affiliate Fraud (First Party Fraud) (Third Party)	The creation or facilitation of bad transactions in order to receive commission payments.
Friendly Fraud (First Party Fraud)	Transactions where fraud is claimed but the consumer is actually the legitimate account holder.

These four categories are just the beginning; as you read through this section, you will get more specific descriptive discussions on schemes and fraudster personalities. The main reason I begin with these four categories is to give you a starting context for describing fraudsters so you can start to tie historical fraud knowledge to types of schemes and personalities.

Why is it important that we describe and categorize fraudster activities? The main reason is it helps us detect patterns and develop fraud-prevention techniques to stop these types of fraudulent behaviors. In working in fraud prevention, it is important to build strategies that can not only detect sophisticated fraud activity but also shut the door once you have spotted a fraud pattern. No fraud practitioner wants to be known as the one that could stop the most sophisticated fraudster, but let the dumb ones keep coming back for more. I say this because it is easy to focus on one type of fraudster, one point of attack, so much that we lose sight of the bigger picture. Remember, fraud has always been around. The moment you successfully stop a fraudster's attack, he or she will be looking for a new attack. Likewise, if you don't stop fraudsters, they will keep coming back until you do.

Take another look at the four general categories listed in Exhibit 3.1. Where would you focus your attention to try to spot this type of fraud activity? What would you do to shut the door and stop that type of fraud from reoccurring? Exhibit 3.2 shows some of the places you can look for these activities and how you can shut the door.

If this still doesn't make sense, don't worry. Schemes, personalities, and fraud-prevention techniques will be discussed in detail as we go through the book. The intent of this exercise is to share a mindset. When you read stories of fraudulent activity or share stories with peers, put on your fraud practitioner hat and analyze the activities that let the fraudster gain access and commit fraud (spotting), and then think about how you would prevent that same fraudster from returning (stopping).

EXHIBIT 3.2

	How to Spot and Fraudulent Activities	
	Spotting	**Stopping**
Identity Theft	Large numbers of purchases to one address; unusual purchases like 4 cameras or 5 computers, multiple cards with same address, multiple accounts with one address	Check for multiple accounts, look at purchase patterns over 90 days, use out-of-pocket checks and cross-merchant checks
Social Engineering	Phone calls to CSR team or internal sales with questions about order process, order amounts, use of multiple cards for single purchase, attempts to update shipping or billing information. "I put in the wrong address on my order." "I am on the road, and need you to send it to my girlfriend or friend."	Reprocess all changes through normal risk-prevention processes, conduct a call-back on all en-route address changes, or simply do not allow them
Convenience	Lots of cards with small purchase amounts, purchase of first item on the web site, or doesn't actually take delivery of goods or services	Use velocity of change and velocity of use checks, hot lists
Internal Fraud	Systemic fraud, fraud ring appears to be hitting you, see fraudsters constantly coming in just under your thresholds, or you find a particular identity that seems to keep popping up every couple of weeks that should have been stopped but always seems to get through the process	Strong employment checks, education, accountability and checks and balances, no one person with the keys to the kingdom. Don't allow CSRs to override their own orders.
Affiliate Fraud	Large numbers of losses with associated commission payouts	Strong affiliate monitoring programs coupled with disbursement fraud screening
Friendly Fraud	Historical purchase activity; strong authentication to shipping addresses; delivery confirmation/ signature	Implementation of strong authentication and verification processes, delivery confirmation and signature requirements

History of Fraud Online

Fraud is not new. The taking of property from others has been around as long as man has been on this earth. Fraud is characterized as the taking of goods or services from another by use of trick or device.

In some cases, the concept of fraud is very clear, such as cases in which a fraudster is clearly trying to pass off stolen credit cards or trying to steal goods going to another individual. But not all fraudsters are hardened criminals. In some cases, one who may look like a good consumer is actually nothing more than a fraudster. For example, a consumer may believe he or she is smarter than a merchant and order a product with the intent of using it and returning it. Or a consumer may order goods, receive them, and say he or she didn't receive them. Some consumers, who are normally good consumers, don't believe these types of activities are actually fraud. But to the merchant, the end result is no different than if a hardened criminal had used a stolen credit card.

What motivates a fraudster to commit fraud? Money? The thrill or danger involved? Or is it the test of skill? It really doesn't matter, as the intent is what I am concerned with—the intent of taking goods or services by use of trick or device.

A broad set of consumers and merchants correlate the rise in credit card fraud online with identity theft. In reality, identity theft is one of the oldest schemes in the book. The fact is we are all just hearing more about it in the news today. It may seem that identity theft is a new phenomenon of the Internet age, but in reality, one of the best ways to disappear throughout the ages was to adopt a new identity. What better way to adopt a new identity than to steal it from another? No doubt, fraudsters can acquire a copy of a birth certificate and from that they can get a social security number and other documents to steal a consumer's identity. Identity theft is only a part of the problem—a single mechanism to commit fraud. Identity theft simply offers fraudsters another way to commit crimes and to hide them from detection.

How Has the Internet Changed the Rules?

With the Internet, fraud scams are more efficient because you don't have to travel to physical stores, or potential marks, to test or use stolen credit cards. They are easier to hide because the fraudster is transparent—you don't see who you are doing business with when doing business online. With the traditional mail order and telephone order channels, the level of transparency was pretty high, but merchants still had physical communication in telephone orders and longer processing times in mail orders, to work with. Additionally in the telephone order channel, if a customer service representative was suspicious, he or she could always ask more questions with the consumer on the line.

With the Internet, the consumer and the fraudster can mask themselves by faking the data points sent to you, making it easier for them to abuse banks and businesses. With the Internet, there is no live communication with a consumer. If the data looks suspicious, you have to reject the order outright, accept it with the risk of fraud, or have someone investigate the order and try to get back in touch with the consumer—all very costly. Likewise, consumers doing business online expect fast turnarounds on their orders.

How Has Fraud Evolved?

Going back to the mid-1990s, we can see the beginning of real commerce from the Internet. I want to start our discussion here to show how, in a span of only ten years, so many different fraud scams evolved in order to give you a feel for the scope and pace of change.

With the start of e-commerce back in 1994, we started to see the first true buy buttons appear on the Internet. Not long after, we started to see several types of fraud. The first fraud trend to be seen was the use of famous names to commit fraud. In this attack, the fraudster would use third-party stolen credit cards with the celebrity of the day's name.

To understand this attack, you need to remember when you complete an authorization, the name used in the purchase is not checked. The fraudsters knew this and used it to their advantage. They also knew human behavior: Businesses were excited about the Internet—"a whole new world"—and they were too excited about the fact they got an order in the first place to think someone actually might be trying to steal from them. Likewise, how many people actually check the names of each order to see if the name looks real?

It had to be a fun conversation, and an embarrassing moment for all, when they saw how many orders were being placed by Mickey Mouse, Bill Clinton, Lex Luthor, and John Wayne.

So, merchants became smarter and implemented rules to check the name being used. But it was only partially effective, as there are so many possible names and so many people with the same name. Likewise, the fraudsters moved on to new attacks.

Next came the technical attacks in which developers created card-generator applications that could come up with real credit card numbers, and they put them out on the Internet. Credit card generators were available everywhere for download on the Internet, and fraudsters wasted no time using these generators to find credit card numbers they could use to make purchases.

These attacks were typically targeted at the same vendor, meaning a fraudster would focus attacks on a single merchant to defraud over and over again. As time progressed, a new trend emerged in which the fraudsters started to jump from site to site, not staying long and hitting multiple merchants with fewer hits to make their activities less noticeable. This was very disturbing as most of the merchants at this time were relying on homegrown applications and manual reviews to prevent fraud. Merchants had no way to see cross-merchant activity until the card associations reported it, and by then it was too late.

After 1996, fraudsters started to use the Internet as a test bed for stolen credit cards. Before the Internet, fraudsters used to take stolen cards to the local gas station where they could test to see if the card was still active and good by trying to buy a gallon of gas at the pump. If it worked, they went on a shopping spree. The trend now is for fraudsters to use the Internet to test credit cards and then go on shopping sprees.

Up to this point, the fraudsters were still relying on old tried-and-true techniques to get credit card information. They used skimming, dumpster diving, mail theft, actual theft of people's cards, and application fraud. But as Internet commerce grew, you started to see a group of fraudsters using the Internet to harvest credit card information. The fraudsters go out on the Internet to attack merchant sites and get new identities and card information to use to defraud the same, or other, merchants. These fraudsters use a technique called "cracking" as their main method to retrieve this data.

If the Internet boom was a creative boom, the fraudsters were right there with the industry. Groups of fraudsters found more and more clever ways to steal goods and services without the hassle of having to find actual credit cards and trying to mask their identities. Fraudsters started to hijack orders. They would hack into merchant sites, or watch consumers to find out what they ordered and when they placed an order so they could steal the shipment. The fraudster would either wait for the goods to arrive and take them at the point of delivery, or call the merchant or shipping company and change the delivery address while it was en route. As the Internet began to peak in the late 1990s, so did the fraudster's creativity in committing fraud.

As 1998 rolled around, the Internet was filled with e-commerce web sites. Established merchants were climbing all over themselves to get online, and new merchants were trying to set up the next big retail conglomerate. Everyone predicted the fall of the direct retail channels and the rise of the e-commerce world. So what better time for fraudsters to commit more sophisticated securities and property scams?

Fraudsters took this Internet fever and used it to their benefit by setting up dummy merchant sites where they could funnel credit cards through their own sites to create cash flow, and then, before the chargebacks rolled in, they would shut the doors and leave the country. In some cases, the merchants would share credit card information with fraud rings to have them commit fraud at other sites.

Not too long after this, we started to see the mass theft of identities from the Internet through information that is provided online under the

Freedom of Information Act. The most famous example was the mass theft of military IDs from the Internet and then the use of these identities to steal from multiple merchants. Since then, the private sector and government have become more careful about sharing this information. The problem for our government is the Freedom of Information Act, which puts a lot of this information in the public domain. But the sad fact remains that even if this information was not on the Internet, a fraudster could still go to state and county public offices to collect this type of data. Understanding this dilemma, merchants started to look for new ways to verify consumer information.

So merchants online started to think about ways they could stop fraud. One of the methods merchants developed was the use of consumer accounts. The merchant would set up a consumer account the first time the consumer tried to make a purchase. After setting up the new account, the merchant would perform a series of checks to validate that the information the consumer provided was true. Merchants typically asked for more data from the consumer with this method, but they offered the consumer an easier one-click checkout process as an incentive to provide it. The concept was good, and consumers and merchants liked the new account method. This method was very popular at auction and larger e-commerce sites. But fraudsters liked this new method as well. Most merchants were only performing their fraud checks when an account was set up. Merchants weren't performing fraud checks when a consumer changed the shipping address or added a new card. Fraudsters could set up new accounts with one credit card and change the credit card information in their account as many times as they wanted to commit fraud. In a 90-day chargeback cycle, they could process a lot of purchases with a lot of credit cards. Fraudsters could also take over a consumer's existing account and change the shipping address and place a number of orders.

As auction sites like eBay and uBid became popular, a lot of new fraud schemes arrived specifically targeted at this community, from selling bogus goods to misleading the consumer as to the type and condition of goods sold. The online auction fraudster had many more scams they could pull, from setting up a number of auctions and selling goods they don't really have, collecting the payments, and then changing their identity, to using stolen credit cards to buy goods they sell on auction sites. Fraudsters could also use the buyer's credit card information to buy additional goods that they then could sell back to other consumers on the site.

After 2000, we really started to see organization in the fraud attacks. Online gangs and fraud rings started to emerge. From Asia to Nigeria to Russia, we saw a very systematic method of attack coordinated to move goods from the site to a third party to fence and sell them.

We also saw the emergence of social engineering in which fraudsters became bolder in their attacks, taking the initiative to contact the issuing banks, the merchants, and credit bureaus to complete their fraud. Even when flags were raised, the fraudster would have taken initiatives to validate their identity enough to get the merchant to ship the actual goods.

This is only a snapshot of the fraud scams committed over the last 10 years and only focuses on the online aspect of the card-not-present (CNP) transaction. Visa estimates the rate of online fraud to be approximately seven times that of fraud in the card-present world. Some independent analysts have the estimate as high as twelve times.

While payment fraud in the card-present world has seen some declines over the last 20 years, it has risen steadily in the CNP world. Fraud is not going to just stop occurring. The initiatives by the card associations will help curb fraud, but as a merchant today, you have to be prepared to fight this battle; and for some of you reading this, that battle may mean the survival of your business.

Own Your Data

DANIEL ENGLAND, FRAUD PREVENTION MANAGER, MONA VIE

Effective fraud prevention rests on one thing: data. Transaction data, chargeback data, refund/return data, inventory data, and so on. Assembling all your data in one place, and then getting access to it, is half the battle against fraud. Data must be fast and flexible: fast so you can find fraud in time to deal with it properly, and flexible so you can find connections to other fraudulent transactions.

The nature of fraud is always changing. Fraudsters poke and prod, always looking for weaknesses in your system they can exploit. If you plug one hole, another appears somewhere else. Therefore, your data cannot be locked into standard preformatted reports. Your data reporting structure needs to be adaptable to the changing fraud patterns that you're noticing over time. Therefore, if you're not managing your own data, your database administrator needs to be your best friend.

Just How Big of an Issue Is E-Commerce Fraud?

In short, when you combine the transparency, the ease of attempting fraudulent transactions, the cross–border capability, and the low cost and high availability of stolen credentials, the online channel will continue to be a prime target forever increasing fraudulent activity.

According to Digital River, fraudsters online account for 10 to 20 percent of all attempted orders more than $200.[1] For orders less than $200 that are electronic, or easily resold, the fraud attempt rate is closer to 50 to 80 percent of all online orders.

Beyond the order amount, the experience of the fraudster plays a critical part in just how much will be stolen. Inexperienced fraudsters are typically able to steal $25 to $100 per successful attempt, while experienced professional fraudsters typically can steal from $200 to $1,000 per successful attempt.

According to *The Economic Times*,[2] the going rate for stolen credit card numbers ranges from $0.40 to $20, while bank account information ranges from $10 to $1,000 per account. They also indicated that if you were willing to buy in bulk, you could acquire 50 credit card numbers for $40 or 500 credit card numbers for $200. In case you were curious, the same article quoted Symantec Corporation as stating that e-mail passwords sell for as little as $4 to $30, while full identities are selling for between $1 and $15.

In May 2008, Javelin Strategy & Research released a forecast for identity fraud. After collecting data for three-month periods from 2003 to 2007, the company studied trends to predict the future of credit card and debit card fraud. As a result, the study predicts debit card fraud will likely rise in the future. This is a pretty scary fact. Whereas credit cards protect cardholders when fraud occurs, there is no such insurance for debit cards.

IN THE REAL WORLD

What Verticals Are Most Impacted by E-Commerce Fraud?

According to the Internet Fraud Watch, an industry watching group, the top 10 categories of Internet fraud are:

1. Auctions
2. General merchandise sales
3. Computer equipment and software
4. Internet services
5. Work-at-home offers
6. Business opportunities

IN THE REAL WORLD (CONTINUED)

- **7** Marketing schemes
- **8** Credit card offers
- **9** Advance fee loans
- **10** Employment offers

How Are Globalization and Cross-Border Transactions Affecting Fraud?

The ability of consumers to conduct transactions with merchants who are not in the same country as issuance presents a real challenge to merchants in relation to fraud prevention. While merchants are scrambling to take advantage of new potential market share, they must increasingly rely on outside vendors to provide tools for fraud prevention because the tools provided by the card associations don't work, work poorly, or simply aren't available in some of these markets. Not surprisingly, overseas fraud, or cross-border fraud, is significantly higher than domestic fraud. In the United Kingdom alone, 77 percent of the reported fraud in 2007 came from overseas transactions (a U.K.–issued card being used at a non–U.K. merchant location). According to the Australian Payments Clearing Association (APCA), total fraud on Australian credit cards in 2008 amounted to $132 million, of which $73 million was obtained by criminals using the cards in other countries.[3]

What Is the Mind Share with Respect to Responsibility for CNP Fraud Losses?

The debate has been ongoing for years: Who is responsible for the fraud losses associated with CNP fraud? I find it interesting that while the associations, banks, issuers, acquirers, and retailers continue to fight it out, the consumers have already made their opinions very clear: three out of four don't believe that it is the retailers' responsibility to absorb these fraud losses. I base this on recent surveys from CyberSource and

CPP. In CyberSource's 2008 *U.K. Online Fraud Report*, it was reported that 24 percent of consumers believe that retailers are ultimately responsible for fraud losses. CPP, a Life Assistance Firm, reported that 74 percent of the U.K. consumers questioned believe it is the responsibility of banks or credit card issuers to resolve any fraud problems.

EXECUTIVE INSIGHT

What Is Good?

DAVE GLASER, VICE PRESIDENT, GLOBAL SERVICES, CYBERSOURCE

As a fraud manager, you've got a tough job. You're pressured to deliver on multiple—often conflicting—objectives, simultaneously. And, the business dynamics change constantly with new products, business models, fraudster tactics, and staff changes. So, what should you measure? Where should you focus your energies? How do you know if you are "doing good"? We see two common traps. The first is the tendency to focus on one metric, such as chargeback rate, as the singular measure of your success. The second trap is the tendency to adopt someone else's benchmark rate as your own goal. In reality, fraud management is a complex system and is highly sensitive to the very specific context of your business. So you want to be thinking more broadly about (1) your process, and (2) your profile, to really understand what good means.

Thinking about your process means understanding the balance between several key metrics—your fraud rate, sales dollars lost to suspected fraud (reject rate), and overhead costs due to manual review—and how those work together to make you more profitable. In the simplest view, you can aim to be more or less "tight" or "loose" in controlling fraud. Tight is not always good. Tight tends to increase reject rates and review rates. You can be too tight if you are rejecting many good orders in a singular quest to drive down fraud. To find your optimal balance, you need to assess the special dynamics of your individual business. For example, if you have a high-margin business, you may do better being somewhat looser and accepting more good orders and tolerating a somewhat higher fraud rate. But if you have a low-margin business, it takes many more good orders to balance one loss, so you will tend to be tighter on fraud.

Even if you understand the broader process, you are still likely to be hungry for target benchmarks to prove you are "doing good." We run an annual industry survey on online fraud, which points to several possible benchmarks used by best-in-class merchants. But it's important to realize that the value of benchmarks is the questions they cause you to ask yourself, as the answers they present. Benchmarks can help you understand your fraud management profile and how your profile changes as your business grows. For example, as you become more sophisticated in fraud management, you may add more tools and specialized staff, so you can show better results. But at the same time, your business growth may make you a more visible target for fraudsters, who look to hide their activity within the volume of larger merchants, and so you may start to feel spikes in fraud. In fact, mid-sized merchants are sometimes caught in a squeeze of becoming larger targets before they have the tools and process in place to react. If you add new lines of business, or acquire other companies, you may have multiple fraud profiles that require individual strategies. Finally, if you take on international orders, you may find two to three times the fraud challenge, but also that much more growth potential. In all these cases, there will not be a one-size-fits-all metric for you to target. Benchmarks help you understand what is possible, then you need to decide what is relevant for your specific business at a specific point in time.

So success in fraud management does not mean hitting any universal benchmark and holding there. Instead you want to build a process that is tuned to your particular business right now, and then be flexible in adapting your targets to match new opportunities. That is "doing good."

Common Fraud Schemes

I have been working with merchants for years, and I am still amazed at the creativity fraudsters come up with to defraud merchants. These people aren't stupid, uneducated thugs. They are educated, crafty, and patient.

If there is one thing I have learned from my experiences, I know that even if you wanted to, it is not realistic to think you can stop all fraud. There are just too many ways to create a perfect one-use identity. The resources, time, money, and people I would have to put into place to catch these fraudsters just don't make sense.

But the good news is you don't have to catch the perfect one-use criminal. The majority of fraudsters out there are still using the basic scams to defraud merchants because there are still too many businesses that aren't doing anything to stop them.

The purpose of this chapter is to give you an understanding of some of the general schemes that are out there. With this understanding, you can look at your businesses and craft strategies to prevent fraud that most closely represents the type of fraud scheme your site sees.

This chapter will also give you the insight to look at fraud patterns to spot fraud schemes as they are being perpetrated against you. Remember that to be effective at preventing fraud you have to be proactive in the design of your strategy. Don't just model your fraud strategies off what you have been hit with in the past, but look at your vertical market and see what other common fraud schemes may be pointed at you.

Where Do Those Fraudsters Get the Credit Card Numbers?

Have you ever wondered where fraudsters get their credit card information from? The fact is, lists of valid credit card numbers are available on the black market, with different prices for valid credit cards and credit cards with the card security numbers provided. Where do all of these cards come from? From several places.

The major point is from a scheme called skimming, in which card numbers are being harvested in common places like restaurants, bars, hotels, ATMs, and airports. The fraudster places fake devices in these locations where an accomplice, or the entire staff unknowingly, is swiping each credit card that comes in. These numbers are then collected and sometimes sold to be used for fraudulent activity.

Credit card numbers can also come from fake applications for credit, identity theft, account takeovers, and from valid unused account numbers. Because credit card numbers are allotted to issuers in blocks, fraudsters can methodically check each credit card number in a sequence by using a credit card generator to test a bank's credit card numbers. Of all of these methods, identity theft is the most worrisome. In cases of identity theft, a fraudster can look and feel perfect to all but the most sophisticated fraud solutions.

One Hit–One Merchant and One Hit–Multiple Merchants

This is one of the more difficult types of fraud to detect and prevent. In a *one hit–one merchant* scheme, fraudsters will acquire a credit card profile and make a single purchase from only one merchant site and dispose of the credit card number. They will not reuse the site again, or if they do, it will only occur after very long periods, greater than three months. In the case of *one hit–multiple merchants* the fraudsters are making more than one purchase on the credit card itself, but they are making one purchase from each of several different vendors rather than multiple purchases from the same vendor. Fraudsters will also typically be drawn to very highly fenceable goods: electronics, jewelry, mobile phones, computer goods, and gift cards.

Number of Purchases: 1

Billing and Shipping Address: Typically different; the shipping address will typically be a drop point or abandoned point

Shipping Method: Express Shipping

Phone: Bogus, or the real consumer's number

Purchase Amount: High

Fraud-Prevention Techniques: High dollar amount rule with express shipping rule, reverse lookup address and phone, use of fraud screening that does cross-merchant velocity-of-use checking, card security schemes

Consumer-Perpetrated Fraud

This is a scheme in which the consumer or an accomplice of the consumer makes a purchase and then denies the purchase was made, or claims that the goods or services were never received. All of the data points will look good, but the consumer will swear he or she did not make the purchase and did not receive the goods or services. Consumers may also say they placed the order but never received the goods or services.

The consumer calls the issuing bank for the credit card and disputes the transaction for one of these reasons:

- Claims they never made the charge
- Claims their account was abused by someone else
- Claims they never received the services
- Claims that their spouse never made the transaction

If consumers say they never placed an order, take a look at your past records to see if they have ever made a purchase from you before, and make sure you put them on a warm list at least to watch for them in the future.

Number of Purchases: 1 or more

Billing and Shipping Address: Typically the same; if different, a real address with a real person

Phone: Real consumer's number

Purchase Amount: Any

Fraud-Prevention Techniques: Signature required on delivery, use of consumer authentication techniques, Verified by Visa, MasterCard

SecureCode, and out-of-pocket checks, hot lists and warm lists, card security schemes

Card Generator Fraud

In this scheme, fraudsters work a block of card numbers to find one or more that will work on a purchase. They are typically working a specific issuing bank's numbers. They will target smaller banks and ones that are not up to date on the card types and solutions. For example, they may not be up to date on address verification systems or real-time authorizations, or they may have set up automatic authorizations for certain amounts. The fraudster will find the banks meeting these criteria, find out their weakness, and then attempt to hit all the credit numbers with the issuing bank's assigned credit card number range. Once fraudsters successfully receive an authorization from one of the credit card numbers, they will make one or more purchases with it, from your business and from someone else's business if they can.

You can spot someone hitting you with a card generator by looking at the velocity of use and change characteristics of the orders. They will have to try the card multiple times, so you will see the same card with different expiration dates, you will see the same address with a lot of credit card numbers attempted against it.

The software for card generators is very widely available, so you will see activity from seasoned as well as novice fraudsters trying it out. If you catch this activity occurring, look at the data being submitted and hot list any elements that were the same across all of the orders, like the e-mail address, shipping address, and phone number.

Number of Purchases: 1 or more

Billing and Shipping Address: Typically different; the shipping address will typically be a drop point, abandoned point, or temporary address

Phone: Bogus, or the real consumer's number

Purchase Amount: Any

Fraud-Prevention Techniques: Velocity of use, velocity of change, fraud screening

Consumer Satisfaction Fraud

You can please some of the people some of the time, but you cannot please all of the people all of the time . . .

What do you do about those annoying customers who keep charging back their orders, when you know you have done what they asked? They may say, "You didn't send what I ordered," "It didn't arrive when you said it would," or "I changed my mind." The fact is chargebacks are expensive, and you just can't afford to have these customers.

We have all heard, or experienced, customers who purchased something, used it, and then returned it saying they just aren't happy with it. Merchants try to explain to consumers that they cannot take it back because it's used, but they simply complain to their issuer and the merchant is stuck with the bill.

I don't have any magic answer on catching these consumers up front; if I did, I would be a rich man, but there are things you can do to limit your exposure. First, if you are selling goods or services under $50, you should consider a no-hassle return policy. Just take it back; don't mess with a chargeback unless you have an iron-clad case. In some cases, the dollar value of a purchase makes fighting a chargeback a worthless proposition.

Second, implement a warm list or use your hot list and add this consumer to the list. I would recommend a two-strikes-you're-out policy. One chargeback or return of goods or services and you are put on the warm list; two chargebacks or returns and you're on the hot list. Make sure you review your warm list quarterly to see how many good purchases have occurred from these customers; if they have a good purchase in that same time period, remove them from the list. However, if the consumer actually did process a chargeback, wait for two good purchases before you take them off the warm list. Remember the hot list automatically declines the order and the warm list automatically causes a review.

Number of Purchases: 1 or more

Billing and Shipping Address: Typically the same

Phone: Real consumer's number

Purchase Amount: Any

Fraud-Prevention Techniques: Hot lists, warm lists

Credit and Return Fraud

This scheme has slowed down dramatically in the United States as most merchants have already implemented polices to avoid this scheme, but it still is occurring in Europe and Asia.

The scheme happens in one of two forms. The first is where a fraudster working alone will come in and make purchases for goods and services and then return the goods to have a credit given in cash.

The second form of this scheme is where the fraudster works with an accomplice. The fraudster makes purchases with the fraudulent credit cards and the accomplice returns them for cash.

In both schemes, there may be some time between the purchase and credit. On return, they may or may not have the receipt. They will commonly try to do returns without a receipt during times when this is common, such as during holiday shopping seasons.

What does the scheme have to do with e-commerce and MOTO? If your business has a direct retail presence, you could see some of this type of fraud as cross-channel fraud. With the emergence of e-commerce and the buy online and return in-store capabilities, the fraudster can use this scheme to move goods and funds.

With this scheme, you have to be very conscious of patterns of chargebacks on items not typically found to be chargebacks. Fraudsters can target safer purchases with this scheme because they intend to return them to get cash or gift cards to then make purchases of higher end goods that they can sell on the street easier.

Most merchants in the United States have adopted a policy of only giving credits to the same credit card that was used for the purchase, or in the case of gifts they will give a gift card. This has curbed the scheme pretty well, but there is still a susceptibility to this scheme for most merchants because of the ability to make the fraudulent purchases, make the returns, and then purchase another item.

Beyond adopting better return policies you can implement velocity of use and change checks on your credits and returns to catch people who are doing a lot of credits from a lot of different points. Be careful with this—make sure you know your customers. Some of your customers could very well have multiple people making purchases for them at the same store, and they could be looking to consolidate gifts and buy something different.

Number of Purchases: More than one

Billing and Shipping Address: Typically different; the shipping address will typically be a drop point or abandoned point

Phone: Bogus, or the real consumer's number

Purchase Amount: Any

Fraud-Prevention Techniques: Better return policies, velocity of change, and velocity of use

Morphing Fraud—Repeat Offenders

In short, the morphing attack is where a fraudster is hitting a single merchant multiple times using slightly different data points each time. These attacks are typically of short duration with multiple purchases being made and sent to the same address or within a very close proximity. Fraudsters may change every data point except one or two, so you have to be doing some good cross-reference checking to catch them.

This scheme has a couple of different variations. I call them the *bust-out*, the *slow morph*, and the *multiple personality*.

In the bust-out variation, the fraudster will make multiple purchases from your site within a short time frame with a number of different credit cards. All of the goods and/or services will be going to the same location, but all of the other data may change between purchases.

In the slow morph attack, the fraudster will make purchases with elapsed time between purchases to prevent raising any flags and will change the credit card, address, and phone slowly over time, just a step ahead of you.

In the multiple personality attack, the fraudster will set up several different personas with different cards and make periodic purchases over a 30- to 90-day time frame. I have seen cases where the morphing attack was pulled off with two to three hits per month, all spread out over a 90-day period. The fraudster used three different credit cards and personas and made one purchase with each persona per month for a three-month period and then disappeared. The merchant in this case was using velocity of use and change, but was only counting usage and change for a 24-hour period to attempt to catch bust-outs. The merchant finally caught on after doing some research on past chargebacks to see the fraudster was using variations of the same name (i.e., Sara, Sarah, Sam, Samantha, Bill, Bob, William, Willard, and Wilda).

The morphing attack is a little easier to spot if you have good velocity of use and change checks in place. The problem is determining how many purchases or changes constitute actual morphing. As merchants, we all pretty much assume that a repeat purchase transaction is a sign of a satisfied consumer, and want to have our customers come back and buy from us. We never assume fraudsters know this as well and will play us based on this. Making a purchase once a month for three months wouldn't in itself set off any alarms, but what they are buying and how the data points they send us change does.

In catching morphing attacks, you will have to really think about how you can look at previous account activity and how you can look at the products purchased. The velocity of change and use checks are the best mechanisms to catch fraudsters morphing their identity in their attacks.

Here are some of the things you can look for to catch these morphing fraudsters:

- Look at the typical buying patterns for your merchandise. Would someone typically buy the product sold more than once in a day, week, month, or year? For example, if you sell televisions online, how often would the same person buy another television on the same day, week, or month? If you sell jewelry, how often does someone buy the exact same piece of jewelry in a day, week, month, or year?

  If you are already looking at velocity of change and use on a daily basis today to stop bust-outs, don't change it. Add another combined look at velocity of use and change over a six-month period in which you look at the number of purchases on a given credit card, e-mail, phone, and address. And track the number of changes of a credit card number to an e-mail, phone, and address.

- Look at the name associated with a credit number to see how many times it is changing. The name is typically not a good tool for doing fraud checks, but in the morphing attack, the attacker can change the name with everything else being the same. They don't always do this though; in the previously discussed case, the fraudster used the same name, which is how we caught him and stopped him from starting back up the following month with a fresh set of cards.

If you are doing e-commerce, track the IP address being used by the fraudster and check it against the IP address from past chargebacks to see if they are coming from the same points. It is very rare that they will have the same IP address, this typically means a real novice fraudster, but you can see trends to certain proxies or regions.

Number of Purchases: More than one

Billing and Shipping Address: Typically different; the shipping address will typically be a drop point or abandoned point

Phone: Bogus, or the real consumer's number

Purchase Amount: Any

Fraud-Prevention Techniques: Velocity of use, velocity of change, geolocation, consumer authentication, hot lists, card security schemes

Fraud Rings

Nothing strikes fear in a merchant's heart like the dreaded fraud ring. If you are lucky, you have only read about them in the paper or seen a piece on them in the news. If you're not lucky, you have experienced how devastating they can be.

Fraud rings are very good at finding the weak points in your fraud-prevention process and exploiting them quickly and efficiently. They are patient, taking a lot of time to learn about your policies and procedures. They typically perpetrate one or more of the other fraud schemes to find out how you react before they make a more massive attack.

- They will target a merchant and see what channels and purchase instruments they will accept.

- They will research the company via social engineering to see how the business operations work, how data is stored, and how long before chargebacks occur.

- They will look for vulnerability in the site, like dollar thresholds, and rules that are applied.
- They will attempt to hack the site.

What are fraud rings looking for? They want to find out where you really start looking at orders. Are there dollar thresholds you use that you don't do any fraud screening on below certain amounts? Do you use any manual reviews, or follow up with phone calls or reverse look-ups? Do you use hot lists or fraud screening solutions? Each of these gives them a different angle of attack and tells them how to attack. These things also tell them at what pace they can attack a merchant. They will also look at how you change across time—do you have more lenient policies during slow times, or during peak holiday times?

One of the favorite times for a fraud ring to hit is during the Christmas season because they know you can't look at everything, and you probably have temporary help that is not as experienced. They also know you can't take down your systems without affecting the rest of your business. Fraud rings aren't typically greedy about their attacks and will patiently attack your site during a holiday season to take you for a reasonable sum before the holiday season is over. They will be long gone before you can really see what was happening.

In stopping fraud rings, you have to focus on the basics of preventing fraud. The most basic point for fraud rings is catching the similar or common data points that can help you isolate and attempt to stop the fraud ring. Using tools like geolocation, freight forwarder lists, delivery address verification, consumer authentication, and velocity checks, you can isolate these common data points. The most common data points you should be looking for are the use of the same address, phone, or e-mail accounts or very close similarities between them (e.g., 12 Main Ave., 12a Main Ave., 12b Main Ave.).

In the cases where the fraud ring is hitting multiple sites in its attack, use of the freight forwarder and fraud-screening techniques that do cross-merchant velocity checks will help in catching these fraudsters. A lot of the fraud rings will use freight forwarders to move the goods out of the country to places such as Asia, Eastern Europe, Africa, and South America.

The more dangerous fraud rings are typically well thought out, using true account takeovers with long active periods of good purchasing behavior in which everything will look okay before performing a bust-out. You also have to assume they have plenty of valid credit card numbers to use because most are associated with skimming or harvesting activities for valid credit card numbers. There are very well-known fraud rings that operate out of Eastern Europe and Africa. If you check out the U.S. governmental sites for the Secret Service and Federal Trade Commission (FTC), you can usually find advisories about these groups. The only downside to checking out these sites is that by the time you see them in print, you have probably already been defrauded.

Number of Purchases: More than one

Billing and Shipping Address: Typically different; the shipping address will typically be a drop point or abandoned point

Phone: Bogus or disposable mobile phone number

Purchase Amount: Any

Fraud-Prevention Techniques: Velocity of use, velocity of change, geolocation, consumer authentication, hot lists, fraud screening, freight forwarder, rules engines, card security schemes

Affiliate Fraud—Internal Fraud

Affiliate fraud can occur in a couple of different ways. In the first method, fraudsters set up an affiliate account with a merchant and make purchases using stolen credit cards. Fraudsters collect the commission payout from the merchant for the sales they made using the stolen credit cards. In this scenario, fraudsters can use real people's addresses, as they aren't interested in the product; they are interested in the commission being paid out.

The second method attempted by fraudsters is to use stolen credit cards to purchase ad placements in search engines and other web sites to push traffic to the affiliate site to make purchases. In this scenario, the merchant may be getting legitimate traffic, but the advertisers are getting fraud losses associated with the ad listings. The risk to the merchant is brand damage from the negative association to paid advertisements that could affect a valid merchant's standing with search engines and network advertising agencies.

Number of Purchases: More than one

Billing and Shipping Address: Same or different

Phone: Disposable mobile phone number or real consumer's number (not the fraudster's)

Purchase Amount: Any, but usually on the upper end

Fraud-Prevention Techniques: Velocity of use, velocity of change, hot lists, fraud screening, rules engines, implementing affiliate monitoring, paid search monitoring on key search engines

Collusive Fraud—Internal Fraud

Collusive fraud is when a member of the merchant's staff is working with the fraudster. This person could be directly helping the fraudster commit the acts or could be funneling goods.

The most common version of this type of fraud is where the inside person will work in a merchant's call center to learn the fraud prevention policies and procedures. The inside person then feeds this information to the fraudster in a form in which he or she can get around your current fraud policies.

Other variations of this scheme include the staff member actually putting in orders or changing shipping information to have goods sent to other points. Or they are taking down credit card and personal information of consumers and then using this to make other purchases there or from other merchants.

Number of Purchases: More than one

Billing and Shipping Address: Same or different

Phone: Disposable mobile phone number or real consumer's number (not the fraudster's)

Purchase Amount: Any, but usually more on the upper end

Fraud-Prevention Techniques: Velocity of use, velocity of change, hot lists, fraud screening, rules engines, implementing tiered reviews with managers reviewing staff, and making sure you document the name of the staff member who works on each transaction

Identity Theft

Identity theft affected more than 9.93 million people during 2008. It has also cost the victims about $1,200 in out-of-pocket expenses with an average of 175 hours needed to resolve the damage caused by the stolen identity.

According to the FTC, one in every six Americans was a victim of identity theft in 2008, and for seven years straight, identity theft has topped the FTC consumer complaint list. According to Javelin Strategy & Research, "Every 79 seconds, a thief steals someone's identity, opens accounts in the victim's name, and goes on a buying spree."

Identity Theft Statistics

- Cost: $50 billion a year global business. (Source: FTC)
- 9.93 million people had some type of identity theft crime committed against them in 2008. (Source: FTC)
- In 2008, the number of identity fraud victims increased 22 percent. (Source: Javelin Strategy & Research)

- The year 2008 reversed a four-year incidence trend of decreasing fraud. (Source: Javelin Strategy & Research.)

- Only 12 percent of identity theft cases are the result of online identity theft methods (i.e., phishing, hacking, and spyware). (Source: Javelin Strategy & Research.)

- Seventy-nine percent of identity theft cases occurred through traditional methods such as stolen or lost wallets, checkbooks, credit cards, or "shoulder surfing" (when someone looks over your shoulder at the ATM). (Source: Javelin Strategy & Research.)

- Seventeen percent of identity theft cases were through friendly fraud or friendly ID theft. (Source: Javelin Strategy & Research.)

- Thirty-five percent of victims know how their information was stolen. (Source: Javelin Strategy & Research.)

- There has been an increase in attempts at identity theft over the telephone (*vishing*). In this scam, the fraudsters trick the consumer to provide their personal or financial information over the telephone. Between 2006 and 2007, the number of vishing identity theft cases rose from 3 percent of theft to 40 percent (Source: Javelin Strategy & Research.)

- One child in every classroom is already a victim of identity theft. (Source: Debix.)

- The children who are victimized averaged $12,799 in fraudulent debt. (Source: Debix.)

- Twelve percent of children who become victims were five years old or younger. (Source: Debix.)

In the United States, the FTC has been charged with tracking cases of identity theft through the FTC Identity Theft Clearinghouse. In Canada, cases of identity theft are tracked through the credit bureaus.

Every day in the United States, thousands of people are victims of identity theft, and this has been the case for the last 12 years, with a slight increase in the past couple of years. The United States Postal Service reported it will typically take a victim 14 months to find out his or her identity has been stolen.

As you can see, identity theft is a major issue. The fact is a lot of merchants and consumers believe that the Internet is somehow to blame for the rise of identity theft, but in reality, the Internet is not even in the top 10 for methods of acquiring identity takeover information. Database intrusion was the number one method for stealing data followed by dumpster diving. Once a fraudster steals someone's identity, what is done with it? According to the FTC, 42 percent of the time it is used for credit card fraud, 20 percent for utility fraud, and 13 percent for bank fraud.

Fraudsters can very easily take over and create new identities. The CDC puts out an annual book that can tell the layperson how to obtain birth certificates for anyone. The birth certificate is bar-none the best breeder document for identity theft. So where do fraudsters get the basic information on a person to start this process? From dumpster diving, database cracking, and car rental agencies, to name a few. Anywhere you might have to fill out an application.

As of 2002, all 50 states delineated identity theft as a crime, whereas before some states would have to use impersonation, check fraud, and so on to prosecute. California recently passed legislation CA Code 530.8 in the Penal Code stating that when someone reports this type of fraud, banks must allow the consumer or police to have access to all records including the files on the application or changes to applications.

So what can you do about identity theft? First, educate your customer service representatives on the tactics of fraudsters. Perform comprehensive customer validation, namely out-of-pocket checks. Also perform velocity of use and change checks and use third-party fraud screening that combines velocity across merchants.

If you have a case of fraud and a consumer calls you and says he or she is a victim of identity theft, be patient with the consumer. It may be true that he or she is a fraudster trying to social engineer you, but you should be polite and assume it really is a case of identity theft unless you have clear evidence to the contrary. Tell the victim he or she needs to provide you with an affidavit and police report, with the police report number and officer's phone number on it. The consumer can get a sample affidavit from the FTC web site, or they can get an identity theft reporting kit from our web site at www.fraudpractice.com. One note on the affidavit: Technically, the affidavit does not have to be signed or notarized to be legal, but ask for this anyway; if nothing else, it is forensic evidence and could be used as evidence of perjury.

Identifying the Fraudsters

With all of the news on break-ins, stolen information, fraud, and abuse, how do you make sense of all of the different characterizations of fraudsters? *Hackers, crackers, phreaks,* and *hactivists*—it sounds like a bad horror movie. But there are some good reasons to understand what these terms mean.

First, you get a feeling for the motivation of your fraudster. Find out why this person is committing fraud. You also get a feel for how likely the fraudster will be to repeat the crime, or if it will mean others will repeat the crime. Finally, you get an understanding of the tools and places where fraudsters get information on how to infiltrate your site and commit fraud.

The following short business case describes each of the fraudster characterizations. The intent is to give you a high-level view of the motive and potential activity of a particular fraudster characterization. Actual fraudsters could do more or less than the example I give. The examples are not intended to be all-inclusive, but should provide a good reference point.

Business Case—All Electronics, Fraudster Characteristics

ABC Electronics is a well-known electronics retailer with more than 1,200 direct retail stores in nine different countries (the United States, Canada, the United Kingdom, Ireland, Germany, France, Sweden, Italy, and their newest stores in China). ABC Electronics also has very active channels in mail order, telephone order, and e-commerce, with 20 percent of their overall revenue coming from these indirect channels.

While their roots in providing businesses with their computer and office automation equipment have always been the majority of the mail and telephone order sales they receive, approximately 18 percent of their indirect business comes from MOTO, and their web business has been growing at a phenomenal rate of over 500 percent per year. Currently, they receive more than 1,000 orders per day from their web business.

ABC Electronics was a little rushed when they implemented their web site, and they didn't have the time to implement real-time payment processing. They decided to store the order information from their customers and process it in a batch during non-peak hours. ABC Electronics relies on a staff of four fraud reviewers residing in their call center to review all e-commerce and MOTO orders for fraud. Because their web-based business was not really a significant amount of the overall revenue, the web-based orders were typically the last ones to be reviewed, if they were reviewed at all (see Exhibit 3.3).

Hackers

Hackers are individuals who attempt to gain access to computer systems and web sites of businesses or individuals to be able to say they can do it and prove it to their peers. The activity of a hacker is not designed to steal or defraud an organization, but instead to prove the hacker's technical skills.

EXHIBIT 3.3

Electronic Fraudster Characteristics		
Fraudster Type	**Motivation**	**Potential Activity**
Hacker	Prove technical prowess	Hackers may attempt to see if they can access credit card data. If they can, they may add an order or pull a list of orders from your system, which may include personal data and credit card information of consumers.
Cracker	Make money, steal anything possible	The cracker will directly attempt to put in orders, or to pull out the credit card data to use for fraudulent activity.
Phreak	Make money, steal phone-related products and services	The phreak would be the fraudster attempting to steal the company's prepaid mobile phones and their calling cards.
Hactivist	Make a statement	The hactivist is an individual who will gain access to your systems to plant a virus to attack your newest stores in China in order to protest human rights conditions.
Script Kiddie	Excitement, make money	The script kiddies are the ones attempting to use freeware card generators to make purchases on the web site.
Criminal Gang	Make money, their business	The criminal gang would be working orders against the unprotected web site.
White Collar	Greed, make money	The white collar provides individuals or gangs the information about the web site being unprotected.

Hackers will typically leave a calling card in the systems they hack to prove to others they have been there, by leaving a piece of code, or taking a key piece of information meant to prove the hack was successful. Hackers want publicity—that is why they are doing it. They are not necessarily looking for tons of publicity, news and such, but there is a hierarchy of hackers, and they need to publicize their hacks to move up in that hierarchy.

On the web sites dedicated to hacking, you can see this hierarchy and how hackers have to contribute to gain entry into the society. They have to show proof of ability. There are a number of these sites out there such as 2600, PHRACK (Phreaking & Hacking), and WAREZ, as well as magazines dedicated to hacking. Hackers use tools called *warez*, devices they have developed to infiltrate web sites. The fact is the tools for hacking a site are easily available on the Internet, and if your site is hacked, you had better fix the holes they have shown you, or else others will try the hack as well.

The hacker is not someone you should focus on in preventing fraud. Your IT department, responsible for information security, should be focused on stopping hackers. The hacker is not the one who will commit fraud on your site, but the information they gain may be used by others to defraud you.

Hackers may attempt to see if they can access credit card information, a hot thing in the news these days. If they can, they may add an order or pull a list of orders from your system, which may include personal data and credit card information of consumers. They would post parts of this information to prove they had gotten in. With this information posted on a hacker web site, a potential fraudster could find holes into a merchant's or bank's systems to pull all of the personal information, including credit card data, to use for fraudulent activity. They could also find hacks in systems to get in and learn your fraud-prevention processes.

One last note about hackers and the hacking community—if you get the desire to check out their sites, make sure you take strong virus and security precautions, as these sites are notorious for downloading items on your computer just by visiting them. These little gifts they leave behind can collect data residing on your computer, learn your passwords, or even take over a camera that may be attached to your computer, in which the fraudster can sit and watch everything you are doing.

Crackers

Crackers are individuals attempting to gain access to a web site or system with the intent of using that activity to steal from the business or individual. They are not trying to prove anything. They don't want publicity. They want money, goods, or information you have.

The cracker is a fraudster and an individual that both you and your IT information security personnel should focus on. These individuals are using the same sites and materials as the hackers, but have crossed the line from proving their ability to attempting to profit from it.

Phreaks

Phreaks are crackers with a major in telephone, cell-phone, and calling-card fraud. Their intent is to steal telephone time and use it or sell it on the street. Phreaks focus on sites that sell telephone, cell phone, and calling cards. They will target these products and attempt to move as much as they can in as short of a time frame as possible.

Phreaks are very focused on certain product types. Some phreaks will stand in public places and memorize people's calling card numbers to resell on the street. Other phreaks set up fake identities to purchase mobile phones they use or sell on the street. Or they focus on stealing prepaid mobile phones and extra minutes. You may have seen these individuals in big cities selling cell phones, all ready for use, with super low charges. Or on one of the auction web sites selling calling cards and prepaid mobile phones. You would be amazed at just how much telephone time is stolen annually by phreaks.

Hactivists

Think of a hacker with an agenda. These folks are the political activists of the fraudsters. They will attempt to hack or crack under the guise that they are serving a higher cause, and they feel this act is a justifiable means of protest. There are plenty of causes to go around, from stopping fur, animal-tested cosmetics, cigarette sales, use of oil, saving the environment, and simply protesting the government.

Hactivists will gain access to a site or system with the firm intent of malicious activity. Whether they personally profit from the act is not of general importance to them. These are the ones who may not just steal from you, which is typically not their style, but will put in a nice tasty virus to shut you down.

Script Kiddies

Script kiddies are your casual fraudsters. They are not hardened fraudsters, and although the idea of potentially pulling off a fraud and profiting from it is nice, they are also motivated by the excitement of doing the theft.

The script kiddie may be a teenager, college student, or highly technical individual who finds out about a tool or method to commit fraud and actually attempts to use it. Script kiddies are not sophisticated criminals. They will be using tools and methods that are highly published, like card generators. They are typically easy to see and stop in your fraud-prevention strategies. Threats of prosecution, use of third-party branding that shows additional fraud checking, and fake information gathering (such as gathering the card security number, but not checking it) are typically enough to scare them off.

Criminal Gangs

The criminal gang is an organized group who intend to steal money, goods, or services from one or more merchants. The criminal gang has multiple people involved in their scheme and will put as much effort into hiding their activity as they do in actually committing the fraud.

The criminal gang thinks big. They aren't likely to be the ones trying to steal consumer data from your systems; rather, they are the ones using stolen consumer data from skimming to move product from your site. They will set up drop points and fake addresses for coordinated thefts at multiple merchants all going to a single address, which will disappear the next day. They may also use freight forwarders to move product out of the country.

Audacity is a word I would use to describe the criminal gang. One of the scams pulled off by an organized criminal ring was the collection of consumer debit and ATM card numbers and PINs. The gang created realistic-looking ATM machines. They went out to stores with ATM machines and replaced them with the fake ones, which would collect the ATM card information and PINs. The ATM machine would tell the consumer the network is down and the consumer would wander off. The next day, they came back and replaced the old machine. Then they harvested the numbers and started to withdraw money from the ATM cards.

Another excellent scam pulled off by criminal gangs is the set-up of fake web sites that have the exact same look and feel as a real web site on which they can collect logons and passwords. The gang sets up a fake web site with the same web address as the real web site, with a one letter difference that will pull up a web site that looks exactly the same, and then collect the logon and password information and break into the accounts to send themselves money or steal credit card data. There was a very well-publicized case of this with PayPal in which the gangs set up web sites like www.paypalnet.com, www.paypal1.com, and www.paypalsecure.com.

White-Collar Criminals

White-collar criminals are those individuals who attempt to defraud a business from the inside. These individuals are motivated by greed and money, and they exploit inside information and/or access to personally profit. The white-collar criminal could be working with external fraudsters, gangs, or individuals. There are many different definitions for white-collar crime, but for the purposes of CNP fraud, I label white-collar criminals as either active or passive.

Active white-collar criminals directly attempt to steal consumer data to process fraudulent orders against that business or other businesses.

They may directly place orders into the system, or monitor and accept orders that they know are fraudulent.

The passive white-collar criminals pass on information about policies and procedures to external personnel so they can commit the fraud. They are paid by the other criminals, but they are feeding the information they need to stay under the radar screen of the fraud-prevention activities of the merchant.

Reporting Fraud

So what do you do once fraud has occurred? As a merchant, who do you contact to report the crime? How do you try to prove your case to the issuing bank?

When you find that a fraudulent transaction has occurred, you can report it in several ways. One of the ways is to use an online resource called the Internet Fraud Complaint Center (IFCC). The IFCC is a partnership between the Federal Bureau of Investigation (FBI) and the National White Collar Crime Center (NW3C).

The IFCC's mission is to address fraud committed over the Internet. For victims of Internet fraud, IFCC provides a convenient and easy-to-use reporting mechanism that alerts authorities of a suspected criminal or civil violation. For law enforcement and regulatory agencies at all levels, IFCC offers a central repository for complaints related to Internet fraud, works to quantify fraud patterns, and provides timely statistical data of current fraud trends.

What to Do If You Are Suspicious

If you are suspicious about an order, try to verify the transaction by asking the customer for additional information. These requests should be made in a conversational tone so as not to arouse the customer's suspicions. If the customer balks or asks why the information is needed, simply say that you are trying to protect cardholders from the high cost of fraud.

If you are on the phone with the consumer, put them on hold and call your acquiring bank for a Code 10 authorization. A separate phone call to your authorization center asking for a Code 10 authorization lets the center know you have concerns about a transaction. Ask for the name of the financial institution on the front of the card. Separately confirm the order with the customer. Send a note to his or her billing address rather than the shipping address. Upon shipping the goods, make sure you ship them with a signature required.

For addresses in which goods have been shipped and stolen, report it to the postal inspector at the USPS in the area the fraud has occurred. This is important as they track fraud by address and may have had other reports for the same address. They may implement a sting operation and/or be able to help you in a prosecution.

For large cases, contact your local police, FBI, or Secret Service resources to see about pursuing potential investigation. Don't be surprised if your local law enforcement agency doesn't jump in to help you. There are a lot of cases of fraud, and unless you have a substantial loss or proof of a larger ring that would catch the attention of broader investigations, they won't be willing to get involved. Even if they find the culprit, unless the dollars involved are substantial, pursuing a prosecution may be difficult.

Understanding the Law and Fraud Prevention

In developing your fraud-prevention strategy, make sure you consult with your legal department about what information you collect, store, and use to prevent fraud. Likewise, make sure you have a clear understanding of how you need to word your responses to the consumer to make sure you don't have to meet other reporting and legal requirements for notifying the consumer.

So what legislation and legal points should you follow as a fraud practitioner? First and foremost, make sure you understand the ins and outs of consumer data protection. From legislation such as the European Union Privacy Directive on Protection of Personal Data to privacy policies and appropriate use policies, what you do with consumer data can leave you open to very large lawsuits. Likewise, make sure you understand how the Fair Credit Reporting Act (FCRA) and the Homeland Security Act apply to your vertical market and sales channels.

Fair Credit Reporting Act

The Fair Credit Reporting Act mandates that agencies granting credit to a consumer who decide not to grant credit must send notice to the consumer of adverse action. FCRA was originally designed to help consumers understand why they weren't approved for mortgages. The focus of FCRA was to explain to consumers the points of credit worthiness that were used in consideration of a loan and why the credit was not granted.

The fact you decide not to sell someone something because you suspect fraud does not mean you have to send notice or have to follow FCRA. But if you word your denial in such a way that indicates or sounds to the consumer that you are denying him or her credit, you could be held liable under FCRA. If you are granting credit in any form (such as credit cards, same as cash), you should be prepared to meet FCRA requirements.

European Union Privacy Directive on Protection of Personal Data

The European Union Privacy Directive is actually a framework for legislation directing member countries to act upon the framework to state specific country requirements for obtaining consent from consumers on the use and storage of any personal data.

This directive has led to the implementation of country-specific acts, such as the United Kingdom Data Protection Act of 1998. The main point you need to remember about these acts is that each country will have different requirements on how you maintain and secure data associated with consumers from their countries. Privacy is the key concern of these acts.

If you are doing business internationally, make sure you check with your legal department about specific requirements for the countries you do business in.

Consumer Data Protection Requirements

There are a number of pieces of legislation out there about handling consumer data and how you have kept it secure as a merchant. Your legal department is the best place to find specific guidance. Saying that, remember that all of this legislation is dynamic and could change at any time. For example, the McCain Legislation defines data handling and consumer redress mechanisms as exceptions for fraud checks and would override FCRA, but could be years before it is enacted.

The FTC, using existing statutes such as "Safe Harbor" for Internet companies, states that "if you have a policy, disclose what you do with data, and comply with your stated policy," then you're okay. If you don't disclose what you do, or do something you've stated you don't do, you're subject to federal prosecution.

Under statutes, such as the Unfair Trade Practices Act, you will find that you need to notify consumers what will happen with the data obtained in the purchase activity.

The issue of protecting consumer data is directly related to concerns of online privacy. Online privacy can be defined as customers' expectations that their online activities, transactions, and preferences will be kept private, not used, misused or misrepresented, or otherwise used in unacceptable ways.

Consumers, government, and businesses are concerned about the use of personal data. These concerns are the driving force behind the calls for legislation to protect this information. This, in turn, broadens the implications for businesses and scares consumers about identity theft and too much government control.

The government is responding to the people; businesses are worried about implications for expanding e-commerce business, which leaves us all in a quandary. The Internet is not owned by any one country. The laws enacted by one country can affect merchants from other countries, so who has jurisdiction? Who do you call if you have a problem?

In a survey done by Harris/Westin in 1998, over 90 percent of the consumers surveyed were "concerned" or "very concerned" about threats to privacy. Of those surveyed, 60 percent wanted laws to govern how information was used on the Internet and 70 percent would favor industry efforts over regulation if companies and associations could implement effective practices. A 2008 Ponemon survey discovered that 77 percent of respondents claimed to be concerned or very concerned about loss or theft of personal information and 72 percent of respondents believed that their chances of becoming a victim of identity theft was greater than 20 percent. The NYCE 2008–2009 Internet Purchase Study of 2,500 respondents found that 43.5 percent of respondents who don't shop online and 26 percent of respondents who don't often shop online cited security concerns as the primary reason they didn't.

Even with this overwhelming concern, each of us every day agree to give up some of our privacy by trading information online in order to get some other information or service. From registering to view articles to giving age and habit data to see our horoscope, we all make choices. In most of these cases, our intent with sharing information is to get a more personalized experience on the web.

The promise of easier searches, simplified purchasing, free stuff, and group buying power seem to lure us in. But what are these merchants and businesses doing with our personal data? Just how safe is it? Consumers are scared about identity theft, and they are scared about losing their transparency online as well. Who can blame them with the stories in the news and papers today? No one wants to live in a society that is watched 24/7 by Big Brother, but no one wants to be a victim, either.

The fastest way to lose revenue is to not take consumer privacy seriously. No amount of marketing, attractive pricing, or convenience will entice a consumer to conduct business online or offline if they believe that in conducting that business, their personal information will be compromised.

If you do any business online today, you will see that the use of a privacy policy is now the norm. This has not always been the case. As consumer awareness heightened with big stories on thefts of card data, business awareness also increased to make sure they were doing things to ease that consumer concern. Over the last 10 years, there have been a lot of third-party organizations that have entered the scene to attempt to enforce privacy policies, such as TRUSTe, BBBOnline, and others.

Businesses today are concerned not only with soothing consumer concerns to keep them coming back, but also about their ability to use consumer information in fraud prevention and investigations of crime. They are also concerned about the repercussions of using that data. In using it, will it leave them open to future litigation? Will it instigate hacking attacks or spur some type of governmental investigations? None of these activities is good for business.

Consumers and businesses must work together to make protection of consumer data easier and safer for conducting business. As a business today, provide your consumer with choices, and as a consumer, take the time to understand what you are agreeing to when you are exploring the web. We all need to hope that government will take a slow and deliberate path on any sweeping legislation to allow the new commerce channels, such as eConsumer, to grow up.

As for our law enforcement community, they will have to catch up and set up new techniques to combat the growing fraud issues with e-commerce, and all of us as merchants doing business online must be proactive in using the data we do collect to try to prevent fraud and abuse. Those businesses that don't take this step won't be around for long.

Chapter Summary

While CNP transactions offer fraudsters more anonymity than stealing directly from a brick and mortar, they are not synonymous with fraud. Fraud has always been around, and e-commerce has only provided another avenue for fraudsters to exploit.

Not all fraudsters have the same motivation or capabilities; understanding the potential motivation and capabilities of a fraudster can help in the prioritization of work efforts. Beyond motivation and capabilities, fraud prevention professionals should never underestimate the knowledge level of fraudsters; they are evolving and changing constantly, just as you are.

Successful fraud prevention practitioners understand the importance of change as part of their everyday needs to monitor and reassess their fraud prevention strategies. In essence, simply fixing what caused a loss yesterday will not ensure you aren't a victim tomorrow.

Finally when it comes to the collection and use of consumer data for fraud prevention, there are some things you may want to do, and some things you have to do, based on the business and the region in which your company does business. Don't assume someone else in your organization has done the due diligence on legal requirements for the collection, use, and storage of consumer data.

Notes

1. www.digitalriver.com/corporate/pdfs/59951100.pdf.
2. http://economictimes.indiatimes.com/News_by_Industry/Credit_card_numbers_up_for_grabs_at_Rs_16/articleshow/3009404.cms.
3. www.australianit.news.com.au/story/0,24897,24937185-15306,00.html.

CHAPTER 4

Fraud Management Key Concepts

After reading this chapter, you will be able to:

- Discuss the differences between solutions, strategies, techniques, tools, and signals.
- Discuss the fraud-solution provider landscape in terms of what is available.
- Define best practices for technique and vendor evaluation.
- Describe what managed services are and when they should be considered.
- Discuss the anatomy of a fraud strategy.

Fraud Terminology

Rules, strategies, business processes, checklists, weights, techniques, tools, tests, modules, applets, policies, procedures, queries, lookups, investigations, reviews, requests, confirmations, qualifications, signals, audits, compliance, verifications, quality assurance, and quality control. It seems everyone has his or her own vocabulary and language to talk about how they prevent fraud.

I am not trying to define an official fraud-practitioner-speak in this book, but I want to define some concepts so everyone understands context. In working with your peers, don't get stuck on what everyone calls a solution, technique, or process; instead, focus on what it does. I have had more titles than I can remember, and I have had to explain my role and duties to customers on more than one occasion, but I didn't take it personally.

I like to keep my conceptual planning simple—the simpler the better. This is important because if your staff and peers can't understand what you are talking about when you walk them through it, you probably need to rethink how you are presenting it. I have found in some extreme cases that the conceptualizations and processes put into place at a business were so complicated it would take over a week with people from multiple departments just to decipher what was actually being done. This does not instill confidence in your management, and it could cost you valuable time in spotting a fraud trend.

Key Fraud Management Terms

Solution: the physical grouping of tools used along with their supported features and techniques.

Strategy: the logical grouping of techniques and signals used to support a business event.

Tools: the individual applications, SaaS, or data sources used in a fraud solution.

Features: the exposed capabilities a tool provides for accessing and/or customizing data into a usable signal.

Signal: the actual or derived response from techniques (i.e., credit card address verification service [AVS] return value = "FULL MATCH").

Technique: a method for applying business process, experience, policies, and rule logic to evaluate, predict, or determine potential outcome. Techniques can comprise one or more tools to produce one or more signals (i.e., identity authentication, rules, phone verification, modeling).

Event: a business workflow component that directly relates to the management and flow of customer interaction (i.e., purchase, return, account change, chargeback, compliant).

Outcome: the final disposition recommendation of a fraud management solution strategy (i.e., accept, review, reject).

Flow and control: selective processing for certain transaction characteristics (i.e., perform additional checks on orders where bill-to and ship-to addresses don't match and overnight shipping has been selected).

At the highest level is the use of *solution* and *strategy* in reference to your fraud management program. In the context of the Total Risk Management Methodology (TRMM[SM]) used by The Fraud Practice,[1] the term *solution* is used to describe the physical components used for fraud management, and the term *strategy* is used to describe the logical components used for fraud management.

So when a company describes its fraud solution, it is talking about the tools, features, and techniques it uses for fraud management. For example, a company's fraud solution may use rules, velocities, credit card AVS, card security codes, and blacklists. When a company talks about its strategy, it is talking about the events, signals, flow, and terms for outcome. For example, a company may allow first-time buyers only when the credit card AVS comes back with a full match (see Exhibit 4.1).

To understand the differences between tools, features, signals, and techniques, let's look at the credit card authorization process as an example. In terms of definition, the credit card authorization process represents a tool for fraud management. Credit card authorizations expose multiple usable features: AVS, card security code, authorization response, enhanced authorization, and SecureCode/VBV. Each of these features provides one or more signals a fraud professional can use within fraud-prevention techniques like rules and velocities (see Exhibit 4.2).

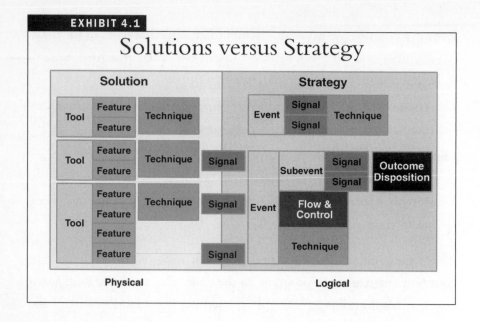

EXHIBIT 4.1 Solutions versus Strategy

Not every company breaks down or talks about its fraud management program with this level of depth. For most fraud professionals, understanding the differences between fraud-prevention strategies and fraud-prevention techniques will be their entire focus. Understanding

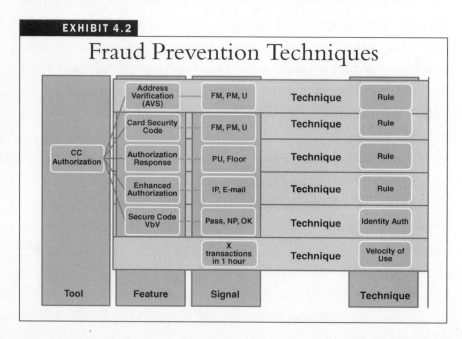

EXHIBIT 4.2 Fraud Prevention Techniques

that, let's spend a little more time refining the differences between these two concepts.

Fraud strategies consist of business processes and fraud-prevention techniques. A strategy is intended to manage fraud losses while keeping administration costs and sales conversion at acceptable levels. A technique is intended to check for a specific condition in an order and to prevent an order from processing if it passes or fails that check. A technique can be used to validate positive or negative conditions, and can be either interrogatory or descriptive.

To illustrate the two concepts and how they work together, I will use an example that most of us have thought about. Most of us have a retirement strategy. We state that we want to have a certain amount of money by the time we reach a certain age so we can retire comfortably. Now there are a lot of different ways we could attempt to reach this goal: We could put money into a 401k, IRA, stocks, bonds, certificates of deposit, or lottery tickets. Each of these is a technique for investing, and each provides different potential returns with varying degrees of risk. Our strategy has to take into consideration our age, our comfort with risk, and our day-to-day needs to survive.

Creating a fraud-prevention strategy is not that different. You have to understand the goals of your business and weigh the value of each technique you implement to understand the associated costs and implications to administration costs, fraud reduction, and potentially lost revenue.

EXECUTIVE INSIGHT

Avoid the Silver Bullet Syndrome

MARK WALICK, DIRECTOR, FRAUD MANAGEMENT SOLUTIONS, GSI COMMERCE

Each transaction or event is like building a puzzle, and each data point and fraud-solution tool is a puzzle piece. Some transactions

Remember fraud-prevention techniques are the building blocks of your fraud-prevention strategy, and your strategy will only be as strong as your understanding of their use.

Anatomy of Fraud Strategy

In this section, I discuss some basics of strategy design to get you started. Again, the goal of this book is to give you an understanding of the fundamentals of e-commerce fraud-prevention techniques, and it does not go into extensive detail on designing a fraud-prevention strategy, as this would render the strategy useless because it would be in the public domain.

Saying that, let's talk about the basics of strategy design. There are five major phases of a strategy:

1. Prescreen
2. Payment
3. Postscreen
4. Review
5. Accounting

Each phase has distinct goals and techniques that can be used to accomplish those goals (see Exhibit 4.3).

The purpose of breaking the business process into phases is to make you look at your business process in terms of goals. For each phase, there

EXHIBIT 4.3	
Phases of Strategy	
Phase	**Activities**
Prescreen	Hot Lists
	Positive Lists
	Velocity of Change
	Velocity of Use
	Rules
	Consumer Authentication
	Verified by Visa
	MasterCard SecureCode
Payment	Authorization
	Address Verification Service
	Advanced Address Verification
	ACH (electronic checking)
	Debit
	Card Security Check
Postscreen	Geolocation
	Fraud Scoring
	Modeling
	Reverse Address and Phone Lookups
	Credit Checks
Review	Call Back Consumer
	Call Bank
	Cross-Check of Buying History
	Query Order Activity
Accounting	Settlements
	Credits
	Chargeback Processing
	Sharing and Updating Information with Peers and Partners
	Educations
	Tuning of Strategy

is a definitive goal of what you want to achieve. By looking at the business process in this fashion, you can look at new fraud techniques and more quickly envision where they fit into your strategy.

The prescreen phase is used to review an order's information to determine acceptance criteria. This phase is typically automated, and it conducts rules and checks in an attempt to eliminate orders you will not do business with regardless of any other checks. In the prescreen phase, you are trying to weed out orders, with the intent of saving time and money. Why process authorizations or other fraud-prevention checks on an order if you know you won't take the order regardless of the outcome? Examples of orders being cut out here are those that are international when the company only does business in the United States, or the rejecting of an order because it contains data on your internal hot list.

In the payment phase, you are conducting the processes and checks required to accept an order. This includes getting an authorization, address verification information, and card security check data.

The postscreen phase is when you perform your advanced reviews on orders that have passed the prescreen and payment phases. This includes using business logic as well as advanced fraud-prevention techniques. Typically the first thing you want to check in this phase is the positive list to see if you can automatically pass all other tests.

The review phase includes all of the postscreening checks you do to attempt to catch fraud or to convert orders. This phase is a manual phase, and it can be as simple as doing spot checks on orders or as complex as having review queues and manual sorting.

The accounting phase starts once an order has been fully accepted and lasts until 12 months after the sale. This includes processing credits, settlements, reauthorizations, chargebacks, and tuning of the overall fraud-prevention strategy.

Typically the prescreen, payment, and postscreen phases are automated and occur in real time. The review and accounting phases will make use of automation tools but are mainly manual processes.

Designing a Strategy Based on Risk Exposure

One approach to designing a strategy is looking at the level of risk your company is exposed to. The higher your risk, the more you will rely on fraud-prevention techniques and the more extensive the checks will have to be.

For some merchants, the level of risk is so small that the standard address verification and card security schemes offered by the credit card associations will be more than enough. For example, the education, utilities, and government sectors can reach out and touch their consumers; they are much less likely to be defrauded. Not that it doesn't happen—it's just not that high of a concern.

Exhibit 4.4 provides a breakout of fraud-prevention techniques by the level of risk a merchant is exposed to. View the three levels of

---

EXHIBIT 4.4

Levels of Risk

Level of Risk	Description
Low Risk	• Looking for lowest-cost solution • Low volume • High margin • Clothing, utilities, tuition, insurance • Fraud rate less than .25% or total losses below $5,000 per year
Medium Risk	• Medium to high volume • Low to medium margin • High fenceability: electronics, toys, games, music, personal services, books, clothing, travel, international business • Fraud rate greater than .75% or total losses exceed $50,000 per year
High Risk	• Medium to high volume • Low to medium margin • Very high fenceability: electronic downloads, high-end electronics, financial vehicles, gift cards, adult, gaming, rechargeable cell phones, travel, international business, credit line or card issuance • Fraud rate greater than 1% or total fraud losses exceed $100,000 per year

risk and determine which category you fall into. In looking at the characteristics, they are not meant to be all–inclusive—you may only meet one or two of the criteria listed. These characteristics are meant to form a guide to determine the level of risk you may be exposed to (see Exhibit 4.5).

EXHIBIT 4.5

How to Determine the Level of Risk

	Low Risk	Medium Risk	High Risk
Authorization	•	•	•
Address Verification Service	•	•	•
Card Security	•	•	•
Consumer Authentications	•	•	•
MOD 10 Check	•	•	•
Smart Cards			
Hot Lists	•	•	•
Warm Lists		•	•
Positive Lists		•	•
Velocity of Use		•	•
Velocity of Change		•	•
Geolocation			•
Age Verification			•
Credit Check			•
Out-of-Pocket Checks			•
Fraud Screening		•	•
Internal Rules	•	•	•
Reverse Lookups		•	•
Return E-mail			
Deposit Check			•
Delivery Address Verification			•
Denied Party Check	•	•	•
Manual Review			•
Neural Nets			•
Rules Engine		•	•
Secure Tokens			•
Biometrics			•
E-Commerce Insurance			•

Understanding the Fraud-Solution Provider Landscape

E-commerce consumer-not-present (CNP) sales are growing year over year at a double-digit rate around the world and still account for only a small portion of total retail sales; in some instances, rates triple in sales. Likewise, actual fraud and fraud attempts are keeping pace with this growth with little effect being cited for association-based initiatives such as AVS, card security schemes, and 3D Secure.

There are three fundamental groups of buyers of fraud-prevention services: merchants, payment service providers, and financial institutions. For CNP-specific services, merchants make up the highest percentage of purchases of these services.

According to surveys done by Digital River, 60 percent of merchants use authorizations as a form of fraud prevention, 10 percent use in-house fraud detection measures, and 30 percent outsource their fraud protection programs.[2]

More than 90 percent of payment service providers and financial institutions utilize one or more commercial fraud-prevention services. According to the CyberSource Merchant survey, more than 50 percent of merchants are using multiple commercial services for fraud prevention, with the largest merchants using the largest number of different commercial services.

In 2000, only a handful of vendors offered fraud-prevention services targeted at the e-commerce channel, but today's market consists of hundreds of service providers offering point to complete solutions. With so many choices for merchants to choose from, the need for a clear and concise understanding of their intended solution is critical, as it can be easy to get lost or sidetracked in the marketplace.

Why Merchants Consider Commercial Fraud Solutions

The reasons that motivate a merchant to implement a fraud solution are different from the reasons to use a commercial solution.

The following are the major motivating reasons merchants, payment service providers, and financial institutions look to implement commercial solutions for the organizations:

- *Development skills.* In-house development skills do not exist or are not available for the project.
- *Fraud expertise.* In-house expertise related to fraud does not exist or is not at a level where the company believes it can build a comparable solution to a commercial product or service.
- *Time to market.* Building internally would take too long.
- *Data availability.* Commercial solutions provide access to information that is not available in-house, even if the solution is built internally.
- *Data breadth.* Commercial solutions offer additional data that in-house solutions would never have access to.
- *Lack of sponsorship for internal projects.* Executive team wants internal development efforts to center on core competency and will not support a major development effort in fraud prevention.

The following are the major motivating reasons merchants decide to implement a fraud-prevention strategy/solution:

- *Financial loss.* The company is being hit by fraud or sees increasing attempts and wants to ensure systems are in place to prevent loss due to fraud due to financial impact (this could be low margins, high price point, or a combination of both).
- *Increasing sales conversion.* The company wants to open sales to new regions or to expand sales by allowing more risky orders to be processed.
- *Legal requirements.* The company has a legal requirement to collect, authenticate, and verify information provided by its customers.

- *Lowering operational cost.* The company is looking to automate or reduce the overall cost of processing fraud screening on transactions.

- *Reducing delivery time.* The company is looking to streamline existing fraud-prevention measures with the intent of shortening the overall time to review purchases before making delivery.

Managed Services—Outsourcing

The fraud service provider landscape has changed tremendously over the past 10 years, and so too have merchants' perspectives on the use of outsourced and managed services for some or all of their fraud-prevention needs. Prior to 2004, merchants were far more inclined to want to manage fraud prevention in-house—if they were doing anything at all for fraud prevention—where today more and more merchants are considering managed services as a real option.

The problem is that while merchants are more open to considering managed services, there is a general lack of understanding about what is available as well as a lot of misconceptions on what managed services really means to a merchant.

The notion that all managed service providers are the same and can be compared in an apples-to-apples comparison just isn't the reality of the market. From a macro perspective, there are a number of different ways vendors can offer managed services to a business in terms of features, functionality, service, and performance. Attempting to evaluate managed services based solely on features and functionality can lead to gaps in performance and disappointment in actual results of the service.

The importance of understanding and evaluating how a managed service will fit into a business's operational processes and customer experience along with the lift and shift it offers in cost or support are critical to successfully moving all or part of a company's risk management requirements to a managed service provider. Unlike the process of selecting a fraud tool or solution, where features and functionality are critical to understanding and evaluating what you are getting, a managed service is supposed to offer the ability to implement and forget—meaning that *how* they do it isn't so much important as *how well* they do it.

There isn't just one reason companies decide to consider the use of a managed service in their organization. Companies considering managed services for fraud prevention are really asking themselves, "Do we want to do this and should we be doing this on our own?" The fact is all companies will at some point in their lifetime consider the use of a managed service for some part of their fraud-prevention efforts. Consider the typical motivators for companies to look at managed services: lack of experience, resource constraints, cost, market timing, lack of infrastructure, or lack of will. They mirror typical product development build–versus–buy discussions. While the motivations may be different from one company to another, the constant similarity with all of these companies is the understanding that fraud is a complex problem and a booming business that will continue to grow during these tough economic times.

In terms of a strict definition, managed services describes the process of offloading or outsourcing day-to-day operational management in order to improve, reallocate, or increase ROI within a company's risk management operation. A managed service provider (MSP) is a term used to describe third-party vendors that offer managed services. Managed services are not the same as hosted software or SaaS. The *managed* in managed services implies human resources working on your behalf to fight fraud and perform operational requirements for running the business.

It is important to realize that merchants don't have to give up control when choosing a managed service. There are many types of MSPs offering low to high control for companies. That being said, while managed service providers take on day-to-day operational duties for a company, they typically don't take on the accountability for the performance of these services. Companies considering managed services should understand they need to build in appropriate oversight and monitoring practices to ensure consistent, optimized, and uninterrupted business operations.

While the definition of managed service is consistent, the definition of what services are actually included in these services is not consistent. In short, managed services in the risk management market will mean companies will need to define what managed services needs mean to them; then, they will need to pay close attention to the scope of coverage from one MSP to another to ensure the MSP meets their definition.

MSPs can be categorized into one of four different groups:

1. Point
2. Hybrid
3. Back office
4. End-to-end models

Each one of these categories offers benefits and limitations depending on what the merchant is looking for.

MSPs offering point solutions are focused on providing companies the ability to offload a specific piece of business functionality that they specialize in.

Hybrid-managed solutions run the gamut and can provide merchants with a plethora of choices. What differentiates a hybrid service provider from a point solution provider or end-to-end provider is the ability to customize a solution to meet a company's specific needs.

Back-office MSPs offer specialized packages of services to offer companies the ability to offload logical groupings of functional responsibilities.

End-to-end MSPs offer companies a turnkey solution for risk management. These solution providers provide operational support for day-to-day operations, strategic risk management, and input into a company's product management efforts to ensure risk management components are considered and integrated appropriately in a company's overall product and channel strategy.

In terms of best practices for preparing to evaluate MSPs, create a solution map of all of your operational risk needs that attempts to display the various business support processes, tools, and systems that can help the company optimize risk operations while making effective decisions. Take this solution map and use it to overlay and evaluate the capabilities of each MSP. This approach ensures a consistent evaluation of the capabilities for each vendor. The Fraud Practice recommends the use of four core categories in a solution map:

1. Front end
2. Service connectivity
3. Fraud screening tool chest
4. Operational capabilities

Having a basic understanding of what MSPs offer and the ways you can categorize them is important, but understanding the best practices for evaluating MSPs is even more important. Not all MSPs are equal, and understanding the right questions to ask can mean the difference between a positive and negative experience.

- Do their services focus on and cover your weaknesses?
- Are managed services really their core business?
- Do they know as much or more about fraud in your vertical market?
- Does their culture match your culture, and are you comfortable working with them?

- Do you share a common vision for customer experience?
- Will they make your life easier?
- Do you believe they can be successful in your business?
- Can they customize their solution to meet your unique needs?
- Does their workflow integrate well with your existing business processes?
- What tools and capabilities do they bring to the table?

The decision to use a managed service is not an all-or-nothing decision, nor is it about giving up control of your risk operations. Companies have choices in today's market to offload as much or as little functionality and control as they would desire.

The idea of managed services can be scary to risk personnel in terms of job security, so based on your company's reason for looking at managed services, make sure you keep your team informed. There are many reasons other than reducing headcount for making the decision to evaluate MSPs.

Regardless of the category of MSP a company chooses to work with, companies will need to have an internal resource to provide direction, liaise, and supervise the MSP.

Managed services are not necessarily more expensive than existing fraud-prevention tools and, in many cases, can be purchased for less than merchants would pay to set up and run them on their own.

Fraud Tool/Solution Categories

To make sense of the competitive landscape and to properly compare tools and solutions, you need to bundle service and software providers into categories, based on similar capabilities and use cases. These categories then allow the direct comparison of vendors on their capabilities and pricing.

The fact is not all vendors offer the same types of services. There can be major differences in what you will get from a tool and its features. Tools and techniques don't offer the same uplift across vertical markets, regions, or payment channels, and the actual applicability to any given merchant's fraud needs must be closely evaluated. When discussing the historical results of a tool or technique, make sure you have a proper understanding of the context in which the tool was used.

Additionally, trying to compare the capabilities and results across categories can be misleading. For instance, comparing an identity authentication provider with an IP geolocation provider wouldn't make much sense because they are fundamentally doing different things for a merchant.

In all, there are eight categories of fraud solution providers. Each category is described below.

Group 1: Guaranteed Fraud-Solution Providers

These solution providers are able to manage merchants' fraud under the association guidelines and are willing to eat merchants' fraud losses. They typically charge more for their services, a percentage in most cases, and have a more invasive consumer experience.

Fraud-solution providers: Fraud Sciences (now owned by PayPal), PreCharge, and Verified by Visa.

Competitive position: With guaranteed payments, merchants have no need for any other solutions; a solution provider would have to be servicing these service providers. This being said, there are two major market forces prohibiting the expansion of these types of solutions: the financial risk and the cost to merchants to use such a service.

The financial risk of such a model is so great that very few fraud-solution vendors have the proper funding to make larger clients comfortable with using them. Additionally, the market is still not ready to spend the money on these services because they still believe they can do it cheaper.

Market penetration: Very low market penetration; they are still priced higher than the fraud losses of most retailers. Some low-margin and high-price retailers do use these services.

Group 2: Identity Providers

These providers offer solutions to perform identity authentication and verification services. They typically are focused on verifying the actual data points of an identity and not the purchase traffic. They are typically low-cost solutions and are really more like tools—alone they generally will not be enough to stop fraud. They are a requirement for application boarding, KYC, and compliance, and would be needed on top of any fraud solution. Verifying an identity is a key component of a fraud solution, but must include verification and authentication. Likewise, identity is not enough for strong fraud protection; you still need to have behavioral indicators as well.

Fraud-solution providers: Experian, Equifax, TransUnion, Idinsight, TargusINFO, Verid, GBGroup (URU), 192.com, Entrust Bharosa (bought out by Oracle), Arcot, Aristotle, CSI Identity, Idology, Strikeforce, Identity to Go, RSA, IDAnalytics, First Logic, Group One, Veratad, Acxiom, InfoUSA, Whitepages.com, Authentify, Service Objects Ltd.

Competitive position: Merchants and financial institutions will continue to need these providers, even with the use of other fraud-prevention practices, internal or commercial. Some players such as IDAnalytics are bending this group into a model more related to data sharing. In general, these solutions are handicapped by the fact that each country has different laws and resources to verify this information; it is very difficult to cross borders with the solution without having to have multiple solutions. Additionally, these solutions are still considered to be consumer unfriendly in the merchants' view, requiring too much data from the consumer and too much interaction, and the merchants blame these services for abandonment.

Market penetration: High market penetration and high usage. Major complexities with these solutions in cross–border application.

Group 3: Fraud-Scoring Providers

These solution providers offer fraud-scoring solutions based on multiple factors that allow merchants to make better risk decisions. They may or may not use shared data. The key thing to understand is that shared data in the context of these providers is typically associated with shared velocities.

Fraud–solution providers: CyberSource, MaxMind, ReD, OrderSpy, Digital Envoy, Fraud Guardian, Bizchord, SafeCharge, Mango, Lexis-Nexis Riskwise, The ai Corporation, TrustMarque Risk Guardian, Digital River.

Competitive position: These are the dominant players in the space today with both mind share and market share. For merchants, if they can pay for a scoring service and it works without needing to do manual reviews, so much the better. These solutions are typically not well suited to high-risk vertical markets, and they suffer from the shortfall that they really work only for specific verticals, if they are really good. By the time you reduce a fraud-scoring service to the level where it can be useful for multiple verticals, you end up watering down the actual results. (For instance, the value of a fraud score to the gambling industry versus the retail-apparel industry is very different.)

Market penetration: Very high penetration with numerous providers in the market today.

Group 4: Shared Network Providers

These solution providers promote, run, and/or facilitate the sharing of customer and transactional data for risk management. These providers can use public and/or private data as part of their solutions.

Fraud-solution providers: Merchant Risk Council, ID Analytics, Early Warning Services, Ethoca, 3rd Man Group, Letix, Hat card File, Click Fraud Network, APACS, CIFAS

Competitive position: Emerging sector; they are all maturing and experiencing the same issues with data quality, critical mass, and legal scrutiny.

Market penetration: Low penetration, a lot of barriers to adoption on this, beginning with legal and flowing through competitive advantage and ending with data quality. Pockets in the United Kingdom and United States have formed but have had mixed results.

Group 5: Technology Providers

These solution providers have developed niche technology solutions to prevent fraud. These solutions face multiple barriers to market adoption, including consumer adoption, invasiveness, difficulty of use, and in some cases lack of a proven track record. They include the use of secure tokens, biometrics, phone verification, device identification, geolocation, certificates, and picture presentment.

Fraud-solution providers: Telesign, Iovation, 41st Parameter, RSA, Authentify, Dynamics LLC, Cardinal Commerce, Cardcops, Orbiscom, Emue Technologies, Identiphi, Digital Persona, VoiceVault, PerSay, Spriv, Trade Harbor, MaxMind, Nuance, L-1, Quova, Digital Envoy, Fraud Labs, Onverify, PhoneConfirm.

Competitive position: Indirect threat; even with the previously listed issues, these are typically very strong solutions and have good adoption. These providers are typically seen more as a tool than a solution, and in some cases, this perception can lead to the view that they are too costly and require time to mature. Geolocation is a good example of a technology play that has gotten enough traction to become a de facto standard in the industry. In the case of geolocation, other solution providers are now integrating this technology into their own solutions.

Market penetration: Low to high penetration depending on the base technology play; a lot of barriers to adoption. Most have found vertical markets they thrive in, but have not been able to duplicate this success when they attempt to go horizontal with the techniques.

Group 6: Analytic Providers

These solution providers focus on providing tools or services related to the analysis of data to create custom models and blended solutions. The key word is *modeling*, and more specifically the building of custom models. These could be simple regression models, neural nets, or Bayesian models. There are several components to this type of solution: the data analysis, design, and the actual building and running of a model-based solution. Providers may offer solutions that perform only one or the other, or in some cases both. These solutions are typically much more expensive than traditional fraud services, and they rely heavily on the availability of clean historical data. These solutions also require a true commitment on the part of the purchaser; to work best, you will need to have skilled resources on staff to tune and maintain them.

Fraud-solution providers: Fair Isaac, Brighterion, Lexis Nexis, Choicepoint, Retail Decisions ReD (Prism), SAS, Alaric, eFunds, EMC, Infoglide.

Competitive position: For financial institutions, these solutions are a must. The cost and complexity of these solutions prevents these solutions from being widely adopted at the merchant level.

Market penetration: High penetration in financial institutions, low penetration in merchant and payment service provider space, a lot of barriers to adoption, and very costly to implement.

Group 7: Data Quality Providers

Data quality providers are focused on providing tools and services for the cleaning, standardization, and viability screening of customer-provided data. These services are typically focused on the address and phone data elements. These services provide organizations several key benefits, including the ability to store clean data, improving velocity checks, and reducing duplication. They can also reduce operational inefficiencies like undeliverable shipments and being unable to contact customers due to fat-fingered data input. From a fraud perspective, these tools provide only rudimentary value, more of an overall uplift due to data quality than creating any ability to catch fraud.

All organizations should be doing data quality checks, but not all use a third-party vendor for this.

Fraud-solution providers: QAS, Cdyne, DataXLTD, Qualified Address, Infosolve Technologies, Correct Address, Equifax, Citation Software, Globalz, APOK Technology, United States Postal Service, Intelligent Search Technology, Experian, CyberSource, ATTUstech, Truth Technologies.

Competitive position: None; they will always be required in the industry.

Market penetration: High penetration, very good adoption.

Group 8: Operational Providers

You can think of operational providers as infrastructure providers. They provide the core systems companies need to build out fraud solutions and strategies. These solutions are typically purchased in addition to other fraud-prevention services and tools, and in most cases don't represent a complete solution in and of themselves (meaning you will have to use some other third-party data source, which may be integrated into their solutions, but still required to achieve optimal use and performance).

Operational providers also typically provide some tools, solutions, and services intended to streamline, automate, and improve manual operational procedures. These solutions may include the review of transactions, manual reviews, chargeback representation, or reconciliation. Most organizations tend to overlook the true financial cost, resource allocation, and time spent on these operational requirements. All organizations are performing these tasks, and most have built home-grown solutions, or are using other systems, such as CRM and merchant accounting systems to perform these tasks. Mature and larger organizations tend to seek these types of commercial solutions when they reach the point that they can't seem to shoehorn the risk requirements into existing systems.

Fraud-solution providers: Accertify, FNIS, SHS Viveon, MasterCard EMS (uses Brighterion for analytics), Retail Decisions ReD Shield, CyberSource (Outsource), Transmedia, Vindicia, Chargeback Experts, (41st Parameter Fraudnet).

Competitive position: These systems are very sticky and have the capacity to become the hub of risk architecture.

Market penetration: Low penetration, still meets resistance in the market as the cost is typically additive in nature to fraud-prevention services.

Now that you have a basic understanding of the fraud tool/solution categories the next seven chapters will focus on introducing the most commonly used types of techniques within these fraud categories.

Chapter Summary

There are a number of key terms associated with CNP fraud management that everyone in e-commerce should know, but the two key terms to understand are *strategy* and *technique*. For most fraud professionals, understanding the differences between fraud-prevention strategies and fraud-prevention techniques will be all they need to focus on. Fraud strategies consist of business processes and fraud-prevention techniques. A strategy is intended to manage fraud losses while keeping

administration costs and sales conversion at acceptable levels. A technique is intended to check for a specific condition in an order and to
prevent an order from processing if it passes or fails that check. A technique can be used to validate positive or negative conditions, and can be
either interrogatory or descriptive.

In designing a strategy for risk management, the first priority is to
understand the level of risk to which your company is exposed. The
higher your risk, the more you will rely on fraud-prevention techniques
and the more extensive the checks will have to be. A fraud strategy can
consist of up to five major phases:

1. Prescreen

2. Payment

3. Postscreen

4. Review

5. Accounting

Each phase has distinct goals and techniques that can be used to accomplish those goals. The purpose of breaking the business process into
phases is to make you look at your business process in terms of goals. For
each phase, there is a definitive goal of what you want to achieve. By
looking at the business process in this fashion, you can look at new fraud
techniques and more quickly envision where they fit into your strategy.

When it comes to buying commercial services for fraud solutions,
there are three fundamental groups of buyers of fraud-prevention services: merchants, payment service providers, and financial institutions.
For CNP-specific services, merchants make up the highest percentage
of purchases of these services. In 2000, only a handful of vendors offered
fraud-prevention services targeted at the e-commerce channel, while
today's market consists of hundreds of service providers offering point to
complete solutions. With so many options for merchants to choose
from, the need for a clear and concise understanding of their intended

solution is critical, as it can be easy to get lost or sidetracked in the marketplace.

To make sense of the numerous tools and solutions available, and to properly compare tools and solutions, you need to bundle service and software providers into categories based on similar capabilities and use cases. These categories allow the direct comparison of vendors on their capabilities and pricing.

The fact is, not all vendors offer the same types of services. There can be major differences in what you will get from a tool and its features. Tools and techniques don't offer the same uplift across vertical markets, regions, or payment channels, and the actual applicability to any given merchant's fraud needs must be closely evaluated. When discussing the historical results of a tool or technique, make sure you have a proper understanding of the context in which the tool was used.

In all, there are eight categories of fraud-solution providers:

1. Guaranteed-solution providers

2. Identity providers

3. Fraud-scoring providers

4. Data sharing providers

5. Analytic providers

6. Technology providers

7. Data quality providers

8. Operational providers

Notes

1. www.fraudpractice.com.
2. www.digitalriver.com/corporate/pdfs/59951100.pdf.

CHAPTER 5

Fraud Prevention Techniques: Identity Proofing

After reading this chapter, you will be able to:

- Describe the benefits and limitations of the card association address verification systems (AVS) and card security code (CSC, CVV) programs.
- Describe the threat freight forwarders have on physical good transactions.
- Define reverse lookups and know when they are used.
- Describe the difference between telephone identification, authentication, and verification.

Address Verification Services

Address verification systems (AVS) is a tool provided by credit card associations and issuing banks to allow merchants to check the submitted billing address to see if it is on file with the issuing bank. The AVS check is usually done as part of a merchant's request for authorization on the credit card. When a merchant makes a request, the address is checked against the address on file at the issuing bank. AVS is supported in the United States, Canada, and the

United Kingdom. Visa, MasterCard, American Express, and Discover Card all support AVS. For other card types, check with your payment processor.

You may see AVS defined as either "address verification system" or "address verification service." Both refer to the same thing and they can be used interchangeably. In general, when AVS is referred to as a system it means the AVS program across association brands, and when it is referred to as a service, it means the technical components a merchant uses to access the program.

How Good Is It?

The reliability of AVS is suspect. There are a lot of viable reasons that the billing address the consumer gives a merchant could differ from what the issuing bank has on file. Reasons range from recent moves or smaller issuing banks that use third-party services who can't keep the records up to date, to frequently traveling consumers who use a family member's address as the address of record. AVS is not a good indicator for fraudulent activity. The fact is if merchants implement AVS incorrectly, they could drop between 5 and 28 percent of their good orders.

Here are other key features of AVS:

- It will help in disputing chargebacks because you have a transaction in which the consumer's billing address on the order is the same as what is on file at the issuing bank.

- It verifies only the first five digits of the address and the zip code. It is still possible to have returned goods if the consumer simply makes a typo when entering his or her address.

- This should be one of the first fraud-prevention capabilities a merchant should implement. If merchants are not using AVS today, they should be. Implementing AVS is easy, and it can help them in prioritizing the orders they want to review.

TIPS AND TECHNIQUES

- AVS is available only from banks. Merchants using payment software or gateways that talk about AVS should understand that these applications and services only support the AVS information flow and cannot offer a merchant the actual AVS check.

- AVS in the United Kingdom is set up differently than the United States. In the United Kingdom, the AVS and card security check are combined in the same request and in the same response code, whereas in the United States, the AVS and card security check are separated.

- If you are a merchant, you should contact your payment processor on the use and implementation of AVS. The AVS check is typically done as part of the authorization call and is done in real time on the e-commerce engine. In implementing AVS, you will have to have logic to interpret the codes that your payment processor sends back to you. You will need to properly route the order based on the information you receive from the payment processor.

- Typically, it takes anywhere from a day to a week to implement AVS into your order process. The keys to quickly implementing AVS are to make sure you have a clear plan on what you want to do with an order, based on the return code from the AVS check.

Estimated costs: Merchants can only get AVS from their credit card authorization request. There is no extra cost associated with getting this information, but merchants will need to make changes to their systems to handle the return codes.

Alternative solutions: Merchants can look at delivery address verification, reverse lookups, or geolocation validation.

Vendors: Any acquiring bank or third–party payment processor.

How Does It Work?

AVS is a tool provided by credit card associations and issuing banks to allow merchants to check the submitted billing address to see if it is on file with the issuing bank. The AVS check is usually done as part of the merchant's request for authorization on the card. When a merchant makes a request, the address is checked against the address on file at the issuing bank. Only the first four to five digits of the address and the zip code are verified—nothing else is checked.

Example:

> Mr. John Doe
>
> 1234 USA Street
>
> Realtown, ST 56789

What would be sent to the issuing bank to be checked would be *1234* and *56789.*

Merchants will get one of six codes back from their payment processor indicating what matched: full match, partial match—address, partial match—zip code, no match, international, and unavailable. Using AVS as part of your risk solution is very beneficial, but relying solely on AVS is very dangerous. If merchants implemented a rule in their solution that said they would only take orders that are a full match on AVS, they would have a very high insult rate, as the information contained in the issuing bank can be old, or the items being purchased could be gifts. Merchants would leave a lot of business on the table if they implemented this type of rule.

Likewise, getting a full match for AVS should tell a merchant something as well: There is less risk. If the order's address information is on file with the issuing bank and the merchant is shipping to the record on file, the consumer would have a hard time arguing that he or she did not make the charge.

Regardless of the AVS return value, a merchant can still get a valid authorization on a card. If a merchant got a *no match,* that would be termed a *soft decline* in the eyes of the banks.

How Do I Use the Results?

In the United States, AVS is the most common tool merchants reported using to help prevent fraud. According to the CyberSource 2002 Merchant Fraud Survey, 71 percent of the merchants surveyed were using AVS, and in the 2008 survey they reported 81 percent were using it.

In general, merchants should anticipate the majority of their orders coming in as a full match—plan on between 40 and 80 percent. Visa EU reported in early 2003 that they were seeing a 75 percent full match rate with those merchants using the new AVS service. Just because a merchant gets a response of partial match or no match does not indicate increased risk in accepting an order. Remember, AVS is not a good indicator of fraud. In case studies, the highest actual fraud losses for any one AVS response code was only 11 percent, meaning 89 percent of the orders were valid and good orders. Some merchants will experience much higher fraud losses than this, but there are other rules and fraud-prediction tools that will better isolate fraudulent behavior without sacrificing sales conversion.

Likewise, getting a response from AVS of unavailable or international does not indicate increased risk either, with most merchants reporting the combined fraud losses for these two response codes being less than AVS full match. Some businesses can and will experience a much higher incidence of international fraud than others. This is especially true for digitally downloadable goods and services.

When evaluating how well AVS is doing for a merchant, don't become trapped by the percent of fraud for any one given AVS response value. If you remember earlier in this discussion we pointed out that the highest percentage of orders will be AVS full match, so the highest concentration of dollars at risk will be there, and typically the smallest fraud percentage of loss will also be found on AVS full match. This gives merchants a false sense of security that AVS full match doesn't need their attention on fraud prevention, when this is the greatest number of dollars at risk, and the easiest way to fool most merchants' internal screening procedures.

There are cases in which merchants do have very specific and significant skews on fraud in international and in no match categories. If the skew occurs, this is typically a sign of a fraud attack on the location, site, or store.

Building This In-House

A merchant can easily implement checks to try and verify the consumer's address, but a merchant cannot build anything that can yield the same check to the bank records. Merchants who really want to verify this information further can perform a manual review by calling the issuing bank to verify the data or doing a reverse lookup.

Advanced Address Verification

Advanced address verification (AAV+) goes beyond AVS and checking the billing address on file with what the cardholder provided to also check the shipping address, e-mail address, and phone number. This service is only available on American Express and is relatively new with the last major changes occurring as recent as March 2009, so check to make sure your gateway or acquirer supports it.

How Good Is It?

AAV+ is a real-time solution for merchants doing e-commerce, mail order, or phone orders. AAV+ is not the same as AVS. AVS is checking the billing address on file with the issuing bank; AAV+ is checking the shipping address, e-mail address, and phone number on file. The service is provided exclusively by American Express and is intended to check the billing and shipping address when the two addresses are different. This service does offer an optional guarantee.

AAV+ allows a merchant to take orders that may have previously been deemed too risky. It reduces the costs for manual reviews for American Express transactions, and most importantly, AAV+ covers a merchant's chargebacks on American Express transactions run through the service.

New Services Offered by American Express

- E-mail address verification reduces fraud by verifying that the e-mail provided by the customer matches the addresses on file with American Express.

- Phone number verification checks the phone number provided by the customer against the phone number on file with American Express.

- Both of these services can operate in batch-mode or real-time environments and can help identify high-risk transactions.

TIPS AND TECHNIQUES

- AAV+ only works for American Express transactions.
- If merchants don't have a direct connection to American Express, they need to make sure their payment processor can handle the new data fields required for this service.
- It does not guarantee customer service chargebacks, only fraudulent chargebacks.

Estimated costs: There are different fees for using the service and getting the chargeback guarantee. The new e-mail and phone number verification systems are offered through American Express's free electronic verification program.

Alternative solutions: Many vendors provide address verification services ranging from delivery address verification to full verification based on credit bureau and government record checks.

Vendors: American Express.

How Does It Work?

To use the service, merchants need to make sure their payment processor supports the new service. If merchants have a direct connection to American Express, they can immediately start looking at how to implement this solution.

Once merchants have decided to implement the AAV+ solution, they will have to notify American Express to get a copy of the AAV+ specifications. American Express will conduct a walkthrough of the specifications if the merchant wants one.

With the specifications, a merchant can begin to modify their authorization format. Once merchants have made the modifications, American Express will have to certify their format and review their ordering system script, and/or checkout page, for their web site. Then a merchant can begin to send orders.

With AAV+, merchants will be sending the following new data in their authorization feed:

- Card member billing information
- Card member billing address, zip code, and phone number
- Card member name as it appears on the card
- Alternate address information
  - Ship to street address, zip code, and phone number
  - Ship to first and last name
  - Ship to country code (ISO numeric)
- E-mail and IP address

How Do I Use the Results?

Merchants will get a response from American Express indicating if the data was a match. If it is and merchants have purchased the guarantee, they can immediately accept the order. If they don't have the guarantee, then they have to decide on the order. If it is a match on the name, phone, and address, the merchant's risk is greatly reduced.

Building This In-House

Merchants can purchase data volumes that give them yellow page–type information against which they can do checks.

Age Verification

Age verification is the attempt to determine the age of the consumer at the time of purchase. Typically, it is used for regulatory compliance in the adult, alcohol, and gaming sectors.

How Good Is It?

The reliability of age verification is directly related to the country in which the consumer resides. Most of the vendors that supply this service rely on public records to determine age. Some vendors rely on credit reports.

Completing an age verification check for consumers:

- Can help merchants ensure that they don't lose their liquor license for selling to underage consumers
- Can ensure a merchant of an adult site doesn't get hit with heavy fines
- Can ensure a gaming merchant doesn't get in trouble with national laws governing the age of consumers playing games of chance or placing bets

 TIPS AND TECHNIQUES

- If merchants are using vendors that use credit reports, they may be required to ask their consumers for their Social Security numbers or for their National Insurance Number if they reside in the United Kingdom.
- Does the service provider offer guarantees or reimbursement for fines or legal fees associated with the use of the service?
- Set up a system of accounts so age verification is run only once per consumer, not for every purchase he or she makes.

Estimated costs: Typically this service is offered on a per-transaction basis. Some vendors offer a subscription-based model for payment.

Alternative solutions: Driver's license fax back; use of an "over 18" or "over 21" web page, in which the consumer has to click on a checkbox that states he or she is over this age to continue on the web site.

Vendors: Aristotle's VerifyMe, Paymentech OnGuard & Verisign (uses Aristotle's VerifyMe, www.verifymyidentification.com), Experian. For card-present operations, check out VerifyIDs.com, AVS.co.uk (Adult only), AdultSights.

How Does It Work?

The typical age verification service requires that a merchant provide the consumer's name, address, and phone number. Some services will require that a merchant also provide the Social Security number.

Depending on the service merchants use, they will get back either an actual age or date of birth. Merchants will still have to do some logic to ensure the age is acceptable, or the service will provide a set of answers such as:

- Over 21
- Over 18
- Under 18
- Unable to verify
- Unavailable

Some service providers will provide financial guarantees for legal fees and fines if the government comes after a merchant and they used the service. Remember a merchant only has to check a consumer once, so make sure to add logic that checks to see if a new consumer has already been checked before.

How Do I Use the Results?

If the age verification service provides a hard age, then:

- Determine which field holds the age, or date of birth, field.
- If date of birth was given, create a formula to determine the age.
- Create a rule to compare the provided age with their age requirements.

If their age verification service provides a descriptive result then check to see which result was returned and make sure it meets the regulatory requirements; for instance, over 18 or over 21.

Building This In-House

Use a process of account set-up in which you ask consumers to provide a copy of their government-issued ID to keep on file. They fax it in to the merchant. A merchant only has to do this once for a consumer, who then can buy any time he or she wants.

Set up a web page that asks the consumer to certify they are over 18 or 21 by clicking on a certification button on the page that won't let them continue if they don't certify. Make sure you keep a record of this acceptance on file.

Card Security Schemes

The CV number is a tool for merchants to verify that the consumer is in possession of the card. This helps prevent fraud in which the fraudster may have acquired the credit card number in the trash or online, but is not in possession of the physical card and therefore cannot give this extra set of numbers. This number is a three- or four-digit number located either above the credit card number for American Express cards or on the back for MasterCard and Visa.

These numbers have been in place for a while and have been slowly adopted by merchants. You are more likely now to be asked for this number when trying to complete a MOTO transaction than you would have been a year and a half ago. The Discover card was one of the last cards to implement this technology. At this time, all of the issuing and acquiring banks should support this technology, but a few smaller holdouts may still exist.

How Good Is It?

Implementing card security checks, such as CV, CVV2, and so on, has shown the ability to reduce the number of fraudulent attempts. It has also shown that it will cause a nominal reduction in sales conversion for online transactions. Merchants do not have to actually check the card security number to get the reduction in fraud attempts. Merchants should expect an increase in call center calls when they implement card security for the first time. The use of card security schemes by merchants is on the rise, and the majority of merchants do use card security. MOTO has had a higher take-up on card security schemes than e-commerce. A couple of key concepts about card security schemes to keep in mind:

- In the United Kingdom, card security schemes are not recommended for use by e-commerce merchants by Visa EU.
- The intent of card verification is to attempt to verify that the consumer using the card is in possession of the card.
- They are good for catching fraudsters attempting to use stolen credit card information from online or through other means like the trash, or through other card activity.
- They are good at catching fraudsters who gained access to cards via skimming.

Adoption of card verification has increased dramatically in the last 12 months; call center–based operations have picked up the use more heavily than e-commerce.

TIPS AND TECHNIQUES

- When merchants implement this check on their web site, they will have to change their credit card submittal screen to show a picture of the credit card and where to find this number because a lot of consumers have no idea what this number is. It can cause some confusion and some additional customer service calls to complete an order when first implemented, but this is only a temporary effect.

- It does not actually verify that the cardholder is making the purchase.

- Not all consumers understand what this number is on their card.

- Make sure all payment processors or banking institutions in use for payment support the card security check data elements.

Estimated costs: There are no extra costs to run the card security check.

Alternative solutions: None.

Vendors: Any banking institution.

How Does It Work?

The card security code is a three- or four-digit value. It has been implemented as a security feature to help stop counterfeit cards and use of card numbers without the physical card. The value provides a cryptographic check of the information embossed on the card.

The three-digit number is derived from the card account number by means of an algorithm and a seed. It is possible to have repeat numbers—about every 900 cards there is a repeat. There would never be a number of all zeros or all zeros and a single one.

The card security value is printed on the signature panel on the back of Visa cards immediately following the Visa card account number or on

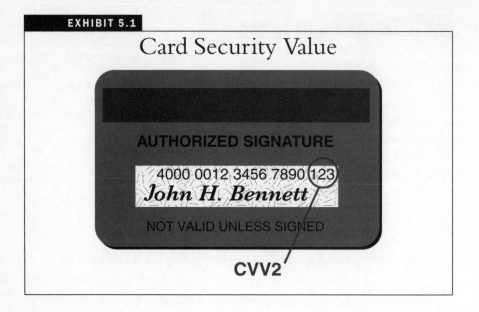

Card Security Value

the front of American Express and Discover cards just after the account number (see Exhibit 5.1).

The card security scheme validates two things:

1. The customer has a card in his or her possession.

2. The card account is legitimate.

The card security number is not contained in the magnetic stripe information, nor does it appear on sales receipts. Using the card security scheme helps prevent merchants from receiving counterfeit cards or being a victim of fraud.

For transactions conducted over the Internet, you may ask cardholders for their CVV2 online. Their Internet screen might include elements shown in Exhibit 5.2.

Authorization requests must include at least:

- Account number
- Expiration date
- CVV2 value
- Transaction dollar amount

EXHIBIT 5.2

Example of CVV2 request

Visa Account Number: [_____]

Card Expiration Date: [MM/YY]

3-Digit Value: [XXX]   ○   Click here if your card
                              has no three-digit number.

Please enter the 3-digit value at the end of your account
number printed on the **back** of your Visa card.

To learn more about the benefits of CVV2 and CVV2 technical requirements, contact the card association.

How Do I Use the Results?

When merchants processed their authorization call, they will get back a
match or *no match* response. If they receive a no match, I recommend an
auto decline. Merchants should tell the consumer they cannot validate
the card security number they submitted, and ask them to call in their
order to the call center. This allows the merchant to coach a legitimate
consumer to find the card security number.

Building This In-House

Implementing this service as part of the back-end process is not a major
initiative and requires mostly data element changes. Updates need to be
made to the front end to allow consumers to input the new data points.
Merchants will have to provide some visual aids for the consumer.

Charge Verification

This is used by merchants to validate card member information from the
issuing bank or card association by physically contacting them and asking
them to validate the cardholder information.

How Good Is It?

The charge verification services available today do not offer any kind of guarantee for fraudulent transactions. They provide extra security for accepting orders, allowing you to confirm more of the consumer's data. There is a significant difference between the card types and the ability to call and confirm consumer's data. This ranges from the Visa and MasterCard Code 10 procedures or American Express's Charge Verification Program to manually contacting the issuing bank of the consumer's credit card for validation. Merchants are really just trying to confirm if the cardholder information they have is the same data the bank has on file. If merchants can confirm the billing data with the issuing bank, they should still confirm the order with the consumer to create the complete loop.

Charge Verification

- Offers no guarantee on chargebacks
- Cannot be automated
- Has different rules and levels of service for each card type and bank
- Will not always contact the card member on file to validate the order—only American Express's program offers this at this time

TIPS AND TECHNIQUES

- Time-intensive process—it adds at least 24 hours to the processing time to accept the order.
- Who will place the calls?
- How will responses from the banks or institutions be handled?
- How will orders be selected for this process?

Estimated costs: The merchant will have to have staff ready to handle the calls. Costs will be directly in response to the number of orders taken and the number of orders that will require callbacks.

Alternative solutions: Use an automated process such as fraud screening, Advanced Address Verification Plus by American Express, or third-party consumer authentication services. Reverse lookups.

Vendors: American Express, Visa, MasterCard, Discover Card.

Typical Usage Method: Manual review.

How Does It Work?

Technically merchants are only supposed to call these numbers if they suspect fraud, but that is a very qualitative standard. So as a general rule, if merchants weren't going to take the order due to the checks they already did, then they should perform this check so they can at least try to convert the order.

Each credit card type is a little different on their rules for charge verification, so check with an acquiring bank on what processes they recommend for each.

American Express offers a Charge Verification Group that will attempt to verify the purchase for a merchant. The purchase can only be for physical goods with a value greater than $200, and must be a consumer-not-present transaction.

American Express will contact the card member to confirm the sale. The American Express representative will reply to the merchant with a yes or no response. (Note: If American Express cannot reach the card member, the merchant will not get a response.)

How Do I Use the Results?

Based on the response, merchants will have to decide if they want to accept the order. Remember they cannot validate shipping information, only the billing information. If they used American Express and they got a confirmation from the card member, they should accept the order. If they were able to confirm the billing information with the bank, then call the card member directly and validate the purchase with them. Don't call the card member first; they may have given bogus information in the order. When calling a consumer where you suspect fraud, always confirm the phone number with the issuing bank and use only that number to contact the consumer.

Building This In-House

Set up a person or team of people to conduct the charge verification process. Be sure to document the process and steps the team members should follow in doing the charge verification. Documenting the process and steps for verification is important, even in a one-person shop, to make sure nothing is overlooked. As a general rule, fraud review personnel can always do more than what is written down, but never less.

Check Verification Services

Check verification is a process that screens checks and check writers to assess the risk of the check being bad. These services typically will check to make sure the account is open, determine if the account has had bounced checks before, and check a negative database of bad check writers.

How Good Is It?

Check verification is a good way to verify that the account information provided is valid, with no typos, and it can help reduce your overall costs by reducing your NSF returns. Check verification is not a good fraud check. These services don't verify the name or address information on the account. With ACH and electronic checks, the cost associated with an NSF return is typically double the cost of processing the original transaction.

Typical information check verification can provide includes:

- Account closed

- Stop payment

- The account is currently in an NSF balance

- Non–DDA account

- Invalid account number

- Invalid routing number

- The account doesn't exist

- Stolen/forged/fraud

TIPS AND TECHNIQUES

- When accepting checks and debit cards, a verification service should be all that you need. Check guarantee services, in addition to using a verification service, can actually cost you more money to process. Unless you yield a high sales volume each month to cover the extra cost for using a guarantee service, just stick with verification.

- *Check verification with conversion* means that the check is not only verified but also converted into electronic funds; this means you do not have to deposit the check into your checking account; the funds will be deposited into your checking account for you automatically.

Estimated costs: Verification transactions usually cost less than $0.50 per item with lower cost for greater volume. There may be a sign-up/application fee. There is often a monthly minimum fee and always a statement fee, especially when dealing with retail check processing accounts.

Alternative solutions: Check guarantees.

Vendors: BetterCheck, National Cash Management Systems (NCMS), TeleCheck.

How Does It Work?

This service is performed using a real-time Internet process to access the account information and compare the new transaction against the list. If customers have a history of bad checks, the transaction will be declined. If they are not in the database for bounced checks, they are approved.

Consumer Authentication

Consumer authentication is a blanket term to discuss emerging tools intended to validate that the authorized credit card holder is the one actually attempting to make a purchase. Visa calls their consumer authentication service "Verified by Visa," and MasterCard calls their service "MasterCard SecureCode." American Express does not offer any similar service today, but has indicated that they are looking into the program.

How Good Is It?

In general the concept of authenticating the consumer is a good one. For the merchant, this is an excellent tool because it is one of the first tools that actually offers some financial coverage if fraud does occur. The card associations implemented these programs to increase consumer confidence in making purchases online and to help protect online merchants from fraud.

The main reason a merchant wants to implement this service is the protection it offers from fraud-related chargebacks. Not everything is protected, so be sure to review the details of the program with Visa and MasterCard. There are significant differences on what is covered in the United States versus what is covered in Europe. Some examples of what is not covered by the program include purchases made with procurement cards, recurring billing, split shipments or back-ordered goods, and "one-click" technology sales and transactions in which the consumer cannot be authenticated.

It also seems that certain high-risk segments, such as adult and gaming, are not going to be covered, so merchants in these vertical markets should check with Visa or MasterCard before they implement this technique. There is no threshold set for risk, but there is wording that suggests a threshold for fraud rates will be set, and merchants will have to keep their losses below that. Also, merchants have to properly set the e-commerce-preferred indicator.

The other major benefit of the consumer authentication tools is the simplification of some of their chargeback resolution activities. For those orders in which the consumer was participating in the program and they did authenticate them, the resolution process would occur between the issuing bank and the consumer, not between the merchant and the consumer.

Consumers may be legitimate even if they can't authenticate. Some examples of reasons good customers may not be able to authenticate include:

- The use of software that prevents pop-up windows will render this service obsolete.

- The pop-up can time out.

- Consumers who were preregistered may not know that they have a password or PIN to authenticate properly.

 TIPS AND TECHNIQUES

- The current consumer authentication tools offered by Visa and MasterCard are meant for, and work only on, e-commerce transactions. Merchants still need to have fraud processes in place to handle MOTO traffic.

TIPS AND TECHNIQUES (CONTINUED)

- For these programs to work, the merchant, consumer, issuer, and acquiring bank must all be participating in the program. Make sure to verify that the acquiring bank supports these programs prior to set-up. Merchants will also need to verify the acquiring bank certification requirements.

- For European merchants, some of the acquiring banks are still not set up to support consumer authentication.

- Merchants still need to perform other fraud checks—this tool does not cover many of the card types on the market today. Likewise, there are legitimate cases in which a merchant may not be able to complete the authentication process with the consumer. Merchants still need to make sure their overall fraud rates are kept within acceptable levels, and industry experts expect to see some fraud shifts to cards not offering this service.

- Companies that do little transactional volume should consider using an outsourced service bureau to perform this service.

- Always check and provide all of the correct data points: Merchants have to make sure they are supplying all of the correct data elements or they may not get the guarantee offered in the program. Confirm that the e-commerce indicator, ECI, is used, and AVS was checked. Likewise, the CAVV/AVV needs to show the order was checked for enrollment. Additionally, the XID (the unique transaction number) must be with the order.

- Merchants will have to get a digital certificate, which takes some time to obtain. Merchants have to get it from Visa or MasterCard. Expect two weeks for this process. The acquiring bank can provide the forms for merchants to start the process.

Estimated costs: Merchants can find this service available as an out-sourced service, or as a software application that can be implemented in-house. The actual cost to purchase the software is fairly low (it costs a couple of thousand dollars to purchase). Merchants will have to pay annual maintenance on the software and will have to make changes to their front-end e-commerce engines.

Alternative solutions: Commercially available consumer authentication.

Vendors: Arcot, Cardinal Commerce, CyberSource, Clear Commerce.

How Does It Work?

The process used by the consumer authentication services to authenticate consumers is pretty simple. The consumer enrolls with the issuing bank and is given a password, PIN, or device. When the consumer makes a purchase online, he or she is asked to give that password, PIN, or device to authenticate.

The purchase sequence can be broken down into five stages:

1. First, consumers go through the check-out procedure, the same way they do today, providing the same data fields they do today.

2. When the buy button is pressed, using the commercially available software on the market, it sends a message to the card association (i.e., Visa or MasterCard) to find out if the consumer is participating in the consumer authentication program.

3. If the consumer is participating in the program, the card association service will send a pop-up window to the consumer. The pop-up looks like it is coming from the consumer's issuing bank.

4. The pop-up asks the consumer to enter the password or PIN.

5. The issuing bank then validates this password or PIN and returns the results to the merchant.

For these programs to work, the merchant, consumer, issuer, and acquiring bank must all be participating in the program. Consumer adoption is slow at best. These programs have not gotten much participation from consumers or merchants in the U.S. market, and while the U.K. has had good adoption it is only because it was mandated that all issuers, acquirers, and merchants participate.

Consumers are being enrolled by self-registration, issuer auto enrollment, and issuer-prompted registration.

The liability shift is different based on the region in which you are doing business, the type of chargeback you have, and the type of card. For the Visa program, you will be covered from chargebacks coded as RC23, RC61, and RC75. For MasterCard, only chargebacks coded as RC37 are covered right now. For the Visa program, you only have to check to see if they are enrolled to get coverage. Remember if they are enrolled and they can't authenticate, you get no liability shift. Currently for European transactions in which the cardholder and merchant are European, you have the liability shift for both card types.

From a security perspective, all communication between the consumer and issuing bank is secured. A merchant will not see or ask for this password. The pop-up window the end user receives contains a secret message that only the consumer knows, showing the consumer that the pop-up window is real and not a fake. This is to reassure the consumer base that someone is not trying to steal the password.

There has been a fraud case in which fraudsters acquired account information and then called the issuing bank and changed the address information and signed up for the Verified by Visa program. The fraudsters then made fraudulent orders on these accounts. The merchants will be covered as long as they followed the rules.

These programs are excellent deterrents, but they are not silver bullets that will end all fraud. In reality, these programs have not stopped fraud but only moved it to other areas, types of transactions, and sales channels. Merchant interest in these programs isn't just about fraud reduction for a number of merchants implementing the Verified by Visa and MasterCard SecureCode programs. It is about attracting new consumers who were not comfortable with using the Internet for making purchases before these services were available.

How Do I Use the Results?

For Visa and MasterCard orders, when merchants are using this technology they should implement the following:

- For orders in which the consumer is participating in the program, the order type is a covered type, and the consumer successfully authenticates, accept the order.

- For orders in which the consumer is not participating in the program, the order type is a covered type, the merchant has checked for enrollment, and the order characteristics are within their normal order tolerances, accept the order.

- For orders in which the consumer is not participating in the program, the order type is a covered type, the merchant has checked for enrollment, and the order characteristics are not in-line with their normal orders, review the order or perform further fraud checks favoring sales conversion.

- For orders in which the consumer is participating in the program but cannot successfully authenticate, and the order characteristics are in line with their normal orders, perform other fraud-screening checks or manually review the order favoring risk aversion.

- For non–Visa and MasterCard orders, perform traditional checks.

Credit Check

The credit check technique is used to check a consumer's identity by comparing information the consumer provided to what is stored on his or her credit report.

How Good Is It?

This is an effective way to verify data a consumer is providing a merchant. In general, the credit report can validate the phone number, address, name, and credit card information provided. Merchants can also use it to verify age. Keep in mind:

- It can be manipulated by a fraudster in cases of true identity theft.

- It can be expensive to use for authentication.

- These reports rely on input from agencies, banks, and merchants, and their data may not be completely up to date.

- It typically requires the Social Security number (SSN), or the last four digits of it, to be provided.

- Depending on the data merchant's access, they may have further legal notification requirements in accordance with the Fair Credit Reporting Act.

TIPS AND TECHNIQUES

- Most consumers are not going to want to give a merchant their SSN and credit card number.
- Can you get data without an SSN?
- Can it support data on international orders?
- What data elements do they require from a merchant?
- Can they tell you about recent changes to the data?
- Don't ever store credit card and SSN information together unless proper security precautions have been put in place. If a merchant gets hacked and this information is compromised, it is going to hurt.

Estimated costs: Moderate, typically a per-transaction fee.

Alternative solutions: Reverse lookups: phone and address, consumer authentication.

Vendors: Equifax, Experian, TransUnion.

How Does It Work?

As merchants are processing an order, they will collect the required data elements from the consumer and will pass them to the credit bureau.

Typically this information is sent through a real-time feed that hooks into their existing order processing or CRM application.

Typically the credit bureaus will have different levels of service as to what type of information they will return back to a merchant. They could have verification-only checks, fraud score checks, and true credit scores. Make sure the information provided by the service will meet the requirements for using them.

Accessing a consumer's credit history is a big deal, so make sure to get legal guidance about what information is being accessed and if there is any new reporting or notification requirements that will have to be put into place.

How Do I Use the Results?

The feed a merchant gets back from the credit bureau may come in one of two forms. The first one is where they simply provide the information on the consumer. For example, the merchant provided a name and an SSN and the credit bureau provided the merchant with an address, phone number, and credit card number.

Or a merchant will provide them with the name, SSN, address, phone, and credit card, and they pass back a pass/fail indicator for each data element. Depending on how their choice of credit bureau works, merchants will have to code their systems to interpret these results. The merchant will have to determine the criteria for accepting or rejecting an order.

Building This In-House

Not applicable.

Deposit Check

Deposit check is used to validate consumers by depositing an amount of money into their bank account and having them validate the amount of money deposited. It is also known as a challenge deposit or bank account verification.

How Good Is It?

The deposit check was primarily used by PayPal for validating customers. As a general rule, this is a good method to validate a person's identity, but it does have limitations. As we all know, true identity theft is a real issue, and in these cases, fraudsters can set up bank accounts that look completely legitimate. More than 700,000 cases of identity theft were reported last year.

This check is not really good for traditional retail or businesses that are looking to have a one-time real-time purchase process. This is better suited to businesses that are establishing long-term arrangements with consumers in which the consumer will be coming back over and over for services, such as subscription services. A few things to consider about deposit checks before you use them:

- They don't catch true identity theft cases.
- They can be costly to set up; merchants have to put money on the line for setting up accounts.
- They take time: merchants introduce a longer time period to close an order because the consumer has to go back and validate the deposit. It can take up to a month to validate a consumer.

 TIPS AND TECHNIQUES

- Will the solution need to support credit cards and bank accounts?
- Does the solution need to be able to credit back the initial purchase amount in future sales?

> - Some consumers want instant gratification; make sure the solution will meet the needs of the consumer base that the merchant services. Also make sure the consumer base feels enough loyalty and desire to use the service that they will still be around to complete this process.
> - From a consumer perspective, this is a very long and burdensome process.

Estimated costs: High.

Alternative solutions: Consumer authentication, out-of-wallet checks.

Vendors: None.

How Does It Work?

Deposit check is a three-step process:

1. When a new consumer comes to do business, a merchant will need to set up a new account. The merchant will get the consumer's credit card information or bank account information, address, and phone number.

2. The merchant will notify the consumer that they will be making a deposit, if banking, and a charge if credit cards. The charge and/or deposit will be between $0.01 and $5.00.

3. The merchant tells the consumer that he or she will receive an e-mail when the deposit or charge has been made and the consumer must then validate the deposit or charge by responding to the e-mail.

Consumers can get this information by accessing their bank or credit card information online, by phone, or when their statements come in.

The merchant will receive an e-mail from the consumer with the amount they received or were charged. The merchant then validates this amount against his or her records. If it's a match, the merchant sets up the account and proceeds. If not, the merchant either declines the business or does a second deposit check.

IN THE REAL WORLD

PayPal was one of the first companies to perform this check on all new account holders. When new customers signed up for PayPal, they would have to register a bank account and then pass a challenge deposit for the account to be listed as verified in the account. This method allowed PayPal to verify that the customer signing up had access to, or was in possession of, the bank account they provided.

How Do I Use the Results?

Whether a consumer passes or fails this test, it is valuable information. Make sure you set up processes to maintain all credit card numbers, bank account numbers, and demographic data to check future account set-up attempts against them. This really helps with prescreening transactions.

Building This In-House

Remember that a merchant needs to have good systems in place to check for consumers that are failing multiple times. Also make sure to implement positive lists, hot lists, and warm lists to prevent fraudsters from working the site to get in.

Make sure to rerun the process on any new credit cards or bank accounts that are added to the account. Fraudsters will set up with a valid card, and then use bad cards inside the account.

Consider allowing consumers to place orders, or use the service, while they are being validated. Just don't allow fulfillment to take place, or for other valid orders to be superseded by these orders.

Put in velocity of use checks to see how many accounts are associated with a consumer's data points such as address, phone number, credit card number, and bank account number.

E-Mail Authentication

E-mail authentication is the process of searching public data sources to determine the age and association of the e-mail with demographic data provided by a person online.

How Good Is It?

It has been an ongoing issue that consumers can get free e-mail accounts easily and quickly. The challenge was to find a way to authenticate that the e-mail address is really associated with the profile data a consumer has presented to you.

So how can you really authenticate an e-mail address like johndoe@hotmail.com? You can perform an e-mail verification, which will confirm that the user has access to that account, but how can you determine if the e-mail address really represents the person visiting your web site?

Until now, the only way to do this would be to conduct your own research using online resources such as social networks to try to find where the e-mail is in use, and to see who is using it.

Now, services exist that provide the ability to look up e-mails across a number of web sources. They offer insight into the profile of the person who owns the e-mail as well as the age of the e-mail account.

 TIPS AND TECHNIQUES

- E-mail authentication is available as a hosted bureau service.
- It works internationally.
- No data doesn't equal fraud. Not everyone has e-mail addresses out on the web, so you won't get hits on everyone.
- Not all responses are real-time responses.

Estimated costs: Typically this service is offered on a per-transaction basis. This service is usually fairly inexpensive.

Alternative solutions: E–mail verification.

Vendors: RapLeaf, Spokeo, Yahoo!

How Does It Work?

Solution providers search social networking sites for profiles that contain the e-mail being sought and compile a synthetic profile of the individual based on the data found from these sites.

How Do I Use the Results?

Use the results in two ways: authentication of name and address to the e-mail, and age of the e-mail.

In some cases, you can also utilize gender or age mismatches from the profile.

Building This In-House

It is possible to perform this manually in–house.

Freight Forwarders

The intent of using freight forwarder checks is to ensure the shipping address where goods are being delivered is not a freight forwarder that may be shipping the goods or services to other destinations.

How Good Is It?

Typically the freight forwarder check is used to make sure the goods or services you are providing are not being reshipped to a third party via freight forwarder. There is a lot of inherent risk for goods and services being delivered to freight forwarders. Fraudsters outside the United States like to use these services to make it look like they are coming from within the United States. Performing a check to determine if a customer is using a freight forwarder is a good way to catch international fraudsters masking themselves as a U.S. company.

TIPS AND TECHNIQUES

- How will the list of freight forwarders be compiled? Will the merchant try to compile it, or will they use an external service to provide this information?
- Does their service keep any data on fraud found with a particular freight forwarder?
- How often is their service updated with new numbers?

Estimated costs: Typically this service is offered on a per-transaction basis, but you can also purchase it as a subscription. There are some very low cost providers online that have hosted screens for you to input data manually as well. This service is usually fairly inexpensive.

Alternative solutions: Fraud scoring solution that includes this capability or delivery address verification service that provides associated phone data with an address. Do geolocation validation on the zip code or area code.

Vendors: First Logic, Group One, Acxiom, InfoUSA.

How Does It Work?

If using it as a manual tool, you would enter the shipping address and phone information into a hosted screen or utility the IT shop has set up for the merchant. The service or application would come back with a response to indicate if the address was a freight forwarder or not.

How Do I Use the Results?

Don't be surprised if the phone number does not match for the address given; this will happen a lot when the fraudster uses a separate number to reach merchants and the address of a freight forwarder for the goods.

This is a good tool to use with tools that provide geolocation data. If the consumer's geolocation information on the IP address showed he was from outside the United States and the address and phone data showed that he was inside the United States and the address is listed as a freight forwarder, you probably have a fraudster. Make sure to hot list addresses of freight forwarders when you do get a fraud attempt or charge-back from their address and/or phone number.

Building This In-House

Try to automate the lookup for freight forwarders, as it is easy to do, and if you use it with geolocation, it can save you a lot of manual reviews.

EXECUTIVE INSIGHT

Data Collection and Identity Verification

PETER MARTIN, DIRECTOR OF RISK CONSULTING, PAYPAL

One of the first rules of doing business anywhere in the world is to know your customer. Unfortunately, knowing who you do business with has become much more difficult as our economies have expanded globally and into the virtual world. Merchants must make many tradeoffs between building high bars of entry and losses due to fraud.

Unlike many financial institutions, PayPal does not ask for large amounts of personal data when a member uses our service, making it easy to use PayPal to transact. That is one of our competitive advantages and a major value proposition for our members.

So without this, we utilize a variety of techniques for identity management both active (asking customers for information) and passive (data verification against internal and third-party databases/name address phone, etc.). The goal is to optimize the risk/reward tradeoffs with customer experience and service.

PayPal's fraud management system uses a risk-based, analytic-driven approach to manage authentication and verification. Most customers may not need additional or higher bar authentication but we do occasionally use tools such as SSN/DOB checks, financial documents, and outbound phone calls if we find that more authentication is needed.

One of PayPal's early innovations in risk management was the use of verification. Our members are verified by adding bank account information to their PayPal account with the use of random deposit or an instant bank password verification service. A customer can also be verified by applying for one of our credit products, which allows us to run a full credit check. Verification in our system helps us lower risk and prevent fraud in our system. It also helps us manage costs because lower fraud rates allow us to pass cost savings to our members. As an additional benefit, our merchant customers can use the verification status with Pay-Pal members as another risk variable in their own risk management programs. And allowing merchants to request less data at checkout increases their conversion rates.

PayPal's verification system is a critical part of a larger management program. We will continue to manage risk in our system, and we encourage our merchants' customers to also manage risk proactively on their side. Stamping out fraud is part of Pay-Pal's DNA and a partnership with our members around the world.

Identity Authentication

Electronic identity authentication is the ability to collect, authenticate, and confirm the personally identifiable information provided by an end user. This could be as simple as being able to match a name, address, and phone number, to verifying more specific data such as date of birth, Social Security number, or national identity number.

Identity authentication not only serves to prevent fraud, but is also a requirement in some cases under the "Know Your Customer" (KYC) requirements of the Patriot Act. In its simplest form, identity authentication is used to cross-check the address and phone information a user has provided to you with a third-party resource to verify that the public records show the same information.

How Good Is It?

Identity authentication is very effective and can provide the most relevant information to a user's identity. It should be understood that identity authentication alone can easily be beaten by a fraudster; performing authentication without verification leaves you susceptible to fraudsters using stolen identities.

TIPS AND TECHNIQUES

Identity authentication is available as a hosted bureau service or you can purchase monthly or quarterly software distribution of data.

- How often will your provider update the information or update their software?
- Will the data include cell phones and business phones?
- Are there any dead spots where information is not provided, such as international, Canada, or Puerto Rico?
- What is the accuracy of the data they have? Try them out: Have ten people's information from around the country and see how well the service validates the information. Include someone who has been in place for a while, one who has recently moved, and one who owns multiple properties.

Estimated costs: Typically, this service is offered on a per-transaction basis, but you can also purchase it as a subscription. There are some very low cost providers online that have hosted screens for you to input data manually as well. This service is usually fairly inexpensive.

Alternative solutions: Out-of-wallet checks, reverse lookups, credit checks.

Vendors: TargusINFO, 192.com, CardCops, Experian, IDAnalytics, iDinsight, Equifax, ChoicePoint, Lexis Nexis, Idology, Veratad.

How Does It Work?

If using it as a manual tool, you would enter the individual's information into a hosted screen or utility their IT shop has set up for you, and the service or application would come back with some mix of the following types of results:

- A full match
- A partial match
- Multiple matches to data element XXXXXXX
- Known negative indicators with data element XXXXXX
- Not found

How Do I Use the Results?

You verify this data and see if it matches.

Out-of-Wallet Checks

Out-of-wallet checks are intended to validate the consumer's identity by asking him or her questions derived from past credit reports or public records. This usually is done using credit reports and includes 5 to 10 questions in a multiple-choice format.

This is also known as out of pocket or knowledge base services.

How Good Is It?

As a general tool, the out-of-wallet checks are very effective at establishing consumer identity. Although you have no guarantees using this service, you do have some good ammunition in fighting a chargeback. Only the most severe cases of identity theft would be able to pass this check.

The pros and cons of out-of-wallet checks are:

- Good tool for establishing consumer identity
- Best practice technique for credit issuance
- Do not require you to get a credit score
- Do not translate well for international orders

 TIPS AND TECHNIQUES

- It can be costly to use.
- It requires a lot more intrusive information from consumers; some may be very reluctant to give this much information unless they are buying something very expensive or requesting credit.
- It does require that you integrate questions directly into your web page checkout process or use of third-party pop-up verification screens.
- It typically requires SSN and/or date of birth. Some of the more recent services are using the last four digits of the SSN with date of birth.

Estimated costs: Typically, this service is offered on a per-transaction basis. Because it requires the use of a credit report, costs tend to be significantly higher than using a fraud-screening service.

Alternative solutions: Verified by Visa, MasterCard Securecode, reverse address and reverse phone number lookup.

Vendors: Experian, Equifax, TransUnion, RSA, ChoicePoint, Lexis-Nexis, Idology.

How Does It Work?

Using the credit report, the service will create questions based on the consumer's past spending history. For example:

What is the name of the bank/financial institution you financed your car with in 1997?

a. Chase Bank

b. Mitsubishi Motors Credit

c. Land Rover Credit

d. Ford Motor Credit

Typically there are 5 to 10 questions with about a 50/50 split on recent versus past activity. Questions usually come from a variety of points such as car loans, home mortgages, and credit cards.

How Do I Use the Results?

The consumer answers all of the questions and the service informs the merchant if the identity was verified (that is, whether he or she passes or fails). It is possible to utilize a service such as this without getting a credit score. If consumers fail, you can route them to another channel to try to convert the order, or you can have them mail in payment.

If someone fails this process, make sure you only send correspondence, either mail or phone, to the address and phone listed from the service you used. Don't send it to the address the new consumer used unless it happens to be a full match to the one on the service bureau record. This is important to ensure you are not aiding an identity theft perpetrator.

Building This In-House

Not applicable.

Reverse Lookups: Phone and Address

The reverse lookup is used to cross-check the address and phone information a consumer has provided to you with a third-party resource to verify that the public records show the same consumer's name is associated with the provided address and phone information.

How Good Is It?

Typically the reverse lookup is used in manual reviews to do an additional verification of a consumer's address and phone information when AVS is not a full match. These checks can be somewhat suspect. Most of the services utilize public records for this information and have to be updated with new information. This type of check can pull up a lot of false positives on fraud, if it is used in a single pass-fail type of scenario. It does provide value in that when you can verify the information through public records and the shipping address is the same as on record, you have far less risk with the order.

Gotchas with reverse lookups include:

- There are a lot of ways to fool this test.
- There are people who move a lot, such as military families, in which multiple phone numbers and address may be in the public records.
- There are lag periods between refreshes of the address and phone data.
- In cases of identity theft, a fraudster can set up these services to look completely legitimate.
- It typically cannot validate unlisted phone numbers.
- More and more people are listing cell phone numbers and business phone numbers.
- If you use it to check the shipping address, there are valid cases in which a consumer could be sending packages or gifts to a relative's home to pick up later.

TIPS AND TECHNIQUES

- It is available as a hosted bureau service or you can purchase monthly and quarterly SW distribution of data.

- How often will your provider update the information or update its software?

- Will the data include cell phones and business phones?

- Are there any dead spots where information is not provided, such as international, Canada, or Puerto Rico?

- What is the accuracy of the data they have? Try them out: Have ten people's information from around the country and see how well the service validates the information. Include someone who has been in place for a while, one who has recently moved, and one who owns multiple properties.

Estimated costs: Typically, this service is offered on a per-transaction basis, but you can also purchase it as a subscription. There are some very low-cost providers online that have hosted screens for you to input data manually as well. This service is usually fairly inexpensive.

Alternative solutions: Fraud-scoring solution that includes this capability, delivery address verification service that provides associated phone data with an address. Do geolocation validation on the zip code or area code.

Vendors: TargusINFO, Whitepages.com, Rootsweb, First Logic, Group One, Acxiom, InfoUSA, 192.com.

How Does It Work?

If using it as a manual tool, you would enter the individual's address and phone information into a hosted screen or utility their IT shop has set up for you, and the service or application would come back with some mix of the following types of reverse lookup results:

- I input the address and phone number, and it gives me the name of the person associated with each piece.

- I input the phone number only, and it gives the address and name associated with it.

- I input an address, and it gives me the phone number and name associated with it.

How Do I Use the Results?

You verify this data and see if it matches. You can do this test on the billing and/or shipping address. It is a good secondary test for checking AVS data when it is not a full match. But beware—there are a lot of valid reasons the shipping address could be different. If, however, you got a full match on AVS and you cannot validate the address, contact the bank. If you got a full match on AVS but cannot match the phone information, contact the consumer for the correct information, or the bank if the number ends up being incorrect.

Building This In-House

Remember you need to make sure you ask the consumer for his or her home phone number and billing address.

Return E-Mail

Return e-mail is used to validate consumers by sending them an e-mail at the time of purchase with a code, password, or link they have to use to validate and complete the sale.

How Good Is It?

The return e-mail was primarily used to validate the consumer's e-mail address. This check is not really good for traditional retail or businesses that are looking to have a one-time real-time purchase process. This is better suited to businesses that are doing digital download or service-oriented businesses that will not physically ship goods to a consumer. In these cases, the e-mail is the most important link with the consumer. Some important limitations to return e-mail checks include:

- They don't catch true identity theft cases.
- They slow down the checkout process.
- It is very easy these days to set up e-mail accounts in free domains.

TIPS AND TECHNIQUES

- Will you use passwords and codes or will you provide a link for the consumer to complete their sale?
- What will the impact be on your business if it takes 1–24 hours more to close a sale?
- How will this affect your order management and fulfillment processes?

Estimated costs: Very low. You can easily set this up within your systems using your existing mail servers.

Alternative solutions: Reverse address and phone number checks.

Vendors: Not applicable.

How Does It Work?

It's a three-step process:

1. When new consumers come to do business, you will need to collect their e-mail address and have them verify it before they close the screen. You will tell consumers to expect an e-mail within a preset time frame that will provide them a password, link, or code they will have to use on their site to complete their sale. When the consumer presses the buy button, you will put the order into a holding status and send an e-mail to the consumer.

2. When the consumer receives the e-mail, it will instruct him or her to use the provided link and to input a code or password to validate the e-mail and the purchase.

3. You then provide the service. For digital download providers, this link could be to the point at which the consumer downloads the software.

How Do I Use the Results?

If you cannot get back to consumers via the e-mail they provided, you should not send or allow them to download goods.

Building This In-House

Remember you should have good systems in place to check for consumers that are failing multiple times. Make sure you implement good hot lists and warm lists to prevent fraudsters from working your site to get in.

Put in velocity of use checks to see how many e-mails are associated with a consumer's data points such as address, phone number, and credit card number.

Telephone Number Identification

Telephone number identification is the process of determining the type of phone being used by a consumer or end user. This technique looks up the phone number to determine where it was provisioned and the type of phone it is associated with.

How Good Is It?

Telephone number identification, or TNI, serves several important functions. First, it authenticates that the number is a real, dialable phone number. Second, it will let you know where the phone was provisioned: the country, region, and city. Lastly, and most importantly, it will tell you the type of phone the number is assigned to.

Gotchas with phone identification include:

- There are very few resources for this type of service, and once outside the United States, the number is increasingly smaller.

- Make sure the service distinguishes fixed VOIP, like Vonage, versus non-fixed VOIP, like Skype.

- On mobile phones, not all prepaid phones will be distinguished as such, and some may look like regular mobile phones.

TIPS AND TECHNIQUES

It is available as a hosted bureau service.

- Common phone types: fixed line, mobile, prepaid mobile, fixed VOIP, non-fixed VOIP, payphone, private number, government line.
- What countries are supported?
- How does the service handle unknown numbers?
- Look into name, address, and phone authentication as well.
- Look into phone verification.

Estimated costs: This is typically an inexpensive service in the United States, and when coupled with other techniques, it can provide a nice return for the money spent to perform the check. However, the price can vary dramatically based on which countries you do business in. It is usually offered on a per-transaction basis.

Alternative solutions: Area code mapping, identity authentication, reverse phone lookups.

Vendors: MaxMind, TARGUSinfo, Telesign.

How Does It Work?

At a minimum, you would provide a phone number and, in some cases, the country where the number is supposedly from. The service then returns information about that phone number. These services are real-time services.

How Do I Use the Results?

Not all phone types have the same level of risk; you will have to determine which phone types indicate higher risk to your organization. We would strongly recommend you combine the TNI results with other forms of authentication.

Telephone Verification

Telephone verification is the process of calling back consumers at the phone number they have provided to verify the phone is working and the person in possession of the phone is the one placing the order.

This is also known as telephone verification, phone verification, automated call-back service, and phone verification services.

How Good Is It?

Typically, phone verification is used in manual reviews to do an additional verification of a consumer's address and phone information when AVS is not a full match. But some merchants are using automated telephone verification services to ensure they have a valid phone number for each customer. The process is simple, and while requiring a little more user interaction, it fits easily into the online real-time process. This has been a popular technique for businesses that are involved with paying out money.

Gotchas with phone verification include:

- Don't forget to do simple phone standardization and checking to prevent wasted verification attempts.
- If you don't do authentication of a phone number before you verify it, then your verification loses a lot of strength. There are two levels of authentication: phone type and phone to name/address.

- This can get expensive if you are doing international business.

- This process does require a change to the user experience.

- Don't forget to perform other redundant checks to catch unwanted behavior.

TIPS AND TECHNIQUES

This is available as a hosted bureau service.

- What countries are supported?
- How does the service handle unanswered calls?
- Can the session be handled from within your site or do you have to pass off to another outside session?
- Look into telephone type authentication, TNI.
- Look into name, address, and phone authentication as well.

Estimated costs: Typically this service is offered on a per-transaction basis. This service is usually fairly inexpensive in the United States, but the price can vary dramatically based on the countries in which you do business.

Alternative solutions: Manual phone verification, area code mapping, pin mailers.

Vendors: MaxMind, Onverify.com, PhoneConfirm, Telesign.

How Does It Work?

Telephone verification works by automatically calling an online end user's telephone number at the same time the end user is making a transaction on a web site. The user, while on the web site, answers the phone and is provided a one-time personal identification number (PIN), randomly generated and presented via the web interface; an otherwise anonymous online end user will be able to confirm that the person who received the phone call and the person who is interacting on the web site are the same person. There are four steps to this process:

1. The merchant requests consumer verification.

2. An automated call is generated to the consumer.

3. Consumer inputs the PIN received on the phone call into the web site.

4. The merchant confirms the PIN, and consumer is verified.

How Do I Use the Results?

If the consumer, or end user, cannot verify through the phone, you should prompt him or her to try again with another phone number. If the consumer cannot pass on further attempts, you should assume he or she is a high risk.

Building This In-House

It is possible to build this technology in-house.

Chapter Summary

While the card associations provide basic tools like AVS and CSC to merchants, these tools have very limited use in identity authentication and verification. Merchants will need to do more if they want to effectively manage their company's risk exposure to fake or stolen identities.

There are a number of tools and techniques available for identity authentication and verification, and merchants should consider their overall risk exposure and customer experience before deciding on which ones would be best suited for them.

When implementing an identity-based program remember to authenticate and verify to get the best results. First, make sure the data makes sense—could it possibly be accurate, is the address deliverable, is the phone number dialable? Second, attempt to authenticate the data the consumer provided by performing authentication checks like reverse lookups. Lastly, perform verification to make sure the consumer is really in possession of the data they provided to you.

CHAPTER 6

Fraud Prevention Techniques: Guaranteed Payments

After reading this chapter, you will be able to:

- Discuss the limitations of MasterCard SecureCode and Visa's Verified by Visa programs.
- Discuss the reasons guaranteed payments haven't been more widely accepted in the marketplace.

E-Commerce Insurance

Merchants use e-commerce insurance to cover their losses on fraudulent orders.

How Good Is It?

Insurance has been around for a long time, and e-commerce insurance certainly does work. However, like any other form of insurance, these companies are in business to make money, so their costs can be extensive, and the orders covered may be limited. Here are some other insurance issues:

- It can be very costly for what you get.

- It may require you to set up elaborate fraud-prevention techniques on top of the insurance.

- It can also affect sales conversion by forcing you to only accept orders that are on the bottom of the risk pile. For example, you can accept orders only when address verification services (AVS) is a full match.

TIPS AND TECHNIQUES

- Are all goods and services covered by the policy?
- What is the notification process? What types of information need to be collected and provided for a claim?
- Does the policy require that the merchant perform collection activities?
- How will future premiums be affected by losses?

Estimated costs: Typically, these services are offered on a basis points system. You will be required to pay a half to five basis points for the insurance on each order you want covered.

Alternative solutions: Some fraud providers offer guarantees and risk sharing. Some fraud techniques offer guarantees as well, such as the Verified by Visa Program, the MasterCard SecureCode offering, and the American Express Advanced Address Verification Service.

Vendors: Start with your merchant business insurance provider.

How Does It Work?

Merchants will enter into an agreement with an underwriter that will require them to pay a preset basis point rate for each order they desire to have insured. Merchants will probably be required to have certain fraud-prevention techniques in place. These could be based on the standard association fraud tools such as AVS and card security schemes, but could also include the use of hot lists, fraud-screening services, and/or the use of financial limits. Typically, these policies will classify merchants by levels of risk based on the cost of their goods sold, the type of goods sold, and the fraud-prevention tools you have in place.

How Do I Use the Results?

The best practice with e-commerce insurance is to combine it with a broader strategy in which you use the insurance for those orders you would normally review, or on those orders that are in the gray area (i.e., not really good, but not really bad). The intent again is to automate the process, so this assumes if merchants take out insurance on all orders they would normally review, they aren't reviewing these orders now that they have insurance.

Building This In-House

Not applicable.

Escrow Services

Escrow services insert into the payment process a middleman who is responsible for collecting funds from the consumer and for paying the seller for goods or services rendered. Escrow services are intended to be a neutral participant in the process, ensuring both parties are protected from fraud.

How Good Is It?

Deciding to use an escrow service is a big decision, with major impacts on the financial side. Escrow services will make your consumers more comfortable with buying from you, and they will ensure you are protected from fraud losses, but there is a cost for this. Beyond the financial cost of the service, this process typically takes 5 to 20 days for the seller to receive his or her money. Unlike the traditional credit card payment, in which payment is received before goods are shipped, in the escrow model, funds are only received once the consumer verifies receipt of the goods or service.

In general, these services are pretty reliable, and they offer a valuable tool for merchants. The best application for this tool is in higher cost goods, nonverifiable identities, or cross-border transactions.

How Buyers Are Protected

- Shipments are tracked, and delivery confirmation is required.
- The seller isn't paid until the buyer accepts the goods or services.

How Sellers Are Protected

- The escrow provider is responsible for confirming the consumer has received the goods.
- The seller doesn't have to ship the goods until the escrow service has confirmed the funds are good.

TIPS AND TECHNIQUES

- Do escrow services support the payment methods you know are appropriate for your business?
- Do they guarantee funds?
- How much padding time have they built into the settlement of funds?
- How does your consumer feel about this process; are you the trusted participant, or is the escrow service?

Estimated costs: Costs will vary based on the vendor you select and the value of the purchase. The costs can range from 4 to 27 percent.

Alternative solutions: Verified by Visa, SecureCode, e-commerce insurance.

Vendors: Escrow.com, iEscrow.com, SafeFunds.

How Does It Work?

1. The buyer and seller agree to the terms of the transaction.

2. The buyer pays the escrow provider.

3. The seller ships the merchandise.

4. The buyer confirms the receipt of goods or services.

5. The escrow service pays the seller.

How Do I Use the Results?

Not applicable.

Building This In-House

While it is technically something you can build in-house, you should remember an in-house service defeats the value proposition for the buyer and makes it a one-way process. If, as a company, you represent both the buyer and seller, like an auction site, then building it in-house is plausible.

Guaranteed Payments

Guaranteed payments use a third party to provide a merchant with a guarantee of payment for fraudulent transactions. These include providers of e-commerce insurance, third-party fraud services, and consumer authentication schemes.

How Good Is It?

This is the holy grail of solutions—merchants are guaranteed that the chargeback will be covered, so it works great. Not every chargeback is guaranteed; only fraud chargebacks are covered. Merchants still have to deal with customer service chargebacks. These solutions will have the right of refusal or require you to provide some stringent data requirements for them to guarantee the purchase. This is not a cheap option, and merchants will pay for the guarantee, but if their margins are low and they need to make sure they don't get hit by fraud, this is one of the best ways to do so.

Note that with guaranteed payments:

- Not all chargebacks are guaranteed (only those that are fraud-based), and there is no guarantee on customer service chargebacks.

- It usually works only for a specific card type, such as Visa or MasterCard.

- It may work only for specific channels, such as e-commerce or MOTO.

- Providers reserve right of refusal, so it can adversely impact sales conversion.

 TIPS AND TECHNIQUES

- Make sure to take time to understand what level of insult rates you will have with the solution. For example, if they guarantee only when they process the order and say yes, how many of the ones they said no to will actually be good orders?
- What channels do they support (e.g., e-commerce, MOTO)?
- Does it require anything extra from their consumer to process the order?
- What credit cards do they support?

Estimated costs: Low to very expensive. Typically involves paying basis points on top of the order. The consumer authentication techniques, Verified by Visa, and MasterCard SecureCode are very inexpensive.

Alternative solutions: Use fraud–scoring services that offer risk sharing.

Vendors: Visa's Verified by Visa, MasterCard's SecureCode, American Express's Advanced Address Verification, and Paymentech's VerifyMe.

Note: For more details on Visa's Verified by Visa program and MasterCard's SecureCode program, see the "Consumer Authentication" section in Chapter 5. For more information on American Express's Advanced Address Verification see the "Advanced Address Verification" section in Chapter 5.

How Does It Work?

For all of the guaranteed payment solutions, except e-commerce insurance, merchants will provide the order information to the vendor. Vendors will evaluate the order data, perform screening, and provide merchants with an answer to accept or reject. Depending on the provider they choose, they may not state that the order is guaranteed.

Merchants have to set up processes that follow all of the vendor's rules to get the orders guaranteed. For example, in the consumer authentication techniques, the merchant will pass an ID with the order showing they got the authentication, but that alone does not mean they're covered. They still have to follow all of the other rules of the program (i.e., marking the transaction correctly, no selling of prohibited products or services, such as gambling or adult content).

How Do I Use the Results?

How you use the results is directly related to the program requirements. Make sure all requirements are being followed exactly as listed and document all of the required elements vendors ask for. It is your choice to accept or reject with most of these services, but if you accept when vendors said no, you are on your own.

Building This In-House

Start with the consumer authentication schemes—they are the cheapest ways to get a guarantee. Then move to the advanced address verification technique. And then finally, if the other techniques are not enough, look for a third party to provide guarantees on goods and services or look for e-commerce insurance.

Chapter Summary

Getting a guarantee may end up costing you more than you are willing to give up. Beyond the higher costs associated with guaranteed programs is the loss of control when it comes to managing sales conversion. Companies considering guaranteed payment services need to fully understand the potential impact to the businesses' bottom line in terms of lost sales, abandonment, and insults.

Visa's Verified by Visa and MasterCard's SecureCode programs sound great, but there are a number of caveats to the guarantee, and there are a number of customer experience issues a company needs to be comfortable with prior to implementing these programs. Companies that decide to use these programs should look at them as layers of the solution, and not the core.

CHAPTER 7

Fraud Prevention Techniques: Fraud Scoring

After reading this chapter, you will be able to:

- Discuss the differences between fraud scoring and modeling.
- Discuss the limitations of fraud-scoring services in terms of evaluating them for best use within a vertical.

Fraud Scoring

Fraud scoring is used by merchants to determine the level of risk associated with taking an order in the consumer-not-present (CNP) marketplace. Merchants use the score to reject, review, or accept orders, as well as to find out information on what other types of preventive checks they should perform on the order.

How Good Is It?

Use of fraud-scoring services gives merchants a much more economical way to use the effectiveness of external checks that could be costly to implement individually, such as delivery address verification, geolocation, credit checks, reverse lookups, shared negative files, cross-merchant velocity, and use of neural nets. It also frees the merchant from training, setting up, and maintaining an internal neural network or fraud solution.

An internal fraud-scoring system will only have limited effectiveness, as the breadth of data being looked at is only a single merchant's data. This will affect any and all velocity checks such as velocity of change and velocity of use. For example, modeling and neural nets built and/or used solely in a one-merchant implementation don't get the benefit of seeing consumer activity outside of their business. For fraud scoring, the more data that go into building the service, the better it will predict and catch fraud.

It is important to know that:

- Modeling and neural nets maintained in-house suffer from breadth of data, missing key information from attempts on cross-merchant data.

- Better fraud-screening services will catch between 40 and 70 percent of fraud attempts, but the higher the catch rate, the higher the insult rate.

- It is only a tool—it provides good information, but merchants have to build the logic into their system to handle the responses.

- It can be very difficult to set up and understand how to effectively weight rules if building in-house. It can require significant intellectual capital.

- It is a great tool to automate manual fraud reviews.

Estimated costs: Costs will vary based on the vendor you select. Typically this service is offered on a transaction basis. There are some providers that offer flat subscription pricing, volume discounts and better pricing for entering long-term agreements. There are also some providers that offer basis points pricing, and these typically offer some sort of risk sharing or charge-back guarantee.

TIPS AND TECHNIQUES

- How often are the underlying models updated? This is important, as the fraud patterns and data points used in a model come from actual good and bad purchases. If a model is a year old, merchants are trying to predict fraud using data elements from fraud that occurred a year ago, whereas a model updated monthly or on every transaction is looking at more recent patterns.

- How often is the data updated and verified by the vendor?

- What types of fraud-prevention techniques does the vendor use (i.e., heuristics, neural nets, external scores)?

- What other components does the service provider include as part of its screening service (i.e., delivery address verification, reverse lookups, geolocation, freight forwarder checks)?

- Do they offer any guarantee on chargebacks or provide any risk sharing?

- Do they offer a pass/fail-only solution or one that provides a true score and range?

- Does the fraud-scoring service support e-commerce, mail order, and telephone order? Remember to look at the data elements they use to confirm the focus of their service. A service designed to predict e-commerce fraud will have less effectiveness in detecting mail order and telephone order fraud, as the data elements are different. For example, the e-commerce consumer will have an IP number and e-mail address.

- For merchants who do a lot of volume, this solution can get very expensive, so make sure you negotiate volume discounts.

- What case studies can they give to show how effective the solution was for other merchants?

- Be leery of any fraud-scoring service that guarantees less than 0.5 percent fraud without explaining what the effect will be on sales conversion.

- One direct measure of the depth of a fraud-screening service is the number of descriptors it can relate back to help you understand why it scored the way it did. These are codes that tell you more about why it scored the way it did (i.e., can't verify address, geolocation inconsistency with country, high velocity of use, currently on a negative list).

- What type of reports does the service provide?

- Does the service provide tools for the fraud-review team to do manual reviews?

- Can a merchant tune or change the service to meet their unique needs?

- Can they tell you what to expect as far as insult rates?

- If the service offers negative files, are these shared negative files or strictly for the merchant putting in the data?

Alternative solutions: Use of a decision engine, application of rules.

Vendors: CyberSource, Clear Commerce, Mango, Experian, Equifax, Fair Isaac/HNC, Lightbridge, Lexis-Nexis (Riskwise), Choice-Point, TrustMarque Risk Guardian, Retail Decisions. CyberSource has a unique relationship and development arrangement with Visa, offering a solution that is enhanced and endorsed by Visa. Cyber-Source is unique in the fraud-scoring market space with its Visa relationship.

How Does It Work?

First, merchants must understand that they can either use an external service for fraud scoring or build their own fraud-scoring engine. In general, you will send an order to a fraud-scoring service, which will provide all of the data elements of the order. Typically, merchants will have performed an authorization prior to making this call, so they can provide information such as address verification results and the card security results to the fraud-scoring service. These services are typically set up to process orders in a real-time environment, but this does not mean merchants can't use them in a batch mode. The service typically takes a matter of seconds to evaluate an order to determine the level of risk associated with it. Once a fraud-scoring service is done, it will provide one of several data points back to the merchant. Make sure to check what the service provider will return: there should be a pass or fail result, a score, and descriptors.

So now that you understand what you will see, what is the fraud-scoring service doing with their order? When you call a fraud-scoring service, it runs a series of data integrity checks on the data you provided to look for things that are unusual or are blatantly fraudulent. Examples of this could be nonsensical input such as a name listed as IUYIOUYIY, or it could be that Mickey Mouse is trying to buy a brand-new three-carat diamond ring. The service can then look at the data elements (such as name, address, phone, e-mail) to see if there are any matches to internal fraud lists. It would then check for issues with velocity of use and change. The service may then look at things such as geolocation and address and phone verification, and combine these in a model to see how well this order compares to previous good and bad orders. The service then correlates this into a score or a pass/fail response. This is only an example. Each service is unique, and most vendors will not share the exact methods they use, as this is their secret sauce.

How Do I Use the Results?

Selecting a fraud-screening service depends on a merchant's sales channels, MOTO, e-commerce, or both. If a fraud-screening service requires data elements from you, you should do everything you can to submit any and all of these data elements. E-commerce fraud-screening services will have less effectiveness with MOTO transactions. But if a solution is 70 percent effective in e-commerce and it is 50 percent effective with MOTO, it will still catch half of the fraud attempts.

If an order fails authorization, merchants don't need to send it out for fraud scoring. This being said, merchants should perform their authorization check prior to a fraud screen.

These services typically don't provide a case management interface, and they provide no means to establish initial settings. Merchants have to base the original settings off their own previous history with charge-backs. Merchants can easily get bogged down in the details of the solution. I highly recommend that merchants have a fraud analyst from the vendor of choice or independent source assist in completing the initial set up and go over best practices of using the fraud-screening service. This can save a merchant a lot of time and money in implementing the solution.

Building This In-House

It typically takes two weeks to set up a fraud-screening service technically: one week of setting up the initial business processes to use the service and one week for completing the integration. Most vendors provide an API that has been designed to be very simple to use and that has a lot of prebuilt plug-ins to major e-commerce applications.

Implementing fraud screening is easy from a technical standpoint, but it is a little trickier from the business side. You need to do a fair amount of analysis on your side to determine what types of risk may be encountered. Also, merchants have to determine how they want to deal with that risk. This information is critical for correctly setting up and using fraud scoring to its fullest potential. Merchants will also have to code in rules to handle return results from fraud-scoring services.

Chapter Summary

Fraud scoring is typically a generic model created to take advantage of a vendor's core data assets. Fraud-scoring solutions can have very different results for merchants in different verticals, and if evaluated, merchants should look for service providers with some viable connection to data that is of use in their vertical market.

CHAPTER 8

Fraud Prevention Techniques: Operational Management (Enterprise)

After reading this chapter, you will be able to:

- Discuss the features and use of authorization responses for fraud management.
- Define a rules engine and what it is used for in fraud management.
- Define the difference between velocity of use and velocity of change.
- Discuss the tools that can be used for manual review.

Authorization (Real Time)

Authorization is a request from the merchant to the consumer's issuing bank to determine if sufficient money is available on the credit card for payment, and to hold those funds for this purchase.

How Good Is It?

There are two methods merchants use to do authorizations: online (which is real time) or batch. If merchants cannot successfully authorize a purchase on a credit card, they will not be able to convert it. Doing real-time authorizations allows a merchant to quickly weed out consumers who don't have the money to make a purchase. It also gives merchants the means to let the consumer know, while the consumer is still on the merchant's site, that he or she doesn't have funds and can try another card. As a positive indicator, the fact a consumer has funds available is positive point in converting a sale, but is not a good indicator for fraudulent behavior.

Authorizations do expire, so merchants need to make sure they are still good when they want to settle their transaction.

 TIPS AND TECHNIQUES

- Exceeding a consumer's card limits: In some cases, merchants can exceed a consumer's credit card limit by mistake because they are running an authorization, and the consumer may fail one of the other checks the merchant requires for processing, and instead of using the original authorization, they run another authorization. This can deplete the consumer's credit line even though the other orders are not going to be processed.

- Some merchants try to cancel an authorization, but this is not really supported by all issuing banks, and usually requires a phone call to the bank. Even with that, there is no guarantee that the bank will reverse the authorization.

- What types of reports do they offer to reconcile transactions on a daily, monthly, and annual basis?

- Do they charge separately for authorizations and settlements?

- Can settlements be done in real time or batch?

- Do they support address verification system (AVS), card security schemes, and e-commerce indicator field?

- Can they process all of the major card types, or do they have to have a separate feed for American Express or Discover? Or if they want separate feeds to keep the costs down, can the application or service support that?

Estimated costs: Costs associated with getting an authorization vary widely. There are service bureaus that offer a transactional fee for each call. This is usually very inexpensive—a couple of pennies to less than 15 cents per transaction. The more volume merchants process, typically the smaller their transactional fees. For small businesses, most major vendors offer special discounted prices for them, but they are limited to the number of transactions they can run. Vendors also provide payment software solutions that will allow merchants to connect to bank or payment processors to conduct their acquiring activities. Merchants will typically pay a moderate up-front cost for the software and then an annual maintenance fee for the software. If they will be using a frame connection to access real-time payment, they will need at least 30 days for the certification process, and the cost of the line should be taken into consideration, as they are significantly more expensive than other options.

Alternative solutions: If a merchant is a small business, I would recommend looking at aggregators. These are businesses that service multiple merchants, called *multimerchants*, and they can provide payment solutions at lower costs for smaller merchants by pooling a bunch of merchants together to keep costs down.

Vendors: CyberSource, Clear Commerce, Paymentech, Wells Fargo, Chase, FDMS, Verisign, Retail Decisions, Retail Logic.

How Does It Work?

The issuing bank checks only the consumer's credit card number for authorization, confirming if it is an active account and if sufficient funds are available and checking AVS.

There are generally two types of declines a merchant can receive with an authorization: soft or hard declines. Soft declines are those declines in which the bank requires further verification. The bank has not given authorization at this time.

The following are reasons the bank may want to be contacted:

- Additional security is in place with banks regarding Internet companies.
- A bank wants to talk with the credit department and then contact the customer to verify the purchase is valid.
- Some banks may have a list of Internet companies for which they will allow authorizations to go through.
- Customers may have a limit for authorization on their card and the bank needs to contact them to verify the purchase before authorization can be given to avoid possible fraud.

Soft declines have a high percentage rate of converting.

A hard decline from the bank is when the return from the authorization is a result of one of the following:

- Insufficient available credit
- Possible fraud—lost or stolen card
- Invalid credit card—number does not exist
- System error
- Time out

System error orders should be actively worked on to try to convert them.

How Do I Use the Results?

Real-time versus batch processing—in general, it is our recommendation that a merchant implement and use a real-time authorization service. Doing real-time authorizations will help merchants cut their overall costs by cutting out those transactions that would not be able to be converted regardless of fraud because the consumer doesn't have any money. If merchants are doing batch authorizations, they now have to store the transaction, run it against the system if it fails, and contact the consumer for another credit card. Had the merchant been doing real-time authorizations, the consumer could have provided another credit card when at the site or on the phone. A merchant will also have a higher number of call center inquiries, as these transactions usually will lead to customer service calls in which the consumer wants to know why his or her orders aren't there yet.

Building This In-House

All banks and processors publish specifications that allow merchants to build their own solutions to communicate payment processing. Merchants will have to get their solution certified with the banking institution. With the number of payment solutions on the marketplace, and the reduction in prices to purchase these solutions over the last couple of years, I would recommend that a merchant not build in-house for the following reasons:

- It is cheaper to purchase these solutions on the open market than build them.

- The payment processing and credit card specifications change constantly, sometimes several times in a year, and merchants don't want to have to keep recoding their solution and getting it recertified.

- Commercial solutions have already been certified by the banking institutions and usually offer multiple links to different banking institutions, allowing a merchant to easily switch between banks for better rates.

- The security found in the commercial solutions is typically more robust than in-house solutions, which provides greater protection from unauthorized access attempts.

BIN Checks

The credit card number can tell you several very interesting things. By using the first six digits, you can determine the card type (e.g., Visa, MasterCard, American Express) and the bank where the card was issued.

The first six digits of the credit card number are known as the bank identification number (BIN). The BIN identifies the consumer's issuing bank.

How Good Is It?

The BIN provides a way to check if the issuing bank is in the same country as the geolocation and to verify address information provided by the consumer. While this alone is not enough to indicate fraud, it provides an additional signal as to the identity of the individual.

TIPS AND TECHNIQUES

- It is not easy to get a BIN list in-house, and it is accessed most often through a third-party service provider or through your acquirer.
- There are two types of BIN list: BIN to country and bank to BIN. A *BIN-to-country list* provides the country of issuance when given a BIN number, and a *bank-to-BIN list* provides the bank name, phone number, and country when given a BIN number.

Estimated Costs: It can be found as a per-transaction hosted solution, or you can potentially get it from your acquirer.

Alternative Solutions: Credit card verification.

Vendors: MaxMind, Service Objects Inc.

How Does It Work?

Credit card numbers are ISO 7812 numbers. As ISO 7812 numbers, they contain:

- A single-digit major industry identifier (MII; the MII is considered to be part of the issuer identifier number)

- A six-digit issuer identifier number (IIN)

- An account number

- A single-digit checksum using the Luhn algorithm

Cards participating in the BIN system include the following:

- Credit cards

- Debit cards

- Charge cards

- Stored-value cards

- Electronic benefit transfer cards

The term *issuer identification number* (IIN) is replacing bank identification number. See ISO 7812 for more information. Exhibit 8.1 shows the prefixes and lengths for the most common card types.

EXHIBIT 8.1

Common Card Types			
Card Type	**Prefix(es)**	**Length**	**Validation**
American Express	34, 37	15	Luhn algorithm
China Union Pay	622 (622126–622925)	16–19	Unknown
Diners Club Carte Blanche	300–305	14	Luhn algorithm
Diners Club International	36	14	Luhn algorithm
Diners Club U.S. & Canada	55	16	Luhn algorithm
Discover Card	6011, 65	16	Luhn algorithm
JCB	35	16	Luhn algorithm
JCB	1800, 2131	15	Luhn algorithm
Laser (debit card)	6304, 6706, 6771, 6709	16–19	Unknown
Maestro (debit card)	5020, 5038, 6304, 6759	16, 18	Luhn algorithm
MasterCard	51–55	16	Luhn algorithm
Solo (debit card)	6334	16, 18, 19	Luhn algorithm
Switch (debit card)	4903, 4905, 4911, 4936, 564182, 633110, 6333, 6759	16, 18, 19	Luhn algorithm
Visa	4	13, 16	Luhn algorithm
Visa Electron	417500, 4917, 4913, 4508, 4844	16	Luhn algorithm

How Do I Use the Results?

Online merchants may use BIN lookups to help validate transactions. For example, if the credit card's BIN indicates a bank in one country, while the customer's billing address is in another, the transaction may require additional review.

Building This In-House

This technique can easily be done in-house, provided you have access to a BIN list.

Case Management

The Case Management, CSR Interface is used by the risk team to review high-risk orders, conduct investigations, and clean up activities related to risk management. This interface is a critical component of the risk tool kit, and is typically the most overlooked part of the organization.

How Good Is It?

Most companies choose to use existing CRM systems, and rely on vendor-specific point solutions. This means they have to open and review multiple different applications to complete a single case. Applications specifically designed for risk management will combine data from multiple different data sources to make it easier and faster for the risk team to review transactions and to perform forensics.

TIPS AND TECHNIQUES

- How well does the application support adding extra data feeds? Is it a black-box approach, or can you integrate other services?
- Can you customize the interface for your business workflow?

Tips and Techniques (continued)

- Does it support queuing and hierarchy?
- Does it support user roles?
- Does it comply with Visa PCI?
- Link analysis is a must.

Estimated Costs: It can be found as a per-transaction hosted solution, subscription price, and software sale.

Alternative Solutions: CRM systems, point-integrated solutions.

Vendors: Accertify, Certigy, MasterCard EMS, SHS Viveon.

How Does It Work?

Typically these systems are running in parallel to existing systems and will allow your existing e-commerce stream to submit transactions to the system in real time or batch mode. They produce the capability for workflow using rule-based queuing and manual routing. A company's operations team can use the interface to manually review risk transactions, to perform analysis on past fraudulent transactions, and to perform forensic analysis.

Chargeback Representment

Chargeback representment is the process by which a merchant can dispute a chargeback with an issuing bank. The representment process allows merchants to present evidence to prove that a chargeback is not warranted.

How Good Is It?

The success rate for fighting chargebacks can vary greatly from merchant to merchant and from industry to industry. Some vendors offering outsourced representment services claim to have an 85 percent success rate on the chargebacks they select to represent. These vendors do not fight all chargebacks; they are selective in which ones they challenge.

TIPS AND TECHNIQUES

- Before you decide to start fighting chargebacks, make sure you analyze your business case. Representment carries a fee from your acquirer, so you may end up spending more money than you will get back from the process. In general, if your loss is less than $25, then you should evaluate the costs of representment first.

- Make sure you are doing the right things in your order process such as AVS and proof of delivery, as these go a long way with representment.

- Be selective on which chargebacks you fight, as not all chargebacks are the same.

- Even if you are selling digital goods, you can still win some chargebacks that are customer service related.

- Don't forget about authentication and verification.

- Check with your acquirer if you are in a high-risk market; they can typically tell you if representing makes sense for you.

Estimated costs: If you are going to pay an outside company to represent for you, the costs can vary greatly. Some vendors offer a pay-for-performance model, which means they are paid only if they win the representment.

Alternative solutions: Chargeback guarantee, chargeback insurance.

Vendors: Transmedia, Vindicia, Chargeback Experts.

Hot Lists, Warm Lists, and Positive Lists

Lists are used to identify returning consumers to determine if they have had good business or bad business in the past. Hot lists (sometimes referred to as *negative lists*) are utilized to reject orders from consumers who have had chargebacks on previous orders. Warm lists are used to either reject or review orders from consumers who have been customer-satisfaction problems in the past. Warm lists aren't used for fraudsters, but for consumers who never seem to be satisfied. Positive lists are used to identify merchants' best customers who have successfully closed business with them in the past and are trying to make a new purchase.

How Good Is It?

The use of lists is one of the most fundamental elements in any fraud-prevention strategy. If merchants are doing nothing today, implementing a hot list is the very first thing they should do. If merchants are doing business today and someone defrauds them, and nothing is in place to prevent the fraudster from defrauding them again, the fraudster will come back. Lists in general can also save a company money by allowing them to cut out certain orders before they have to pay for external calls such as authorizations, fraud screening, credit checks, and the like.

Here are some things to know about lists:

- Hot lists are excellent at preventing repeat fraud and fairly good at catching some forms of identity morphing.

- Warm lists are an effective way to stop those customers who continuously make purchases and then just return the goods or don't make full payments.

- Warm lists are also a good way to track return or credit abuse.

- Positive lists are an excellent way to reduce the number of orders for which you have to call out to external fraud screening. They are also a good way to fast-track orders from the best customers if merchants rely heavily on manual reviews.

 TIPS AND TECHNIQUES

- To maximize the effectiveness of using lists, merchants should make sure they can share data from and be checked from all channels (i.e., e-commerce, MOTO, and card-present), if possible.

- Merchants can exponentially increase the effectiveness of lists by having access to shared fraud lists.
- The data fields a merchant uses for these lists are critical, so make sure you can add data elements as well as import and export data into the set. Also, make sure you have methods to purge old records.
- Plan on maintaining data in a hot list for at least 12 months—I recommend 18 months.

Estimated costs: Costs vary based on the method you implement. Merchants can get basic hot list capabilities from most fraud-screening services, and they can get them as part of most decision engines. They can also build them internally very easily.

Alternative solutions: None.

Vendors: CyberSource, Clear Commerce, Retail Decisions, HNC/Fair Isaac.

How Does It Work?

List checks are fairly simple: Merchants designate a set of fields to maintain in a database, and they populate it with records where they want to take some action. When they process a transaction, they check it against the list.

Typically the data element used for list checks are address, state, zip code, phone number, credit card number, and e-mail address. Name is not recommended, as there are too many people with similar names, which could really kill their sales or fill their manual review BINs.

When checking new transactions against the database, a merchant is looking for a match on any of the data elements, not just one of them. For address checks, merchants will have to use some normalization to be effective. Make sure states are represented in the two-character designation, zip codes are five digits or five-plus-four, and all blanks are stripped out of the address line. Look for matches on parts of the address line, not exact matches, as some individuals will change just one digit or letter to make it look like a different address. Set up a process that mandates that all chargebacks related to fraud must be input into the hot list.

How Do I Use the Results?

- Always perform the hot list check first, before any call for an authorization. If a consumer is on the hot list, reject the order.

- If using warm lists to catch customer service issues, check this second, before authorization. If a merchant's policy is to reject all warm list customers, simply cancel the order; otherwise, if it is to review, then check this after you do the authorization.

- Positive file checks, unlike the warm list or hot list, must be a 100 percent match. Address, phone, and e-mail—everything—must match before a merchant decides to skip any other fraud checks.

One of the interesting ways warm lists have been implemented is to catch customers who are constantly returning goods. They can also be used to catch internal fraud rings that do credits to third-party credit cards. The method calls for a connection to their applications that process credits. Using a velocity of use technique, they count the number of credits based on each of the data elements discussed earlier. When they reach a preset number (e.g., more than three in 30 days), have that data populated into the warm list.

Building This In-House

The main thing a merchant needs is a database. Have a database administrator set up a database to use, adding the data elements previously discussed. Working with the credit or finance group, compile a list of previous chargebacks using the data elements to fill it in. You can put the data into a comma-separated file or into a spreadsheet application such as Microsoft

Excel. With the spreadsheet or comma-separated file, the database administrator should be able to easily import the data into the database.

The next step is to set up a call to the database from the e-commerce engine if a merchant is processing orders in real time, or from their order-processing application if they are operating in batch. The database administrator can set up the lists so they are optimized for fast queries by presetting stored procedures. Remember, although it is easy to add this directly to the e-commerce engine, I recommend that you create a fraud-prevention strategy first and implement this and other techniques with the end-state strategy in mind.

Internal Rules

Internal rules are built into e-commerce engines, payment processing systems, or order management systems to attempt to catch potentially risky orders. Sometimes called *heuristics*, these are simple logic statements that look to see if a condition is present.

They usually take the form of pass/fail, true/false, or yes/no types of questions, and are normally used to find risky or negative conditions. It doesn't have to be that way, but that is the typical application approach.

How Good Is It?

In writing rules, you must remember that it is only natural to tend to write them to catch risky behavior. If you attempt to only write rules that are based on previous fraud attempts, you will find that your risk solution and catch rules will be relative in nature, causing you to have to put in fixes and updates regularly. Be proactive in building rules—look at and profile good orders and base rules on that behavior to let these orders flow freely.

Here are some other things to know about rules:

- Rules form the basis for heuristics and catching negative characteristics of orders.

- With a well–thought–out strategy, rules can offer the lowest cost solution to keep fraud losses in check.

- Most manual checks can be implemented as rules.

- Within the rules discussion, I have not discussed building rules based on other fraud–technique tools such as card security, AVS, hot list, or velocity, as these rules and techniques are discussed in their own sections.

TIPS AND TECHNIQUES

- Implementing rules requires that merchants keep a good overview of the intended overall strategy. This will ensure they don't create more work for themselves by creating rules that cause them to review more orders than they really need to.

- Rules should be based on quantitative data, so make sure that you can prove that the majority of the transactions the rule will weed out really are fraudulent.

- Make sure only one entity is responsible for adding, changing, or deleting rules to ensure multiple parties in a business are not canceling each other's rules out.

- Make sure checks are done consistently.

- A lot of e-commerce engines have some built-in ability to add rules, such as the pipeline object in the Microsoft e-commerce platform.

Estimated costs: Implementing rules in–house is very inexpensive to do. You can have an internal resource directly code the rules in, or you can hire a third party to input the rules. Merchants can purchase commercially available decisioning software that will allow them to build rule logic.

Alternative solutions: Use of third-party service to build a custom set of rules for a merchant.

Vendors: CyberSource, Clear Commerce, Retail Decision, HNC Fair Isaac.

How Does It Work?

- *Dollar amount.* Reject or review all orders over an order amount of $X. This is a dangerous rule, as most fraud rings will work a merchant site to determine the threshold and submit orders just below that. The merchant moves its threshold, and then the fraudsters move theirs. To be effective, this rule cannot be under the average order amount for the business or within 15 percent of the average. The amount rule should be coupled with other rules such as shipping type, product type, quantity, or region.

- *Shipping type.* Look at the order to see if overnight or express shipping has been requested. In itself, this does not indicate fraud, but in conjunction with other rules, it does and can indicate higher risk.

- *Product type rule.* Set up a list of SKUs, product names, or codes for high-risk items or things routinely stolen, or that have a high incidence of theft.

- *Quantity rule.* Set up a rule to catch orders in which unusual numbers of items are being ordered (e.g., more than one laptop or more than two CDs of the same type).

- *Regional rule.* Set up a rule to catch orders from a high-risk region of the country (e.g., NY, FL, CA, or down to the city level).

- *International rule.* Set up a rule to catch all orders that are not from a desired country by looking at shipping address, billing address, card BIN, or geolocation check.

- *Different billing and shipping addresses.* Set up a rule to catch all orders in which the billing and shipping addresses are different.

- *Profanity rule*. Set up a rule to review all text input fields, especially name, address, and e-mail to check for profanity. These words are not typically found in real names or addresses and indicate high risk.

- *No vowels rule*. Set up a rule that looks at addresses, e-mail, and names to check for gibberish words with no a, e, i, o, u, y characters. It is very rare for this to occur in legitimate information. Merchants can also vary this to check for more than six consonants with no vowels.

- *Famous names rule*. Early fraud online used famous names or common names to perpetrate a crime. Create a list to check against this such as John Wayne, Marilyn Monroe, John and Jane Doe. Not a dead indicator of fraud, but I would check twice if Mickey Mouse was ordering 10 CDs.

- *Card security number rule*. If merchants are taking in the card security number, they can perform a quick test on the numbers the consumer provides to look for suspicious patterns. This check is very important if a merchant is collecting the card security number and isn't actually checking it. Look for "000," "001," "123," and "111," as these are all highly suspicious numbers for the card security number. If a merchant has the ability to do velocity of change checking on additional data fields, perform a velocity of change check on the card security number as well.

- *Home-built area code rule*. Using your phone book, build a list of all area codes by state and set up a rule to check the area code given with the phone number to the state of billing and/or shipping address. If they don't match, review or reject the order.

- *Private mailboxes (PMB)*. In the past, fraudsters have used mail drop locations such as mailboxes and so on as delivery points for goods ordered fraudulently by telephone or the Internet. Such a delivery address might appear as though it were a business:

TO: John Doe
My Company
123 Any Street, Suite 333
Mytown, State ZIP

Recently the U.S. Postal Service established a requirement that mail-drop addresses be identified as such. Effective April 2000, the Postal Service may refuse to deliver to private mail-drop locations unless the mailbox is included in the address and identified as PMB. The preceding address would then be legitimately displayed as:

TO: John Doe
My Company   '
123 Any Street, PMB 333
Mytown, State ZIP

- *Business hour check.* Create a rule to check the time of day for the order in the geographic zone the order is coming from to see if it matches the normal business hours. Business hours can be extended hours, but you are looking to see if an order is being placed at 2 A.M. in the area where the person is placing the order. Then decide if that makes sense when you look at typical customers. Typical time envelopes are 8 A.M. to 5 P.M., 6 A.M. to 8 P.M., 6 A.M. to 11 P.M., and 11 P.M. to 6 A.M.

How Do I Use the Results?

There are three accepted methods of utilizing rules within a strategy:

1. *Rule list.* Merchants implement their rules as a set of checks with each one indicating fail or review. If any one condition comes up true, the list is stopped and the result is returned as review or fail. Typically, all fail conditions are put at the top of the list with review conditions put afterward. On the plus side, this is the easiest method to implement. On the negative side, merchants only get

one return value, so they don't know if multiple conditions failed or what required review.

2. *Weighted list.* Merchants implement a set of rules, with each rule having a weighted score for true or false. A score range is established and within the range, subranges are set for pass, fail, and review. On the plus side, they can mix positive and negative factors and get quite sophisticated with scoring. On the negative side, this requires a lot of research and maintenance to ensure it doesn't hurt sales. It typically has a longer learning curve.

3. *Decision tree.* Merchants implement a set of rules that follow a path based on each preceding rule. For example, if condition A is true, then do this; if not, then do that.

Building This In-House

Building an in-house rules engine is very easy to do, and most merchants have implemented some form of rules engine already. It is recommended that, unless merchants have a fairly sophisticated technical group, they use a commercially available rules engine to implement rules. This ensures that they can easily see what rules have been put into place, and it allows them to ensure that the solution is being maintained from someone other than their internal resources.

Manual Reviews

Manual review is a technique in which merchants use staff members to perform manual checks on orders to determine which orders are fraudulent.

How Good Is It?

In general, this is not a very good fraud-prevention technique. The quality and effectiveness of manual reviews is directly proportional to the knowledge and experience of the review staff as well as the tools and process that they have established to perform manual reviews.

According to a merchant survey conducted by CyberSource Corporation in 2008, more than 80 percent of the merchants surveyed use some level of manual review. The survey also shows that the more sales merchants made, the more likely they were to be using some sort of manual review.

This represents a big issue when it comes to scalability. If merchants are relying on manual review, what do they do when their business grows or when they have peaks? As a quick fix, or as a tool to look at for sales conversion, manual reviews are very effective. When it comes to fraud prevention, merchants need to be very careful how much they rely on them.

If merchants are going to rely on manual review, they need to use it to review the orders they were going to reject anyway. This allows merchants to have the possibility of converting an insult instead of trying to catch fraudulent orders.

Drawbacks of manual review include the following:

- It does not scale well; the only way to grow is to add new staff.

- The more people do reviews, the more unpredictable the results, as each will have varying levels of experience and will adopt their own styles for looking for fraud.

- There are good reasons to do manual review, but it should be done to catch those orders a merchant wants to try to keep instead of trying to find fraudulent orders.

- It typically lacks formal training of reviewers.

 TIPS AND TECHNIQUES

- Determine how many orders your fraud reviewers can process in a given day.
- Before implementing manual reviews make sure you understand how much time will it add to the fulfillment process.

TIPS AND TECHNIQUES (CONTINUED)

- Make sure you understand what percentage of fraud they have to catch to make up the difference in their pay.

- Set proper expectations and talk about how many customers will be falsely rejected by the process (insults).

- Manual reviews require tools; before hiring a team make sure you know what tools will be provided to the team to conduct the manual reviews.

Estimated costs: Moderate to expensive.

Alternative solutions: Rules engine, fraud scoring, hot lists, warm lists, positive lists, and consumer authentication.

Vendors: Accertify, Certegy, CyberSource.

EXECUTIVE INSIGHT

Don't Overlook the Basics— It Could Be Costly

MICHAEL LONG, COFOUNDER, CHIEF PRODUCT STRATEGIST, ACCERTIFY, INC.

After more than a decade of experience fighting fraud and helping merchants successfully prevent fraud, I've learned there are several key steps involved in managing data to prevent online retail crime. Some key components that are often overlooked but critical to a cost-effective approach for reducing fraud include the following:

1. Don't forget about manual reviews and case management. Optimize your case management and transaction review process by ensuring you have tools for customizing workflow, streamlining reviews and investigations through to completion. This includes the ability to customize and empower your risk teams' ability to manage rules, transaction display, and other key features. Focusing on case management will

ensure higher throughput, accuracy, and consistency in manual reviews as well as lower customer insults.

2 Maintain negative files based on fraudulent returns or other bad transactions that resulted in credit card chargebacks and automatically update them. Also, keep positive files and leverage positive screening rules so good customers are not flagged for review when their buying habits innocently make them appear suspicious.

3 Measure outcomes. When companies are faced with so many budget priorities, being able to measure your success will help you justify anti-crime investments. Your risk team should have access to robust reporting tools that can be customized to their needs.

How Does It Work?

Merchants set up a fraud-review team. Typically, this team will work under the call center or the finance department. This team will be charged with reviewing all of the company's orders to determine which ones are fraudulent.

The team may have built sorts or queries that put the order data into views in which they can look for suspicious activity. They may look at activity by region, credit card number, or order size. In some cases, they will have queues built to provide them with the orders that need to be reviewed.

When the team finds a suspect order, they may simply reject the order or they may follow up to try to determine if the order is good. Following are some of the common tools used in conducting a manual review:

- Call the bank to verify the shipping and billing information.
- Use a lookup tool to check the consumer's address and phone information.

- Check historical purchase records to see if there is any other activity from this consumer in the past.

- Call to verify the order data with the consumer.

- Have the consumer fax or mail in copies of their driver's license, a utility bill from the address, and/or a credit card statement.

How Do I Use the Results?

As a best practice, it is a very effective way to maximize sales to set up automated processes to weed out the orders a merchant would not automatically accept, and then use reviews on what is remaining. This also allows merchants to scale better because they are only reviewing orders they were going to reject anyway.

Building This In-House

Not applicable.

Rules Engine

The rules engine is a middleware application that allows the creation and prioritization of rules to be used in managing fraud. These engines allow merchants to create rules that will be evaluated on orders as they come in. The rules engine can have many different names, such as *decisioning software*, *management software*, or *order management*. Most payment, CRM, and order management systems will have some of the capabilities to build and apply rules.

How Good Is It?

You can use a rules engine to help you prevent fraud. The rules engine gives you the ability to perform pre- and post-authorization tests and rules, so you can have logic on how and when you want to call for an authorization and you can have rules to handle the return results from authorization.

Merchants have been applying rules to their order flow for years. The concept of a rules engine does not derive from the growth of fraud; merchants have had to build rules to process the order. For example, merchants need rules to add tax based on consumer location and to add shipping based on consumer preference. With fraud, merchants have reacted to losses by having their IT departments add rules to their order management system to weed out orders they may not want to take or to separate orders that they may want to manually review (e.g., all orders over a certain dollar amount).

The intent of the rules engine is to provide business owners with a way to add new rules to their order process to look for fraud. Good rules engines allow technical novices to apply their fraud expertise to add very complex rules that can automate the review of orders without manual intervention.

Good rules engines also provide a mechanism to more quickly make changes to the order flow if you are getting burned by fraud. This is crucial to being successful at minimizing the impact of a fraud ring. Think about it: If your company was being hit by a fraud ring, and you could see the characteristics to look for, and you were in the peak holiday season, how long would it take to get your IT department to implement a new rule to prevent these orders from processing? Could they even do it without bringing down the business for a time period? In reality, I have seen that it can take as long as a month to implement a new rule without a rules engine in place.

Rules engines also:

- Put the control of the fraud-prevention process back into the hands of the fraud-prevention owner
- Allow you to more quickly react to new fraud schemes, by applying new rules in real time
- Allow you to automate the separation of orders more quickly and efficiently, reducing the number of orders to manually review

- Give you better insight into the processes in place
- Have a high cost to get started
- Require someone to manage the fraud business processes
- Add additional software and hardware burdens to ongoing costs.

TIPS AND TECHNIQUES

- How does the solution integrate into your current business flow?

- Do you have to have a technical background to operate the solution?

- Could anyone looking at your business process in the rules engine understand it? Or do you have to learn how to interpret it?

- How fast can you add or change a rule?

- Does the engine manage only a list of rules or does it allow you to set up a business process flow?

- Does the solution integrate other fraud-prevention techniques such as geolocation, velocity, and/or hot lists?

- What type of graphical user interface does the solution come with?

- Do you just get back a pass, fail, or review, or do you get the results of all of the tests?

Estimated costs: Moderate; you will typically pay for a software purchase. A couple of providers offer all of these services on a hosted and managed basis.

Alternative solutions: Fraud scoring.

Vendors: CyberSource, Fair Isaac, Retail Decisions, Clear Commerce.

How Does It Work?

The rules engine concept is pretty simple to understand. You write some rules, and the engine will run those rules against an order when it is submitted. But in actuality, there are different ways this can be done, and you need to make sure you understand that the solution you are looking at is the type of engine that will do what you really want it to do.

Type 1. The rules engine allows you to add rules into a list of checks, and then when an order is processed against the engine, it will evaluate the rules one at a time. The first rule to fail fails the entire transaction. No other rules beyond the first failed rule will be run. This type typically will not allow for very complicated comparisons.

   This type of rules engine is simple to set up and maintain, and it produces a pass or fail type of answer. One of the major shortfalls of this solution is that not all of the rules are run, so if you try to look at a failed order, you will only see the first rule that failed, making it more difficult to determine which orders you should spend more time trying to convert. This type also is hard to interpret what is actually being checked. So if you have high turnover of staff, this solution can be a little more difficult to understand for staff coming in.

Type 2. The rules engine allows you to add rules into a list of checks and apply weights to each of the rules to allow for some rules to be treated as more risky than others. When an order is processed against this type of rules engine, all of the rules are run, and weights are applied to each and the rules engine then creates a score that will determine the outcome of the order. This type can support pass, fail, or review outcomes. This type is the hardest to interpret what is actually being checked. So if you have high turnover of staff, this solution can be a little more difficult to understand for staff coming in.

   This type of rules engine is a little more complex to set up. You will have to understand how to weight certain conditions to get the effective results from the solution. It will require more intensive management.

Type 3. The rules engine allows you to add rules into a business flow, indicating which outcomes or rules need to be run based on the outcome of any one particular rule. When an order is processed through this solution, the number of actual rules run against the order could be different for every order processed because the number of rules run is based on the outcomes of each rule and the order's data points. This type can produce a pass, fail, or review response.

This type of rules engine is a little more complex to set up, but offers a much easier way to view and describe the business flow. This type offers the greatest flexibility for adding or changing the rule logic, by allowing you to blend the rules for fraud prevention with the business processes you use to make a decision on an order.

Type 4. The rules engine is designed to be an all-encompassing engine that provides a merchant with the ability to set up and manage all of the fraud-prevention tools under one application. This gives the merchant the capability to write and edit rules and integrate new prevention tools more rapidly and effectively. With this type of rules engine, you can alter your risk-prevention capabilities on the back end without having to touch the code in your front-end systems each time you need to make a change.

The rules engine evaluates orders via a previously deployed strategy. This part of the rules engine provides a way to encompass other business processes and fraud techniques into the solution, such as payment processing, fraud scoring, geolocation, credit checks, and age verification.

Inside the rules engine, you will have the ability to set up business strategies that represent your risk management decisions and consist of workflows and rules. The workflows represent a collection of rules and a rule compares data points of a transaction to a set of conditions, or it can compare data points to other data points. Think of them as *if/then* statements that you are writing and that express what elements you look at for predicting risk.

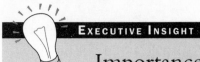

Importance of Real–Time Control on Risk Strategies

TIMOTHY LAUDENBACH, CREDIT RISK MANAGER, BESTBUY.COM

Doing business online is all about being able to do business in real time: the customers expect it, the fraudsters exploit it, and you have to own and plan for it as a fraud professional. Whether you are a small or large company, fraud attacks will come at you quickly and they will change frequently and you need to be prepared to react immediately. Fraud programs need to not only have the right tools, they need to have the ownership and ability to make changes as situations dictate.

Companies that rely on their IT department to make rule changes or perform data inquiries are handicapping themselves and can still take heavy losses in peak traffic periods. Fraud professionals need to have tools that allow for direct interaction and management by the fraud team. *When you respond to a fraud trend is just as important to how you respond to it.*

How Do I Use the Results?

Rules engines are great at automating the fraud–prevention business process. Make sure you take this into account when you are deciding the outcomes you want from the solution. Try to maximize the number of orders going into the *accept* and *reject* buckets, while minimizing the number of orders you want to review.

Make sure their calling applications don't contain any rules or logic. If you set them up to look for the pass, fail, or review, you free yourself up to add and manipulate rules in their rules engine and not in their production system.

Building This In-House

Not applicable.

Velocity of Use

The intent of velocity of use is to look for suspicious behavior based on the number of associated transactions a consumer is attempting. It works based on counting the number of uses of a data element within a predetermined time frame. The theory is the higher the number of uses on a data element (e.g., credit cards) in a predefined time period (e.g., 24 hours), the higher the risk of taking an order.

For example: How many times in the past 24 hours has credit number "111111111111111" been used?

How Good Is It?

Velocity of use is a building block of any serious fraud-prevention solution. Keeping track of the number of uses by different data elements allows you to spot unusual trends and run-up activity. Most major fraud-screening solutions have this type of functionality built into them.

- Velocity of use is good for detecting fraud rings, multiple fraud attacks from the same perpetrator, and some forms of identity morphing.

- The more data elements for which you can track velocity of use, the more effective the tool is. Good data elements to perform this test on are credit card number, address, phone number, e-mail address, and account number.

- If you establish accounts for your customers, perform velocity of use on the number of accounts associated with a particular individual.

TIPS AND TECHNIQUES

- Decide up front on the data elements you want to perform velocity of use checks on. You will also need to know the number of uses you want to flag and the time interval in which you want to look.

- You will have to perform some normalization on the addresses if you are doing this in-house to ensure you get matches.

- Make sure you are logging usage for all attempts, not just completed or valid orders.

- Plan on maintaining data for at least 12 months. I recommend 18 months.

- Will you want to have a pass/fail velocity of use check or a graduated-scale type of solution? The graduated scale adds more risk as the number of uses increases. So, a set of three orders happening in five minutes would have more risk than a set of three orders happening over 30 days.

- There is a distinct advantage to using a third-party service that combines data from multiple merchants or banks to track velocity of use, as you get a much fuller picture on activity by a potential fraudster and have a better chance at picking up on run-up activity.

Estimated costs: Costs to implement a simple velocity of use tool are low, as long as you already have database resources you can utilize and the applications you use to process orders are easily integrated into. A lot of ERP, application servers, decision servers, and the like on the market have this technology integrated into them.

Alternative solutions: Fraud–screening services have velocity of use already built in. Be sure to check if you can add your own custom fields. If you are looking at doing this check based on their account numbers, you will have to look at purchasing in–house solutions or building this service on your own.

Look at velocity of change as well, as these two forms of velocity complement each other.

Vendors: CyberSource, Clear Commerce, Retail Decisions, HNC/ Fair Isaac.

How Does It Work?

The velocity of use technique requires a supporting database and two calls to work. One call increases the count on a data element while the second call does a lookup to see what the count is. If you are using a commercial solution or you are getting this functionality from a commercial fraud-screening service, you will see only one call to acquire this information as the solution will hide these calls from you

Based on the lookup call, you will get a pass or fail type of response and have to decide to reject, review, or pass the order to another sales channel, such as telephone order.

There are three components to performing a velocity of use check: the data element, the count, and the time interval.

Typically, the data elements used for velocity of use are the address (street address, state, zip code), phone number, credit card number, and e-mail address. Name is not recommended, as there are too many people with similar names, which could really kill sales or fill manual review bins. The address has to be looked at in whole, not in parts; counting the number by state or zip code can raise a lot of false alarms. If you typically don't do a lot of business in one location in a short time frame, you may want to look at zip code or state. Likewise, if you have identified a hot spot by zip code, you should apply a rule to perform further fraud-prevention tests on that order.

The count and time frame are very tightly joined. There is no hard, set rule on what number of changes and time frame to look at. In general, you need to understand your good customers, know if you get a lot of repeat business, know if is it typical for your customers to make more than one purchase per day, week, or year. You also need to think about when it becomes completely unrealistic. For example:

- *I sell printer ink, paper, and refills.* I would expect my customers to be repeat customers, and I would assume on non–bank-to-BIN orders that consumers would not typically make more than one purchase per day, but it would not be unusual for a consumer to do two orders in one day, but three or more orders in one day would be highly suspect.

- *I sell laptop computers.* I would expect my BIN-to-country customers to have more one-time purchases with at least 12 months' time between orders. I would be suspect of any BIN-to country customer making more than one order per day on computers. This does not mean ordering more than one computer in an order; this means placing two separate orders for computers in one day or week.

- *I sell jewelry.* I would expect my BIN-to-country customers to only make one purchase a day and would be very suspect of two or more orders in a day. I would be somewhat suspect of more than one order in a week or month and would want to take a closer look, and I routinely have BIN-to-country customers who make more than one purchase in a year.

- *I sell rechargeable cell phones.* I would be highly suspect of more than one recharge in a day. I would be slightly suspect of more than one recharge in a week and expect a recharge every other week or once a month.

The better commercial solutions, usually fraud-screening services, don't simply pass and fail on velocity of use. They actually increment the level of risk by the number of uses until they reach a point that they reject the order. This is usually only found in solutions that allow weighting of tests. For example: If I am looking at a time interval of 15 minutes and a credit card number with only one use comes up, I would get no added risk, but if the same credit card showed up twice in five minutes, I would give it high risk. The more attempts in the time period, the higher the risk goes. Likewise, the more time that passes between attempts, the lower the risk.

Set up a process that mandates that all attempted orders are logged into velocity, not just valid sales.

How Do I Use the Results?

- Log all attempted transactions, not just valid orders coming into the system.

- You can set up velocity of use tests to look for orders to review or reject, but if you are going to reject based on velocity of use, make sure they fail other fraud tests as well. If the only test they fail is velocity of use, we would recommend you call the customer to validate the purchases.

- The magic number before chargebacks appear is 90 days, which means they won't appear on a hot list until up to 90 days. Some fraudsters will time their attacks so orders are coming in at odd intervals: one order today, next one in three days, the next in one week, the next in four days, and so on. Make sure some of your velocity of use tests are looking at activity within the 90-day window. You can do this real time or to save processing time in the upfront orders; set up an offline batch routine that looks at activity by accounts or orders to establish counts over the 90-day window.

- If someone fails this test and you are looking at a time period less than 24 hours, *make sure you cancel or put on hold* the original orders.

Building This In-House

The velocity of use technique requires a supporting database and two calls to work. One call increases the count on a data element while the second call does a lookup to see what the count is.

Database. Have your database administrator set up a database resource for you to use. They will have to set up the database structure and design to store the data elements and to maintain counts on the data elements.

Call 1: Add records and increment. Have your IT team set up calls from all applications and channels that touch those data elements, so e-commerce, MOTO, and card-present channels will add new entries into the data set or they will increment the counts on the data elements if they already exist. You have to enter a date time stamp with every new record you put into the data set.

Call 2: Look up activity. Have your IT team set up calls from all applications and channels that touch these data elements, typically done as part of your fraud-screening procedures, to check the number of uses this person has. This is typically done by use of stored procedure. In the event you are using only one record per data element and are incrementing the count and date time stamp, you would only have to call the supporting data set and look up the data element. This call is doing the look up on each independent data element you have determined to do velocity of use checks.

Velocity of Change

The intent of velocity of change is to look for suspicious behavior based on the number of changes between data elements on new transactions with previous transactions. It works based on counting the number of changes with associated data elements within a predefined time frame. The theory is the higher the number of changes on a set of data elements, such as the number of phone numbers or addresses associated with credit cards in a predefined time frame, the higher the risk of taking an order.

For example: How many phone numbers have been used with credit card number "111111111111111" in the last 24 hours?

How Good Is It?

Velocity of change is one of the mechanisms to catch identity morphing. As a general fraud-prevention tool, there is a high correlation to risky behavior with those transactions that fail this type of test. Most major fraud-screening solutions have this type of functionality built into them.

- Velocity of change is good for detecting stolen card numbers, multiple fraud attacks from the same perpetrator, and forms of identity morphing.

- The more data elements you can track velocity of change on the more effective the tool is. Good data elements to perform this test on are credit card number, addresses (billing and shipping), phone number, e-mail address, and account number.

- If you establish accounts for your customers, performing velocity of change on the number of accounts associated with a particular individual data element or in the opening of new accounts can help catch fraudsters before they can place a fraudulent order.

 TIPS AND TECHNIQUES

- Decide up front on the data elements you want to perform velocity of change checks on. You will also need to know the number of changes you want to flag and the time interval you want to look in.

- You will have to perform some normalization on the addresses if you are doing this in-house to ensure you get matches.

- Use the shipping address, and not the billing address, for velocity of change. See guidelines and samples under "How it Works."

- Make sure you are logging usage for all attempts, not just completed or valid orders.

- Plan on maintaining data for at least 12 months. I recommend 18 months.

- Will you want to have a pass/fail velocity of change check or a graduated-scale type of solution? The graduated-scale adds more risk as the number of changes increases. Typically, with velocity of change, the pass/fail method is used.

- There is a distinct advantage to using a third-party service that combines data from multiple merchants or banks to track velocity of change, as you get a much fuller picture on activity by a potential fraudster and have a better chance at picking up on bust-out activity.

Estimated costs: Costs to implement a simple velocity of change tool are low, as long as you already have database resources you can utilize and the applications you use to process orders are easily integrated into. A lot of ERP, application servers, decision servers, and the like on the market have this technology integrated into them already or through third–party modules.

Alternative solutions: Fraud-screening services have velocity of change already built in. Be sure to check if you can add your own custom fields. If you are looking at doing this check based on account numbers, you will have to look at purchasing in-house solutions or building this service on your own.

Vendors: CyberSource, Clear Commerce, Retail Decisions, HNC/ Fair Isaac, Trustmarque.

How Does It Work?

The velocity of change technique requires a supporting database and two calls to work. One call increases the count on a data element while the second call does a lookup to see what the count is. If you are using a commercial solution or you are getting this functionality from a commercial fraud-screening service, you will only see one call to acquire this information as the solution will hide these calls from you.

Based on the lookup call, you will get a pass or fail type of response and decide to reject, review, or pass the order to another sales channel, such as telephone order.

There are four components to performing a velocity of change check: two data elements to compare, the count, and the time interval.

Typically, the data elements used for velocity of change are the shipping address (street address, state, zip code), phone number, credit card number, expiration date, and e-mail address. Name is not recommended, as there are too many people with similar names, which could really kill sales or fill manual review bins. The address has to be looked at in whole, not in parts; counting the number by state or zip code can raise a lot of false alarms. If you typically don't do a lot of business in one location in a short time frame, you may want to look at zip code or state. Likewise, if you have identified a hot spot by zip code, you should be applying a rule to perform further fraud-prevention tests on that order by looking at changes within that zip code.

The count and time frame are very tightly joined. There is no hard, set rule on what number of changes and time frame to look at. In general, you need to understand your good customers: Do you get a lot of repeat business? Is it typical for your customers to make more than one purchase per day, week, or year? You also need to think about when it becomes completely unrealistic.

To see change, you have to be comparing two data elements to count the number of times one piece of the information changes. This forms the basis of the technique.

As an example, if your customers typically buy your products or services as gifts for other people, you would want to do the following checks:

- *Credit card number to expiration date.* Check to see how many times the expiration date changes with a credit card number.

- *Credit card number to shipping address.* Check to see how many shipping addresses are associated with a credit card number.

- *Credit card number to phone number.* Check to see how many phone numbers have been given with a credit card number.

- *Credit card number to e-mail.* Check to see how many e-mails are given with a credit card number.

- *Phone number to shipping address.* Check to see how many shipping addresses are given with a phone number.

- *Phone number to credit card.* Check to see how many credit cards are given with a phone number.

- *Phone number to e-mail.* Check to see how many e-mails are given with a phone number.

- *Shipping address to credit card number.* Check to see how many credit card numbers are associated with a shipping address.

The better commercial solutions, usually fraud-screening services, perform these velocity of change tests.

Set up a process that mandates that all attempted orders are logged into velocity, not just valid sales.

How Do I Use the Results?

- Log all attempted transactions, not just valid orders coming into the system.

- You can set up your velocity of change tests to look for orders to review or reject.

- The magic number before chargebacks appear is 90 days, which means they won't appear on a hot list until up to 90 days. Some fraudsters will time their attacks so orders are coming in at odd intervals: one order today, next one in three days, the next in one week, the next in four days, and so on. Make sure some of your velocity of change tests are looking at activity within the 90-day window. You can do this in real time, or to save processing time in the upfront orders set up an offline batch routine that looks at activity by accounts or orders to establish counts over the 24-hour window by under the 90-day window. For orders over 90 days old that have not been charged back, you don't need to perform active checks.

- If someone fails this test and you are looking at a time period less than 24 hours, *make sure you cancel or put on hold* any other orders from this identity.

- The following are meant as starting points only; you have to look at your customer base to determine what time intervals and number of changes really are best for you.

  - *Credit card number to expiration date.* More than two changes in 24 hours; they could make one typo, but to see three changes indicates guessing.

  - *Credit card number to shipping address.* If your products are normally sent as gifts, you should set this high, if you use it at all. This is really better for businesses that don't normally have consumers buying gifts.

  - *Credit card number to phone number.* More than two changes in 24 hours shows guessing and high usage and is considered risky.

  - *Credit card number to e-mail.* Most online consumers use the same e-mail address for making purchases. If you start to see more than two e-mail addresses, you should do further review.

  - *Phone number to shipping address.* Again, if you do a lot of gifts, you should not use this test, as you will get a lot of changes with this indicator. It is usually a good indicator of bogus phone numbers.

  - *Phone number to credit card.* Most online consumers use one to three credit cards for online purchases. If you see more than four associated with a phone number, you need to review or reject the order.

- *Phone number to e-mail.* Again, more than two changes indicates you need to do some other checks.

- *Shipping address to credit card number.* Typical online consumers use between one and three credit cards for purchasing online, so look for more than four changes.

Building This In-House

The velocity of change technique requires a supporting database and two calls to work. One call increases the count on a data element test while the second call does a lookup to see what the count is.

Database: Have your database administrator set up a database resource for you to use. He or she will have to set up the database structure and design to store the data elements, and to maintain counts on the data elements as changes are documented.

Call 1: Add records and increment: Have your IT team set up calls from all applications and channels that touch those data elements, so e-commerce, MOTO, and card-present channels will add new entries into the data set or they will increment the counts on the data elements if they already exist. You have to enter a date time stamp with every new record you put into the data set.

Call 2: Look up activity: Have your IT team set up calls from all applications and channels that touch these data elements, typically done as part of their fraud-screening procedures, to check the number of changes this order has. This is typically done by use of stored procedure, or in the event you are using only one record per data element and are incrementing the count and date time stamp, you would only have to call the supporting data set and look up the data element. This call is doing the lookup on each independent data element you have determined to do velocity of change checks on.

Chapter Summary

Operational management providers provide the infrastructure companies need to run a fraud operation independently of their IT departments. These solutions allow fraud programs to make use of real-time decisioning as well as providing access to third-party data within a structured system. Structure is key; it is the ability to implement the basic fraud techniques such as rules, lists, velocities, and authorizations that make these systems central to the operational performance of a fraud program.

As a basic building block for fraud management, understanding the role of velocities is an essential learning point. Velocities are one of the simplest ways to catch repeat fraudsters. Velocity of use will help find the repeat offenders using the same information over and over, while velocity of change will help find the fraudsters attempting to morph their identity by changing pieces of their identity.

For some merchants, the need to perform additional fraud screening in the form of manual reviews makes good business sense. In the case where manual reviews do make sense, companies need to make sure their reviewers are given the additional tools they need to make the determination to accept or reject a transaction.

CHAPTER 9

Fraud Prevention Techniques: Analytics

After reading this chapter, you will be able to:

- Describe limiting factors for creating models
- Describe the difference between "what if" and shadowing analytical capabilities

Neural Nets

Neural nets are a form of modeling in which a computer attempts to predict good and positive outcomes by use of previous and current activity. Neural nets are not unique to fraud or fraud prevention; they are used in many different industries today. The neural net is typically the primary engine behind more sophisticated fraud-scoring applications.

How Good Is It?

Neural nets are very complicated to set up and maintain. They require very educated and experienced personnel to set up correctly. The value of a neural net is directly proportional to the people and data that went into making it. Generally speaking, neural nets are very effective tools for predicting risk.

The casual merchant is not going to go out and implement his or her own neural net solution. First, it is very expensive, requiring very experienced and highly educated personnel to set it up and maintain it. Second, to build an effective neural net, you need to have a lot of quality data to make sure it can accurately predict the positive and negative behavior, and this data must be refreshed often to be effective.

TIPS AND TECHNIQUES

- How often is the data in the neural net updated: per transaction, per quarter, semiannually, annually, or more often?

- Where did the data inside the neural net come from? Did it come from the same type of sales channel you are using (e.g., e-commerce, MOTO, or card-present data)? Does it include data from multiple card types or mainly just one type?

- How many orders and how many other merchants or associations are feeding the data?

Estimated costs: Very expensive.

Alternative solutions: Fraud scoring that offers neural nets modeling as part of its solution.

Vendors: Fair Isaac.

How Does It Work?

The neural net is based off underlying models. These models attempt to make predictive correlations between data elements. For example, a correlation may be as follows: "The more credit cards you see associated with an address, the higher the risk." The neural net takes several of these correlations. Then, as an order is presented to the system, it runs all of the correlations to come up with predictions about the outcome of the order.

In building a neural net, you build a number of models and correlations and then feed in a set of data to train the neural net. By training the neural net, you are telling it the actual outcomes on known orders, and this becomes its basis for making future predictions. You are also showing the neural net how to weight certain correlations, because they are not all equal when it comes to predicting a desired outcome. This is why the quality and breadth of the data you use in your neural net is critical to accurately predict required outcomes.

Once you have trained a neural net, you have to test it with known test cases that you didn't feed into the model build in order to see how well it predicts the required outcome. Likewise, you should do analysis at least once a quarter to determine the effectiveness of the predictions of the neural net.

Once the neural net is ready for actual use, it is typically set up to provide a ranged score (say, 1 to 100 or 1 to infinity) that indicates the level of risk with an order. Needless to say, you also have to do analysis on the scores that get spit out of the neural net to understand what a score of 10 versus 10,000 really means to you.

Accumulating the required data and making sure it is clean and accurate takes a lot of time. Training the neural net also takes time, so updating a neural net is not a trivial process. This is why most vendors that offer a neural net have limited refreshes on it. It is not a small undertaking to set up and administer a neural net, so it should be well thought out.

How Do I Use the Results?

The neural net will typically provide a ranged score. In some cases it will provide a pass or fail answer. You will have to set up the system to interpret these results.

Building This In-House

One of the biggest questions you will have to ask yourself in building a neural net is whether you want to base the neural net and modeling off good or bad behavior. I believe you should use heuristics and rules-based checks for bad behavior and use neural nets for trying to predict good behavior.

If you look at a typical business, you will find that the majority of orders that come in are good orders, not fraudulent. In modeling, you need data, and lots of it, to build an effective predictive model. If a typical merchant did 100 orders and had a fraud rate of only 1 percent, would you rather build the model off 1 order or 99 orders?

Furthermore, fraud is a moving target—new schemes and techniques are constantly being developed to get around these fraud techniques. If you base modeling on bad behavior, you are only going to catch the types of fraud you already know about. What about the schemes you have never heard of?

By focusing on good behavior, I can look at an order and attempt to predict the answer for "How much does this order look like the other orders I have had that successfully processed without fraud?"

Data is king when it comes to modeling. If the volume is not very high, think about working with a group of other merchants in the same vertical space to share data and to help make even more predictive models.

Don't lose sight of the insult—you could build a solution that will catch all fraud attempts, but at what cost? How many good consumers will your solution peg as bad or risky consumers when the order is just fine? This is a major thing to consider as it can cost your business millions of dollars. In studies I have done on tools such as address verification, if you relied solely on AVS as the decision maker on risk, you could insult up to 25 percent of your good consumers.

EXECUTIVE INSIGHT

Utilizing Statistical Models as Part of Your E-Commerce Fraud Prevention Toolkit

CHRIS URIARTE, CHIEF TECHNOLOGY OFFICER, RETAIL DECISIONS

While various types of fraud detection models that are based on advanced statistical and mathematical algorithms (neural networks, Bayesian, etc.) have been successfully used by card issuers over the last 20 years, it is only in the past five years or so that these models have proven themselves valuable in the detection of e-commerce fraud when deployed by merchants as part of a comprehensive CNP fraud detection strategy.

For many years, such models have been at the forefront of fraud detection systems utilized by issuers, who often rely on their fraud scores as the dominant indicator as to whether fraudulent activity has occurred on a card within its portfolio. Issuers have the ability to model on a rich set of cardholder spending patterns, which help paint a comprehensive picture of how each cardholder uses his card. Merchants, however, only have access to a limited view of how a cardholder utilizes his card, and thus, it is challenging to create effective CNP fraud detection models for merchants by modeling on cardholder behavior alone. This presents a unique challenge when building merchant CNP fraud detection models and also forces merchants to give careful consideration as to what role the model should play and what level of model effectiveness is acceptable. Unlike the heavy reliance on these models in the issuing world, merchants must couple their use with a strong suite of additional fraud detection tools and techniques in order to achieve acceptable overall detection rates—statistical models alone will not get the job done.

However, while models may not be comprehensively effective in and of themselves, good models should provide a level of fraud detection "lift" above and beyond all other tools and technologies used within the fraud detection suite. Therefore, merchants should focus less on overall model detection rates and, instead, focus on the level of fraud detected by the model that was not detected by other techniques. A model that detects only 4 percent of overall fraud within a universe of transactions can still be considered to be very effective if, say, 2 percent of that fraud would have gone otherwise undetected. Furthermore, the overall fraud rate detected in a comprehensive, multidimensional fraud-prevention system can be further boosted by relational linking of transaction data associated with those transactions that were uniquely flagged by the statistical model. For example, linking other e-mail or shipping addresses associated with transactions flagged by the model may result in the uncovering of additional fraudulent activity.

Merchants should be aware that fraud detection models require constant care and feeding in order to maintain an acceptable level of effectiveness. The evolving nature of fraud, coupled with the ongoing evolution of a merchant's product and service suite, means that, in addition to the up-front investment required for model creation, merchants must also budget for ongoing model maintenance, as well as refresh and rebuild activities. There may also be peripheral work required to begin the modeling process, such as ensuring that all historical fraud data is accurately associated with original transaction data, or cleaning up historical data in order to ensure consistency across all data elements. The time and cost associated with these activities should be considered within the "total cost of ownership" required to operate the model, which, of course, should be compared against the monetary savings that the model brings to the enterprise.

The construction and maintenance of these models can often be complex and costly, but if executed correctly, they can bring additional fraud detection capabilities above and beyond other fraud detection tools, techniques, and technologies used by merchants today.

Other Key Analytical Concepts

- *Bayesian models.* Bayesian models are a different approach to modeling where behavioral characteristics are input to create predictive outcomes. A good practical example of this approach is the way a physician diagnoses an illness by looking for certain characteristics or symptoms. From a fraud perspective, the model attempts to diagnose fraud by looking for certain symptoms or characteristics of fraud.

- *Regression analysis.* Regression analysis compares the relationship between two data elements with one being fixed and the other changing in relationship to the fixed data element (e.g., how many different names are associated with a given phone number).

- *Monitoring.* Monitoring is the act of actively reviewing transactional or account history to detect anomalies and outliers for review and investigation. Monitoring also includes the benchmarking of exiting fraud controls for accuracy and reliability.

- *Historical analysis—"what if."* This is an analytical tool to create new rule sets or strategies to run "what if" analysis against known outcomes on historical data.

- *Shadowing.* Shadowing is an analytical tool to create and put a strategy or rule set in live production to run in parallel to existing processes to determine the effectiveness of a new fraud strategy.

Chapter Summary

Modeling can be a very effective tool for fraud prevention, but it typically requires access to a lot of historical data along with highly experienced staff to make it work correctly. The investment in modeling can be substantial, and it is typically associated with larger, more established companies.

There are shell models that can be adapted to different companies within a similar vertical market, and models should not be ruled as an option for mid-sized companies looking for higher returns. The more data signals a company collects, the more likely models will be of use.

Analytics isn't just about modeling; it is a core part of any fraud operation, and the capability to perform what-if and shadow strategies can mean the difference between a successful change to a strategy and a real disaster. What-if and shadow capabilities allow fraud teams to test new strategies and rule sets before they roll them into production.

CHAPTER 10

Fraud Prevention Techniques: Data Quality

After reading this chapter, you will be able to:

- Describe the differences between address authentication and delivery address verification.
- Discuss the role of a MOD 10 check.
- Discuss why denied party checks are needed.

Delivery Address Verification

Delivery address verification is used to check the consumer's shipping address to make sure it is a deliverable address.

How Good Is It?

The systems used to check addresses are typically the same ones the United States Postal Service (USPS) uses to deliver mail. So, they are good. Remember, this service does not check to see if the consumer actually lives at that address; it just verifies that the address exists. The main use for this check is to ensure you don't have goods returned because the address is not deliverable. But this is also a good way to see if the consumer is using a real address or not. Some important things to consider about delivery address verification are:

- It doesn't validate that the consumer lives at the address; it just confirms that the address exists.

- There is a much higher value for digitally delivered goods to make sure the consumer is not giving the merchant a bogus address.

- It is good for fulfillment and for issues with lots of returned shipments due to undeliverable addresses.

- Some of these services will autocorrect addresses to make sure they work correctly.

 TIPS AND TECHNIQUES

- Does the service provider support all of the countries required for the merchant's business?

- Address data changes constantly—how often is the data updated?

- Does the service know all of the actual numbers for post office boxes or private mailboxes? Does it capture suites?

- Does the service do address cleanup?

- Does their provider give the merchant the following:
  - Validation of the incoming address
  - Address standardization
  - Zip correction and Zip+4 code appending
  - Line of travel (LOT) coding
  - Delivery point bar coding
  - Distinguishes residential and business addresses
  - Carrier route codes and carrier
  - Advanced name and address parsing

Estimated costs: For service bureaus, you will pay for each transaction. For software services, you will pay quarterly or monthly subscription fees for updates.

Alternative solutions: Get address verification from credit bureaus or consumer authentication services.

Vendors: CyberSource, Group One Software, USPS, Intelligent Search Technology (CorrectAddress.com).

How Does It Work?

The service takes the shipping address information provided and checks to see if the address exists. It checks the street, city, state, zip code, and country. Make sure to do the test in real time for the best results. Doing it in real time allows the merchant to immediately ask the consumer to correct the shipping data. For digital goods providers, use the billing address.

Some delivery address verification services will actually attempt to auto-correct the address. It will put the zip into five-plus-four, and it will check the numbers and letters on addresses that have multiple units.

How Do I Use the Results?

If the delivery address verification check fails, make sure to ask the consumer to reconfirm the shipping address.

Building This In-House

Purchase software with address data, and then create a call to the data to check the address. Or, if merchants want to check this manually, they can go to the USPS site to check the address as well.

MOD 10 Check

The MOD 10 check takes the credit card number the customer submitted and validates that the number is in the correct range and format to be a credit card number and it is the type of credit card the consumer says it is.

How Good Is It?

When consumers decide to buy on a site, merchants are relying on them to input their information correctly the first time. If you think about this, it may seem simple, but in reality, things do go wrong. Consumers could transpose numbers in the sequence, forget one of the digits, forget to input the expiration date, or say it's a Visa card when it's really an American Express. These things slow down their order processing and clog up the system. And if you don't do anything to correct this information up front, you open yourself up to the most basic forms of attempted fraud by simply plugging numbers into their site.

Items to note about MOD 10 check:

- It does not tell you if a credit card number is active or not, just that it is in the correct format.

- This test is used on a web site to validate that the credit card submitted is a recognizable credit card number.

- High value: It helps prevent merchants from processing credit card authorizations on numbers that could not possibly be credit cards.

The fact that people get their credit card number wrong on the buy page does not mean the order is fraudulent. They could have done any of a number of legitimate things to affect the information. If someone repeatedly cannot pass through the MOD 10 check, then it is an issue.

TIPS AND TECHNIQUES

- Implement first: This is one of the lowest-cost and easiest things to implement on your web site, and you should implement it now if you are not using it already.

- Many development sites online offer free snippets of code for completing the MOD 10 check.

Estimated costs: No costs for doing the check, just the initial costs for setting up the code.

Alternative solutions: None.

Vendors: None.

How Does It Work?

The MOD 10 check is usually implemented right on the web site in the web page that contains the buy button and credit card information. The code is a client-side script, so when the customer puts in his or her purchase information and presses the buy button, the MOD 10 checks are done. The order is only sent to the merchant site when the MOD 10 check passes successfully.

Implementing it this way saves you processing time to go back and forth with the consumer in the order processing. For merchants doing off-line authorization, it saves manual intervention time and callbacks. It also saves you money if you are paying each time you call for an authorization.

How Do I Use the Results?

Because it is a client-side script, you don't have to do anything with the results. You should not see consumer orders unless they can pass the MOD 10 check.

Building This In-House

Determine the proper code for your web site and add the MOD 10 code to your customer order page on the submit button.

Denied Party Checks

Denied party check is used to check the federal listing of parties that merchants in the United States are prohibited from doing business with. The intent is to automatically cross-check consumer information in real time against lists provided by the U.S. government of designated parties for whom it is illegal to ship, trade, or sell goods and services.

U.S. regulations prohibit the sale (trade) of goods and/or services to certain entities and individuals, such as known terrorists and other restricted parties, contained in lists issued by various U.S. government agencies. The Office of Foreign Assets Control (OFAC) in the Department of Treasury publishes a denied party list of restricted entities and individuals.

How Good Is It?

There are providers of automated services and software to check for denied parties, and merchants can do this on their own. In general, these solutions are fair, so make sure the solution that is chosen is using fuzzy logic. Fuzzy logic is the ability to see if the consumer data is similar to an entry on the denied party list. This is good to catch things such as abbreviations, misspelled words, or variations.

Using a service means you don't have to maintain the list of denied parties; instead, you are paying for each use of the service.

Important considerations for the denied party check include:

- Using a third party service provider is a way to screen orders with the posted listing without having to do significant coding.

- Have an automated way to update the information in the listing.

- Make sure there is a means for doing fuzzy logic matches.

- There are a number of denied party lists, and the requirements for the level of verification can be more stringent based on the goods or services a company provides. If you don't understand the requirements for your business, make sure you use a provider that does.

- International companies will likely require multiple service providers as service providers typically don't have all denied party lists in the United States, Europe, and Asia.

TIPS AND TECHNIQUES

- What lists does the service get information from? For example, U.S. Government Anti-Terrorist, Embargoed Countries, International Traffic in Arms Debarment and Sanctions lists, and Specially Designated Nationals (SDN) and other Denied Persons lists, which may include terrorists, narcotics traffickers, and blocked persons and organizations.

- How often are the lists updated?

- Medical, drug, and some high-technology requirements differ greatly and merchants will have to put in significant updates to be compliant with these requirements for ensuring that they are not violating any laws.

- Does the service employ fuzzy logic for making matches?

- Is the service standalone or part of a broader export compliance solution?

Estimated costs: For service bureaus, merchants will pay for each transaction; for software services, they will pay quarterly or monthly subscription fees for updates.

Alternative solutions: Some payment gateway services provide this service for free as part of their authorization services.

Vendors: Actimize, eCustoms, Intelligent Search, Lexis Nexis, Experian, CyberSource, Quova.

How Does It Work?

Typically, this check is done before the authorization or fraud screen is executed. There are several lists maintained by the U.S. government of persons or companies in the United States, and abroad, with which U.S. businesses are not allowed to conduct trade. Lists include the following:

- *Specially Designated Nationals* (SDN) list, including terrorists, narcotics traffickers, and blocked persons and vessels. Issued by the Department of Treasury, Office of Foreign Assets Control.

- *Denied Persons List* (BXA) issued by the U.S. Department of Commerce Bureau of Export Administration, includes individuals who have violated export laws, shipping prohibited goods to.

- *Entity List*, issued by the U.S. Department of Commerce Bureau of Export Administration, includes foreign end users involved in proliferation activities. These end users have been determined to present an unacceptable risk of diversion to developing weapons of mass destruction or the missiles used to deliver those weapons.

- *Embargoed Countries List*, U.S. Department of Commerce, issued by the Bureau of Export Administration.

- *International Traffic in Arms Debarment List*, issued by the Department of State, includes individuals convicted of conspiracy/violations of the Arms Export Control Act, who now are subject to statutory debarment from participating in arms export transactions.

- *Sanctions List*, Department of State, Office of Foreign Assets.

How Do I Use the Results?

Should a match occur, the requested transaction would be stopped before execution. It is recommended that a customer service agent review the order before any communication is sent to the customer or the product is shipped.

Building This In-House

You can easily build a system to check for these addresses yourself. Just remember you have to constantly look for updates and make sure they are loaded into your system.

For more information on recent export regulation news, go to www.bis.doc.gov/dpl/default.shtm.

Chapter Summary

Performing data quality checks is simply a no-brainer for companies to perform. On the highest level, data quality checks ensure only good data is being stored in the data warehouse, and they increase the likelihood of a good customer experience with your customers.

The purpose of data quality checks is to make sure the data provided by a consumer makes sense and is properly cleansed and standardized before storing it. Data quality checks are not a form of verification; when a company runs a delivery address check, it is making sure the address provided is deliverable, not that the consumer using it actually is connected to it. Likewise, performing a MOD 10 check will not tell you that a credit card is owned by a consumer, but it will tell you if the number provided could even pass as a credit card number.

A part of data quality is the running of any policy-based checks that would preclude you from doing business with an individual. This could be a self-imposed policy or a legal requirement like OFAC or denied party checks.

CHAPTER 11

Fraud Prevention Techniques: Technology

After reading this chapter, you will be able to:

- Discuss the most popular technology-based tools in the marketplace.
- Describe the difference between geolocation and geolocating.

Biometrics

Biometrics are used to verify a person's identity by a unique physical attribute that distinguishes that individual from any other person. Common physical elements used include (but are not limited to) fingerprints, retinal scans, voiceprints, and DNA matching.

How Good Is It?

Biometrics are very effective as a tool to authenticate a person's identity. The problem is that it is very expensive to implement and requires the consumer to have equipment to produce the authentication. For today's marketplace, it is very unlikely that this type of fraud technique will be implemented in any kind of mass scale. If you have a defined set of consumers who constantly make purchases, you may entertain this option. But more than likely, you are in a very high-risk regulated sector if you are entertaining this fraud-prevention technique. For example, the pharmaceutical sector would be well suited. Some important things to consider about implementing biometrics include:

- Merchants may still have application fraud in which the account is set up in the fraudster's identity with his or her biometric readings.

- It is very expensive to implement and a very small-scale type of solution.

- It requires the consumer to have specialized equipment to perform the authentication check.

- Most solutions still store authentication data on hard drives that could be hacked.

- A lot of devices give the option of defaulting to a password instead of a biometric authentication.

 TIPS AND TECHNIQUES

- Are the merchant's consumers setting up accounts? How will the merchant collect the initial biometric data from their consumer?

- What type of equipment will the consumer need to perform the check?

- Are the devices portable, or will they only work on the one system on which they are installed?

- How do they work for MOTO?

- What happens if the system cannot authenticate, and it is the real consumer?

- What are the insult rates of the solution?

- Who supports the consumer in getting the technology to work?

- There may be hardware compatibility issues.

Estimated costs: Very expensive.

Alternative solutions: RSA tokens, authentication schemes with passwords or codes.

Vendors: Identix, BioLink, Ethentica, Touchcredit.

How Does It Work?

These devices compare a stored image or value that is calculated by the unique characteristics of consumers with the value they use when they make a purchase. For example, with fingerprints they may be counting the number of identical points from a saved image of the consumer's thumb.

How Do I Use the Results?

These tools can be implemented in a number of different ways. The merchant could send the consumer the device and have him or her install it upon registering with the merchant's solution provider. Then when the consumer attempts to make a purchase, the system would do a validation and pass the information on to the merchant.

Another method is to have the device perform the authentication and produce a one-use number for the purchase, like a disposable credit card number. In some cases, the device actually performs the authentication as a means for gaining access to the site or material for making a purchase.

Building This In-House

Not applicable.

Geolocation

Geolocation services provide detailed information about a consumer's worldwide location, line speed, domain, and so on. It is used primarily to verify the consumer's data to determine where he or she is at the time of purchase. Geolocation services can be used for fraud prevention as well as export and regulatory compliance.

For fraud prevention, geolocation shows a merchant if the consumer is trying to hide his or her identity. For example, it flags the result if the consumer is making the purchase from a location vastly different from the billing or shipping information, such as if a consumer gives the merchant an address and phone number in New York, but the IP address is showing that the consumer is coming from Russia.

For regulatory compliance, industries such as gaming, digital software download, and certain export industries would use this service to validate that consumers are really in the location they say they are in. Merchants can also ensure that they don't provide goods or services to consumers in countries where it may be prohibited.

How Good Is It?

In general, these services are pretty reliable and offer a valuable tool for merchants. The best application for this tool is in the regulatory compliance arena. For fraud prevention, it provides a valuable tool but cannot stand alone in making a decision to accept or reject an order. Purchasing this solution can be more expensive than most fraud-scoring services, which typically provide this type of a check as part of the scoring service.

Pros and cons of geolocation include the following:

- Pro: It is easy to implement.
- Pro: It is the best method to validate regulatory compliance on country.
- In general, if merchants do business only in a certain country, this is a great tool to catch those consumers from outside the country before they get into the order-processing stream.
- Con: It is good for catching large discrepancies between the data provided and the actual location of the consumer, but due to the

nature of the web and people traveling, merchants do have to be careful about how they implement this as a fraud-prevention tool.

- Con: It is useful only when you have an IP address, so it will not work for other consumer-not-present (CNP) transactions such as phone-based orders.

TIPS AND TECHNIQUES

- Can the solution see through proxies and through services such as AOL to determine where an order is coming from?
- Can the solution tell how reliable the information is when you get it (e.g., level of confidence by country or region)?
- What other types of data does the service provide as part of the solution such as geographic information (continent, country, time zone, state, city, zip, area code, longitude/latitude, DMA, MSA, PMSA), proxy information (AOL, anonymous proxies, cache proxies, corporate proxies), and/or network information (domain name, network connection type, network speed, autonomous system number, backbone carrier name)?
- How often is the data updated and verified by the vendor?

Estimated costs: Costs will vary based on the vendor you select. Nslookup, Whereis, and Whois are utilities that provide this information in a basic form for free. You can also find vendors that offer more sophisticated services as in-house software solutions with subscription fees, or on a completely outsourced model with a per-transaction fee.

Alternative solutions: You can also look at trying some of the fraud-scoring services that offer the geolocation check as part of the score.

Vendors: CyberSource, Clear Commerce, Quova, Digital Envoy, Akamai, SamSpade.org.

How Does It Work?

Geolocation services provide detailed information about a consumer's worldwide location, line speed, domain, and so on. These services rely on the IP address. Merchants can get the IP address from the HTTP header on the order that comes into the site. This IP address can be compared to the location the consumer says he or she is at and a determination can be made if the order is fraudulent or not.

Geolocation services can offer a variety of information at varying degrees of depth, but the information can be lumped into three major categories:

1. Geographic information, such as continent, country, time zone, state, city, zip, area code, longitude/latitude, DMA, MSA, PMSA.

2. Proxy information, such as AOL, anonymous proxies, cache proxies, corporate proxies. See the "Proxy Detection" section in this chapter for a more detailed discussion of proxies.

3. Network information, such as domain name, network connection type, network speed, autonomous system number, and backbone carrier name.

TIPS AND TECHNIQUES

Make sure your provider is using a technology that can dig out a consumer's location even through proxies and services such as AOL. Quova is one of the services that can dig out the consumer location even for AOL users.

Many vendors offer geolocation services, but many have not created their own solutions and are actually using the technology of a handful of technology providers like Quova.

The core of an IP geolocation service is the mapping of IP addresses to global locations to create a global data collection network. The system, provided by Quova, uses multiple automated techniques and algorithms to collect, map, and analyze the billions of IP addresses that make up the Internet, plus international teams of expert analysts to review the data, refining and developing new, more powerful algorithms. This unique combination of processing power from a large collection network and analysis from human experts allows the system to accurately keep up with the Internet's complexity and rapid rate of change. The result is levels of data quality and accuracy that are unsurpassed and constantly improving.

How Do I Use the Results?

In using a geolocation service, merchants can feel more confident in accepting orders in which the IP address geolocation check matches up with the *ship to* or *bill to* address.

In using a geolocation service, if merchants find a major discrepancy with the IP geolocation match to the *ship to* or *bill to* address, then they should review or decline the order.

If the geolocation service provider gives country or city information, merchants can create rules to decline these orders for regions in which they do not do business. They can also prevent business in regions where they have had a high incidence of fraud in the past.

If the geolocation service provider gives information about proxies, the merchant can build rules to do further fraud screening for orders in which anonymous proxies and cache proxies are evident.

If merchants run the geolocation service on every transaction and store the data results, merchants can build a very targeted marketing profile of their customer base, including demographics on region, time of day, and methods of getting to their site.

Building This In-House

There are several methods merchants can use to build their own geolocation capability in-house. Building these types of services in-house means they have to be committed to maintaining them going forward, which can be extensive.

- *Area code check*. Using a phone book, build a list of all area codes by state and set up a rule to check the area code given with the phone number to the state of billing and/or shipping address. If they don't match, review or reject the order.

- *Zip code check*. Using commercially available mailing services, build a list of all zip codes by state and country, and set up a rule to check to see if the data matches.

- *IP address check*. Using freeware services available online such as BigIP, check the incoming IP address to see where it is coming from. A merchant must have a listing showing where these addresses reside. This has a lot of issues, as proxies and services such as AOL will mask a lot of the transaction's real origins.

- *Credit card BIN check*. Create rules to weed out orders coming from the same credit card bank identification number (BIN) range with nonmatching geolocation data. Look for the same credit card BIN range with deliveries being billed to a specific city, state, or zip code.

Digital Signatures

Digital signature services provide the merchant with the ability to capture real-time signatures over the Internet for a variety of applications and verticals (i.e., financial, mortgage, travel). Digital signatures are the digital equivalent of traditional handwritten signatures. Digital signature schemes use cryptography, and if implemented correctly, the digital signature is more difficult to forge than a traditional handwritten signature. Typically, consumers can sign their name with their mouse or some type of hardware (i.e., electronic pen, tablet PC, touchpad) through a pop-up window during checkout. Merchants then have a conventional signature they can show, if needed, for chargeback representment.

In terms of recovering money from CNP fraud chargebacks, digital signatures may provide the merchant with important evidence during disputes that the consumer was authenticated with an intent to purchase. It should be noted that trusted time stamping can make the merchant's case more compelling against friendly fraudsters attempting to backdate.

Encrypted digital signatures have become more widely used in e-commerce and regulatory filings, but their widespread adoption and success still remains to be seen. Consumers have found that their online signature using a mouse are usually nothing like their actual handwritten signature. While digital signatures may provide added security to the consumer, the value of digital signatures to merchants in fighting chargebacks is still not clear.

How Good Is It?

In general, digital signature services have been around for a long time with no significant widespread acceptance. These services have the ability to bridge the gap between the consumer-present (CP) and CNP world, but there is a low probability of that happening.

Pros and cons of digital signatures include the following:

- Pro: A signature marks a legal transaction has taken place and can be used as evidence in chargeback disputes.
- Pro: Digital signatures can be used to authenticate the source of messages.
- Pro: Increased security against fraudsters trying to steal information in transit because when encrypted messages are changed the signature becomes invalid.
- Con: Hardware such as a mouse, electronic pen, tablet PC, or touchpad will be required (depending on the service).
- Con: A digital signature *does not imply* that the person who is signing is in fact the cardholder.

- Con: Digital signatures cannot provide certainty about the time and date for the document that was signed. In this instance, back-dating may become a problem. To avoid this, use trusted–time stamping in addition to digital signatures.

- Con: Nonrepudiation may become complicated if the consumer's private key was compromised. A nonrepudiation service requires the establishment of a public key infrastructure (PKI), which can be complex and costly to establish and operate.

- Con: The possibility of a hacker capturing universal signature access represents a huge potential problem for the merchant.

 TIPS AND TECHNIQUES

- Can the digital signature be utilized effectively with trusted-time stamping?

- Does the region or country have specific laws relating to digital signatures and the implications associated with chargebacks? Will the evidence hold up in court?

- Is the public-key algorithm insecure? Some are known to be insecure.

- Does the digital signature disrupt business processes with additional work?

- Does it comply with the merchant's auditing process requirements?

- How will the private key remain private?

- Does the consumer possess the necessary hardware for digital signatures? If not, what are the costs to provide them with the needed hardware?

- Is the public key owner verifiable? How much time and money does it cost to operate and establish the public key infrastructure?

Just because you have a digital signature does not mean you are going to win your chargeback representment case. The rules for documentation and proof of cardholder authorization are different for CP and CNP transactions. Presenting a digital signature as evidence is not something covered by the association, and the interpretation of its value will come down to the issuing bank in question. This means in the U.S. market you will have more than 40,000 different opinions on whether digital signatures are acceptable for proof of purchase authorization.

Estimated costs: Costs will vary based on the vendor you select. The additional cost of a public key infrastructure can be costly and time consuming. There exist several commercial PKI operators but many have suffered publicly due to data breaches. The effort required to establish and monitor a closed PKI system is usually too costly and time consuming for merchants to do on their own.

Alternative solutions: There is no clear alternative to digital signatures, but consumer verification can provide the merchant with the ability to authenticate the consumer.

Vendors: AlphaTrust, ARX (Algorithmic Research), AssureSign, DocuSign, Signature Link, SoftPro's SignDoc, Topaz Systems Inc.

How Does It Work?

Merchants use digital signatures to capture a signature from a consumer through some device on the computer (e.g., electronic pen, mouse, tablet PC, or touch pad). Essentially, the consumer will be prompted during the checkout phase with a box on the screen with a small x next to a line (e.g., x_____). Once the signatory has signed, the signature is captured as an image and encrypted for the consumer's protection. The encrypted message is sent to the merchant and the consumer is verified and authenticated. The digital signature can then be used for proof that a legal transaction has occurred. However, digital signatures are complex and require many processes and techniques to come together to become cost effective for the merchant. Data encryption, hashing, cryptography, digital certificates, private keys, public key infrastructure, and verification must all come together to provide the merchant with the genuine consumer authentication desired.

How Do I Use the Results?

If the consumer is verified and authenticated through the digital signature, then accept the transaction. However, it will be impossible for merchants to know if the transaction is fraudulent when the fraudster has access to the private key. In this instance, digital forgery can become a major concern.

Building This In-House

It is very expensive and time intensive to build the required PKI needed to securely retrieve the consumer's public key. Merchants are better off integrating a third party's digital signature method to deliver this payment method to the consumer.

Device Identification

The concept of device identification is not new; cookies have been around for a long time, but the problem is a user can delete and manipulate a cookie. Device identification has grown into a very sophisticated science, with versions that are completely transparent to the user, to some that load applets or other programs to serve their purpose.

This is also known as device ID, device identification, device authentication, and device signature.

How Good Is It?

Device identification is not fool-proof, and fraudsters can get around this technique, but the commercial solutions available today make the effort on the fraudsters' part very time and resource intensive to do so.

Device identification is an excellent subsequent visit authentication mechanism, to be able to say the user in a subsequent visit is using the same computer as the last time he or she came to the site. Additionally, it provides strong tools for linking multiple accounts to the same device.

Device identification works well for digital products, where a fraudster doesn't have to alter any information stolen from a victim. In these cases, the identity information you would receive looks good and would pass all authentication methods. If you were using device identification, the next time the fraudster attempted to make a purchase with a different identity, you would be able to catch them.

TIPS AND TECHNIQUES

- How many different variables are being used to identify a device?

- Exact matches are easy to track and manage; the art and science is in the ability to apply partial matches to an existing device.

- Device identification is better suited to catching repeat fraudsters, habitual friendly fraudsters, and, in some cases, fraud rings.

- Device identification is an excellent mechanism for account login authentication.

- Does the vendor allow for sharing device information with other similar companies?

- Device identification is a tool, and you will need to do other fraud checks, authentication, and verification techniques to create a complete solution.

- It is normal behavior for a consumer to have more than one device.

Estimated costs: Solutions are available on a pay-per-transaction or subscription fee basis.

Alternative solutions: Cookies, activeX tracking controls, tokens.

Vendors: 41st Parameter, Iovation, RSA, Blue Cava, Kount, iPASS.

How Does It Work?

Device identification uses some to all of the passive data collected when a user interacts with your web site. There are a number of discrete pieces of information that can be collected and used. In some cases, these solutions will use a piece of code that a user must accept to tag the device. Just remember, if users know they are adding a piece of code, and they are fraudsters, then they also know they need to remove it.

How Do I Use the Results?

The primary use is to catalogue and maintain velocities on the number of devices associated with an account, and the number of accounts associated with a device. Additionally, you should blacklist devices and prevent any device associated with fraud from doing future business.

Building This In-House

While it is possible to build this in-house, the tricky part is modeling and building out the partial match capability. Any solution that relies solely on full matches will be short lived and will provide very little uplift.

EXECUTIVE INSIGHT

Bot, Bot, Bot, Bust

ORI EISEN, FOUNDER, 41ST PARAMETER

The nature of e-commerce fraud is changing. The "other side" is becoming increasingly sophisticated and efficient, as their tools become widely available. The reach and anonymity of the

Internet are being exploited more effectively than ever, and our response to it has to be as sophisticated and efficient as our adversaries. Two places where e-commerce fraud detection will sink or swim over the coming years are our ability to consistently recognize browsing client devices and our ability to detect botnets.

To the extent they can be consistently recognized, client browsing devices are the best proxy we have for the human being behind a transaction. Within the context of a customer account, transactions are several orders of magnitude safer when we know that they came from a client device that we have a positive history with; in context, account takeover or unintentional customer insult are highly improbable. When we are facing new customers, effective client device identification (CDI) can yield great efficiencies on our side, stopping repeat offenders and exposing the common device behind an otherwise perfect fraud where every order attribute is different for each of a hundred orders.

Detecting botnet-based attacks will become another essential ability for e-commerce fraud prevention; as botnets become more readily available as a for-hire service, their use as an attack vector will grow. Botnets will allow any weakness found to be attacked on a massive level, with a potential for a correspondingly massive loss. Fortunately, botnets leave trails and provide signals, and to the extent we are armed with technology to detect these now and as over time as they morph, we will be able to defend ourselves in this battle.

Proxy Detection

Proxy detection web services allow instant detection of anonymous IP addresses. While the use of a proxy is not a direct indicator of fraudulent behavior, it can be a useful indicator when combined with other data elements to determine if an individual is attempting to hide his or her true identity. The fact is, some of the most-used ISPs, like AOL and MSN, are forms of proxies, and are used by both good and bad consumers.

How Good Is It?

The fraudsters know it is very easy to make their IP geolocation information look like it is coming from the region where their stolen credentials originated. This ability makes them look authentic, when in fact they are using a proxy to mask their true location.

Again, not all proxies are equal; some are very reputable, and to cut them off would be a death-nail to your sales conversion. The goal is to use this technique to distinguish which proxies are derived from compromised computers, or from proxies that are known to be highly used by fraudsters. The generic ability to identify an anonymous proxy provides little value.

- IP address spoofing

- Anonymous proxy detection

- Anonymous proxy risk ratings

 TIPS AND TECHNIQUES

- Can the solution see through proxies and through services such as AOL to determine where an order is coming from?
- Can the solution tell how reliable the information is when you get it? For example, how risky is the proxy?
- How often is the data updated and verified by the vendor?
- Does the service detect and map corporate proxies?
- Does the vendor provide post event alerts to let you know if an IP has gone bad?

Estimated costs: Costs will vary based on the vendor you select. There are several utilities that provide this information in a basic form for free. You can also find vendors that offer more sophisticated services as in-house software solutions with subscription fees, or on a completely outsourced model with a per-transaction fee.

Alternative solutions: You can also look at trying some of the fraud-
scoring services that offer the proxy detection check as part of the
score.

Vendors: FraudLabs, MaxMind, Quova.

How Does It Work?

These services rely on the IP address. Merchants can get the IP address
from the HTTP header on the order that comes into their site. This IP
address can be compared to known lists of good and bad IP addresses.
These services use public information as well as in-house resources to
map out and catalogue these proxies.

The value of looking at the proxy information is that proxy servers
can hide the actual location of a consumer. If consumers are using a
proxy server on the West Coast of the United States and they live on the
East Coast, their IP address will make you think they are coming from
the opposite coast from where they actually are.

This same ability to hide where they are coming from can also be
used by potential fraudsters in Asia or Europe to make it look like they
are coming from the United States. Anonymous proxies were intended
for privacy reasons so users could mask where they are coming from.
AOL consumers are one of the biggest issues in determining where the
consumer really is because they all look like they are coming from
Virginia.

Many vendors offer proxy detection as part of their geolocation services, but many have not created their own solutions and are actually
using the technology of a handful of technology providers.

The core of an IP geolocation service is the mapping of IP addresses to
global locations to create a global data collection network. Solution providers can use multiple automated techniques and algorithms to collect,
map, and analyze the billions of IP addresses that make up the Internet.
They can also use people to review the data, refining and developing new,

more powerful methods to determine if an IP address is an endpoint or a midpoint proxy being used to complete a transaction. The ability of a service provider to collect this type of data and the breadth of their capability to harvest it are the core strengths by which they should be measured. This unique combination of processing power from a large collection network and analysis from human experts allows the system to accurately keep up with the Internet's complexity and rapid rate of change.

How Do I Use the Results?

If the geolocation service provider gives information about proxies, the merchant can build rules to do further fraud screening for orders in which anonymous proxies and cache proxies are evident.

Building This In-House

There are several methods a company can use to build its own proxy detection service in-house. Building these types of services in-house means they have to be committed to maintaining them going forward, which can be extensive.

Secure Tokens

Secure tokens use a device to create a unique number to authenticate the end user. Typically these devices have been used in network security, but there are vendors now offering this type of solution for consumer authentication.

How Good Is It?

Secure tokens a good way to ensure that consumers are who they say they are. To use this solution, you have to have the consumer and merchant participating for it to work. It requires the consumer carry a *fob*, a device the size of a key that creates a unique number every minute. And it requires the merchant to have the ability to authenticate the number the fob created. It is not likely that a fraudster will be able to mimic or copy the number, as they change every minute, but the device can be stolen by a fraudster.

Typically, this solution is offered by a particular merchant or bank and the consumers can use it at any of the participating merchant locations. If they go outside of the supported merchant base, the tool is useless, and the regular fraud-prevention techniques come into play. Market adoption of this type of solution is extremely low.

Secure tokens as a fraud-prevention technique:

- Don't catch true identity theft cases.

- Require the consumer carry a fob.

- Require all merchants to support the validation of the number.

- Are a good method to get nontraditional e-commerce or MOTO customers to make purchases through these channels.

TIPS AND TECHNIQUES

- What type of device or fob does the solution offer?
- Will the device work with any other merchant site?
- Who provides customer support if the fob is defective?
- How long is the fob going to last?
- Does the device use a unique PIN combined with the fob to increase the security?

Estimated costs: Moderate.

Alternative solutions: Smart cards, consumer authentication.

Vendors: Cardinal Commerce, RSA.

How Does It Work?

The merchant or bank issues the consumer a fob. These fobs come in different sizes and shapes, and you can get them as key rings or credit cards. The consumer is also issued a PIN to use with the unique number.

When consumers are ready to make a purchase, they go to merchants that support the technology and they choose what they want to buy and then start the checkout process. When going through the buy process, consumers will be asked to give the PIN and the unique number generated by the fob. The merchants will likely be going to a third-party service that has an application that can match the exact number the fob will create to see if the number provided by the consumer matches or not. If it does, you have authenticated the consumer; if it does not, you would then reject the order or attempt another authentication technique.

How Do I Use the Results?

If the consumer can authenticate via the secure token, then you would accept the order. If the consumer cannot authenticate, you would reject the order. If a consumer comes in who is not using the secure token, you will have to have processes in place to catch fraud with these orders.

If you support this type of solution, you should also set up a process to confirm a card is not supposed to be using a secure token. This will prevent you from processing an order for a consumer who had his or her card stolen, and is being used fraudulently.

Building This In-House

Not applicable.

Smart Cards

Smart cards have implanted chips that can be read by specialized devices to authenticate that the card is authentic. They don't authenticate the consumer; they authenticate the card is real. Some implementations called *chip and PIN* actually use the combination of a chip to authenticate the card and require consumers to enter a PIN to authenticate.

How Good Is It?

Smart cards are a great concept, and they are pretty reliable when it comes to fraud prevention. Currently there are a few card issuers with smart cards, such as the American Express Blue Card. But for the most part, adoption is still very low.

The biggest downside of the smart card is the reader required to check the chip. Until the time comes that a chip reader can be put on all computers, phones, and terminals, this technology will be slow to be adopted. To the consumer, there really is no incentive to use this technology unless he or she is simply scared of having the card or number stolen.

The fact is, most merchants are not set up to handle these cards either, and they are simply using these as normal credit cards in their process, thereby stripping any fraud-prevention value the technique may have offered.

Smart cards:

- Are good for preventing counterfeit cards
- Rely on physical card reader to work the secure check
- Work like a normal card when no reader is available
- Are not highly adopted today
- Are part of major initiatives in Europe to switch to this technology

 TIPS AND TECHNIQUES

- Make sure your company's processor supports the services.
- Make sure you can get card readers to their consumer.

Estimated costs: Low to high.

Alternative solutions: Consumer authentication.

Vendors: Visa, MasterCard, American Express, Discover.

How Does It Work?

The issuing bank issues a branded credit card that has an embedded chip that is unique. When a consumer makes a purchase in which the merchant has a specialized reader that can read the chip, the chip and magnetic strip data are checked when the card is swiped.

Readers are available for CP transactions and for computers. Some issuers actually send out a card reader to the consumer with the card. The basic use of the card is the same as a standard credit card; the chip is just a means to make sure the card is authentic.

How Do I Use the Results?

If the consumer can authenticate via the smart card, then you would accept the order. If the consumer cannot authenticate, you would reject the order. If a consumer comes in who is not using the reader, you will have to have processes in place to catch fraud with these orders.

If you support this type of solution, you should also set up a process to confirm that a card is not supposed to be using a reader. This will prevent you from processing an order for a consumer who had his or her card stolen and used fraudulently.

Building This In-House

Not applicable.

Mobile Phone Geolocating

Mobile phone geolocating is the ability to compare the physical location of a customer's mobile phone in relation to the location given by a consumer (IP address, billing address, shipping address). Mobile phone geolocating is a technique that can be used for CP and CNP transactions and can be applied worldwide.

How Good Is It?

When you can directly tie the phone number to the consumer, mobile phone geolocating can be a great tool for new account authentication and verification that a consumer is who he or she claims to be. It also provides excellent ongoing authentication that the legitimate account holder is the one initiating transactions. Consequently, it has applicability for preventing first- and third-party fraud. When you combine mobile phone geolocating with device identification or account credentials, it also offers a strong two-factor authentication platform. Mobile phone geolocating can help you to:

- Detect the fraudulent use of authentic profile data.
- Detect the use of proxies to hide actual location.
- Detect real consumers who deny they initiated transactions.
- Tie the transaction to a shipping address.

Pros and cons of mobile phone GPS include the following:

- Pro: You can tie physical location to geolocation.
- Pro: It is great for authenticating repeat consumers who travel frequently.
- Pro: It can reduce manual review costs for ongoing authentication that a transaction is coming from the legitimate account holder.
- Pro: It still requires consumer authentication of data to be effective.
- Con: The technique is still in its early phases, so global and regional coverage are an issue.

TIPS AND TECHNIQUES

- What countries are supported?
- How does the service handle unknown numbers and prepaid cell phones?

- What is Global System Mobile (GSM) versus Code Division Multiple Access (CDMA) network compatibility? Services that only support GSM will only be able to authenticate a small number of U.S. residents, as the majority of U.S. cell phone networks are not GSM.

- Most services require at least a one-time opt-in from the consumer; some require permission every time.

- How does this address consumers' privacy concerns?

- Is it installed on the wireless provider's network?

- Not all service providers give the same level of location detail; some only offer country, while others will go down to the address.

- If you are using it for first-time authentication, you still need to perform authentication that the phone number is tied to the consumer.

Estimated costs: Typically this service is offered on a per-transaction basis. After the service is installed, a fee would be paid to the service provider for each transaction verification.

Alternative solutions: Phone verification, IP geolocation, telephone number identification, or device fingerprinting.

Vendors: Spriv, Ericsson, Google Mobile.

How Does It Work?

A company sends in a mobile phone number and receives back a physical location of the mobile phone. If the service provider requires opt in by the end user, the end user would typically receive an SMS message requesting permission to send the location data. With the location data the company can compare it to transaction data or existing profile data to determine if the end user is authentic.

How Do I Use the Results?

On new accounts, make sure you have authenticated the phone number that is tied to the end user, and match the location of the phone with the location of the end user at the time of purchase or signup.

On existing accounts, with the understanding you know the number is tied to the end user, match the physical location of the end user with the location of the transaction.

Building This In-House

Not applicable.

Chapter Summary

The popularity of IP geolocation and device identification in the market make them the best-known techniques in the technology category. IP geolocation has become a de facto standard for e-commerce transactions and is widely used in other category solutions.

There is a large diversity of technology-based tools in the market today, and companies will likely find that the majority of them will not be a good fit for their business. But don't despair; while many of these won't be a good fit, the ones that are typically are a very good fit. Learn about what your peers and competitors are doing in your vertical to best understand which technologies work best for your business.

CHAPTER 12

Fraud Prevention Techniques: Data Sharing

After reading this chapter, you will be able to:

- Discuss the market factors limiting the adoption of data sharing in the fraud space.
- Describe the potential benefits of data sharing.

Data Sharing

Data-sharing bureaus are organizations that collect and aggregate information from multiple companies to improve fraud detection through breadth of data. These services aggregate information across merchants allowing them to create, detect, and inform any one merchant about potential fraudulent information before they could detect it themselves.

Data-sharing bureaus can operate in one of two roles: a trusted source for identity authentication, like a credit bureau, or a fraud service.

How Good Is It?

Nobody in this business is ever going to say that sharing information isn't a good concept that could help prevent fraud. The problem isn't the concept, it is how do you get companies to share their data? This is a critical component to determining how effective a service provider is, because the service will provide value only if the vendor is able to get enough companies to participate.

Achieving critical mass is not a small problem to overcome, as there are a number of barriers the vendors have to overcome to get a company to agree to share their data and for the vendor to make it of value to the other participants.

In short, the value of data-sharing bureaus is their ability to build models based on a much larger data set than any one merchant has. A single merchant's internal fraud scoring system will have only limited effectiveness, as the breadth of data being looked at is only their data. This will affect any and all velocity checks such as velocity of change and velocity of use. For example, modeling and neural nets that are built, and/or used, solely in a one-merchant implementation don't get the benefit of seeing consumer activity outside of their business. For data-sharing bureaus, the more data that goes into building the service, the better it will predict and catch fraud.

It is important to know the following:

- Modeling and neural nets maintained in-house suffer from breadth of data, missing key information from attempts on cross-merchant data.

- It is only a tool: It provides good information, but merchants will still have to perform other fraud checks.

- Merchants should verify the vendor's validation of negative information; in some cases, certain participating companies could purposely flag their best clients to prevent competitors from doing business with them.

 TIPS AND TECHNIQUES

- How many companies are participating?
- What information is shared, and how is it standardized?
- How often is information provided by the companies?

Estimated costs: Costs will vary based on the vendor you select. Typically, this service is offered on a subscription pricing plan, but some offer it on a transactional basis. As with most services, volume and the length of your agreement can greatly affect your cost.

Alternative solutions: Use of fraud scoring, identity authentication.

Vendors: Ethoca, IdAnalytics, Early Warning Services, Merchant Risk Council (MRC).

How Does It Work?

Vendors collect information either in real time or batch mode from the participating merchants. Vendors clean the data and update their core data sets. The merchants call the vendor when they are processing a transaction to get a real-time check on data associated with a consumer.

The merchants also have to periodically notify the vendor when they get information indicating a past transaction has gone bad. The vendor updates the core data set with the negative information, so all participating merchants can make use of it.

EXECUTIVE INSIGHT

What Is the Problem with Sharing?

ANDRE EDELBROCK, CEO, ETHOCA

Data sharing has been in practice in many industries and applications for decades. And up until recently, in the world of online commerce, it has been done informally by sharing of information, sometimes by sending clear text information or in files over e-mails.

But a lot has changed in the past few years with independent third parties, like Ethoca, stepping in to facilitate the development of technology and methods for collaboration among online merchants. The objective of sharing data goes beyond the simple concept of data sharing, and looks to create a global community of merchants of all sizes, vendors, banks, payment providers, and other stakeholders, working together to assemble a global data resource to fight fraud.

According to Andre Edelbrock, Ethoca's CEO, the biggest challenges faced in building out collaboration for fraud management purposes centered around getting the foundational infrastructure right, such that merchants could trust each other and the independence of the repository management, and then "getting the fire started"—reaching critical mass such that there was a sufficient level of participation to create value in being a member to entice others to join.

The biggest benefits, according to Andre Edelbrock, Ethoca's CEO, are that merchants can share their transaction experiences in real time, safely, while ensuring adherence to the strictest global standards for data privacy, governance to manage data integrity, and compliance with community rules, conformance to all industry standards (including PCI, DSS, and AICPA rules, etc.), and data security beyond the highest expectations of any one merchant. By empowering collaboration across merchants, companies like Ethoca are powering a cross-merchant, cross-industry, and cross-platform global solution for anti-fraud collaboration, enabling merchants who may be in direct competition with each other, or using services from competing fraud vendors or payment service providers, or in completely dissimilar lines of business, on opposite sides of the world, to benefit from access to each other's information to make better fraud decisions in real-time based on the massive repository of data.

How Do I Use the Results?

The results from this type of a service should be used to augment your fraud-prevention strategy. Getting a negative hit with this type of service is a strong indicator, but a "no hit" or "high velocity hit" is not necessarily a strong indicator of fraud.

Building This In-House

Any company can set up its own data-sharing relationships with other companies.

Chapter Summary

Sharing data is not a new concept; the role of credit bureaus is to make it possible for merchants and financial institutions to share data on consumers and merchants. In the fraud space, data sharing can be limited to negative experience or to all data.

One of the largest barriers to data sharing is concern over data privacy and potential backlash from a data breach or negative consumer event based on the data provided. This fear is meaningful in light of the numerous data breaches occurring worldwide.

Beyond concerns for data breaches is the basic trust merchants have in the data being provided. In early attempts by the gambling verticals, merchants were found to be marking their best customers as bad so other competitors would not accept them.

Lastly, shared data is great, but if there isn't enough data being shared, its usefulness is greatly diminished for all parties involved. Even with all of these barriers to sharing data, the concept of data sharing is a long-term given, and companies should continue to evaluate options in this space.

Protecting Yourself from Identity Theft

The following checklist will help guide you through the steps you can take to protect yourself from being a victim of identity theft.

1. Never leave receipts at bank machines, bank counters, trash receptacles, or unattended gasoline pumps. Keep track of all your paperwork. When you no longer need it, destroy it.

2. Memorize your social security number and all of your passwords. Do not record them on any cards or on anything in your wallet or purse.

3. Call the three credit reporting bureaus listed as follows and get copies of your credit report at least once a year, or if you are using one of the credit notification services that most credit cards offer, just order a copy of one.

    You don't have to pay for a credit report if you have been denied credit, are on welfare, have been a victim of identity theft, or are unemployed.

Equifax
P.O. Box 105873
Atlanta, GA 30348
Report Fraud: 800–525–6285
Get Credit Report: 800–685–1111

Experian (formally TRW)

P.O. Box 2104

Allen, TX 75013-2104

Report Fraud: 800-301-7195

Get Credit Report: 888-397-3742

Transunion Corporation

P.O. Box 34012

Fullerton, CA 92834

Report Fraud: 800-680-7289

Get Credit Report: 800-916-8800

4. Empty your wallet of extra credit cards and IDs. Better yet—cancel the ones you do not use and maintain a list of the ones you do.

5. Never give personal information over the telephone, such as your Social Security number, date of birth, mother's maiden name, credit card number, or bank PIN code unless you initiated the phone call. Protect this data.

6. When you open new accounts, create a real password; don't use your mother's maiden name.

7. Promptly remove mail from your mailbox after delivery.

8. Deposit outgoing mail in post office collection mailboxes or at your local post office. Do not leave it in unsecured mail receptacles.

9. Shred preapproved credit applications, credit card receipts, bills, and other financial information you don't want before discarding them in the trash or recycling bin.

10. Order a copy of your free personal earnings and benefit statement at the United States Social Security Administration by calling 800-772-1213 or by using your online estimate tools at www.ssa.gov.

11. Notify the Direct Marketing Association that you want to remove your name from the direct mail and phone lists:

Mail Preference Service
P.O. Box 9008
Farmingdale, NY 11735

Telephone Preference Service
P.O. Box 9014
Farmingdale, NY 11735

Or visit their web site at www.the–dma.org.

12. Sign all new credit cards upon receipt.

13. Save all credit card receipts and match them against your monthly bills.

14. Be conscious of normal receipt of routine financial statements. Contact the sender if they are not received in the mail.

15. Notify your credit card companies and financial institutions in advance of any change of address or phone number.

16. Never loan your credit cards to anyone else.

17. Never put your credit card or any other financial account number on a postcard or on the outside of an envelope.

18. If you applied for a new credit card and it hasn't arrived in a timely manner, call the bank or credit card company involved.

19. Report all lost or stolen credit cards immediately.

20. Beware of mail or telephone solicitations disguised as promotions offering instant prizes or awards designed solely to obtain your personal information or credit card numbers.

21. Use caution when disclosing information online. For any personal information or for credit card information, make sure the forms are secure—you should see *https://* and/or a locked key on the screen.

22. When you subscribe to online services, you may be asked to confirm your credit card number to open the account or for your password—do not disclose them to anyone.

23. Only use one credit card for making online purchases.

24. Shred returned checks or store in a secure location.

25. Don't preprint your driver's license number or Social Security number on your checks.

Sample Strategy

The following strategy is meant for illustrative purpose only. It is not meant
to be all-inclusive, nor is it meant to represent any particular vertical market.
I have purposely put in as many fraud techniques as I could to give some
conceptualization to the use of fraud techniques and business flow.

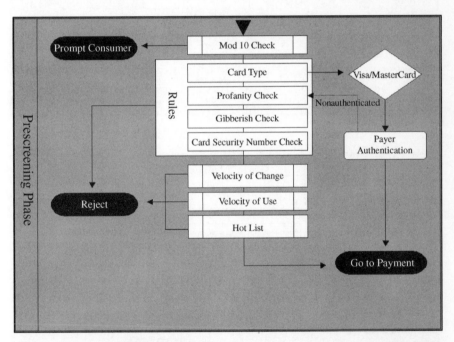

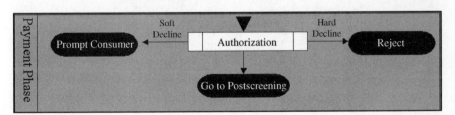

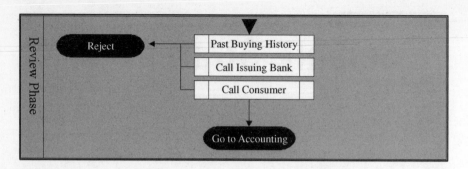

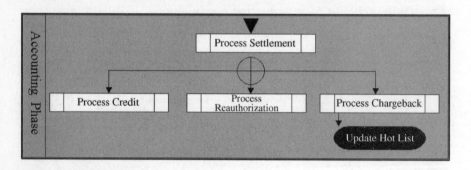

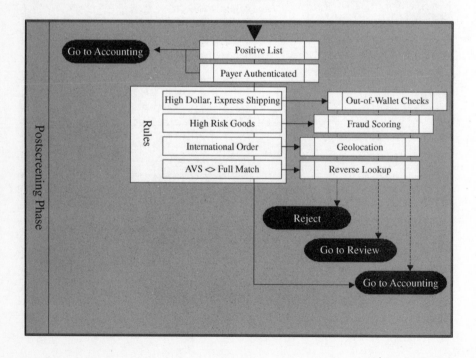

About the Author

Mr. Montague is the founder and president of The Fraud Practice, (www.fraudpractice.com), an independent consultancy firm. He has spent the last 14 years working in the e-commerce space and is well respected for his business knowledge and thought leadership. His background includes an in-depth application of innovative solutions for preventing business to consumer e-commerce fraud. Prior to founding The Fraud Practice, he held positions as the director of risk solutions at CyberSource, Inc., and national principal at IBM Global Services.

Along with a master's degree in information management, Mr. Montague offers extensive knowledge in electronic payments and fraud prevention with more than 10 years of consulting and product development experience specifically related to this space. He has a history of designing, developing, and deploying innovative technical solutions for major e-merchants, payment processors, financial institutions, and solution providers.

Along with being a published author in the space, Mr. Montague speaks regularly about e-commerce fraud at events such as Merchant Risk Council (MRC), Direct Response Forum (DRF), National Retail Federation (NRF), Fraud and Loss Prevention Conference, Retail Week's Retail Solutions Show, Retail Week's United Kingdom Risk Management Conferences, CyberSABOTAGE Conferences, Nestor Fraud Symposiums, Microsoft Tech-Ed, and a host of other seminars and workshops around the world.

Mr. Montague serves on advisory boards for Fididel.com and Spriv LLC and is an active member of the Association of Certified Fraud Examiners and the Gerson Lehrman Group Council.

Index

Account takeovers, 82
Acquiring bank, 35
  Code 10 authorization, 95
  credit card orders, merchant usage, 41
  request routing, 41
Address verification, 45
Address verification services (AVS), 127–132
  features, 128
  in-house construction, 132
  process, explanation, 130
  quality, 128–129
  results, usage, 131–132
  risk, indication, 131
  techniques, 129
Administration costs, management, 3
Advanced address verification (AAV+), 132–134
  American Express, impact, 133
  in-house construction, 134
  process, explanation, 133–134
  quality, 132–133
  results, usage, 134
Advertising/promotional providers, 4
Affiliate fraud, 82–83
Age verification, 135–137
  in-house construction, 137
  process, explanation, 136
  quality, 135–136
  results, usage, 137
  techniques, 135
Alternative payments, 4
  advertising, 18–19
    examples, 18
  growth, probability, 6–7
  options, 4–6
  providers, 21
American Express
  AAV+ services, 133
  card association, 37
Analytic providers, 122

Analytics, 231
Area code check, 254
Authorization, 42, 44–47
  accumulation, 45–46
  amount, 46–47
  expiration, 46
  funds commitment, 45
  reversal, 42, 47
Authorization (real time), 190–194
  in-house construction, 194
  process, explanation, 192–193
  quality, 190–192
  results, usage, 193–194
  techniques, 191
Automated Clearing House (ACH)
  electronic network, 9
  network, growth, 13
  online banking payment rails, leveraging, 11–12
  payment providers
    examples, 10–11
    push/pull method, usage, 9
  payments, 3

Back-office MSP, 115
Back-ordered goods, 147
Bank identification number (BIN) checks, 194–197, 254
  common card types, 196e
  in-house construction, 197
  process, explanation, 195–196
  quality, 195
  results, usage, 197
  techniques, 195
Bank payments, 3
Bank services, 9–13
  costs, decrease, 10
Bayesian models, 236
Bill Me Later, 15

Biometrics, 247–249
    process, explanation, 249
    quality, 247–249
    results, usage, 249
    techniques, 248
Botnet-based attacks, 260–261
Bustout, 78

Card associations, 36–37
Card authentication, 43–44
Card-not-present (CNP). *See* Consumer-not-
        present (CNP)
Card security schemes, 137–141
    authorization, 140
    CVV2 request, example, 141
    in-house construction, 141
    process, explanation, 139–141
    quality, 138–139
    results, usage, 141
    techniques, 139
    validation, 140
Case management, 197–198
    process, explanation, 198
    quality, 197–198
    techniques, 197–198
Cash alternative payments, 16–18
    providers, 16–17
Cash-alternative providers, 4
Chargeback representment, 198–199
    quality, 198–199
    techniques, 199
Chargebacks, 43, 48–53
    categories, 48–49
    coding, 49
    fees, variability, 51
    fraud, possibility, 12
    impact, example, 52–53
    liability, example, 50–51
Charge verification, 141–144
Check verification services, 144–146
    process, explanation, 146
    quality, 144–146
    techniques, 145
Cobranding, concept, 34
Code 10 authorization, 95
Collusive fraud, 83–84
Commercial fraud solutions, merchant
        considerations, 111–113
Communications technologies, impact, 29
Consumer authentication, 146–151
    process, explanation, 149–150
    quality, 146–149
    results, usage, 151
    techniques, 147–148

Consumer-not-present (CNP)
    fraud losses, responsibility (mind share), 68–69
    payments/fraud, 1
    sales, growth, 111
    space, 44
    transactions, credit card fraud, 33
Consumer-perpetrated fraud, 73–74
Consumer-present (CP), credit card fraud,
        33
Consumers
    data protection requirements, 97–99
    online purchase fears, 30–31
    preferences, 5
    satisfaction fraud, 75–76
Crackers, 90–91
Cred-Ex, 15
Credit, 43, 48
Credit card charge verification, 141–144
    in-house construction, 144
    process, explanation, 143
    quality, 142–143
    results, usage, 143–144
    techniques, 142
Credit cards
    associations, 8
    authentication, 42, 43–44
    AVS, 103
    BIN check, 254
    fraudster collection, 71–72
    generator fraud, 74–75
    information, consumer supply,
        40–41
    Internet, impact, 61–65
    market penetration, 9
    money flow, 40, 42
    payments, 7–9
    theft, rate, 67
    validity, 41
Credit check, 151–153
    in-house construction, 153
    process, explanation, 152–153
    quality, 151–152
    results, usage, 153
Credit report, locations, 277–278
Credit/return fraud, 76–77
Credit-term providers, 3
Credit terms providers, 15–16
Criminal gangs, 93–94
    audacity, 93
Cross-border transactions, 24–25
    impact, 68
Cross-merchant velocity, 184
Customer base, 5
Customer service chargebacks, 50

Data availability/breadth, 112
Data collection, 160–161
Data quality, 238
    providers, 123
Data sharing, 272–276
    in-house construction, 276
    problem, 274–275
    process, explanation, 274
    quality, 272–274
    results, usage, 276
    techniques, 273–274
Delivery address verification, 238–240
    in-house construction, 240
    process, explanation, 240
    quality, 238–240
    results, usage, 240
    techniques, 239
Delivery time, reduction, 113
Denied party checks, 242–246
    in-house construction, 245–246
    process, explanation, 244–245
    quality, 243–244
    results, usage, 245
    techniques, 244
Deposit check, 153–156
    in-house construction, 156
    process, explanation, 155
    quality, 154–155
    results, usage, 156
    techniques, 154–155
Development skills, 112
Device identification, 258–261
    in-house construction, 260
    process, explanation, 260
    quality, 259–260
    results, usage, 260
    techniques, 259
Digital signature, 254–258
    in-house construction, 258
    process, explanation, 257–258
    quality, 255–257
    results, usage, 258
    techniques, 256–257
Direct debit services, 9–13
    costs, decrease, 10

E-commerce fraud
    consumer perspective, 27–32
    magnitude, 66–68
    merchant perspective, 32–34
    prevention toolkit, statistical models, 234–236
E-commerce insurance, 175–177
    in-house construction, 177
    process, explanation, 176–177

quality, 175–176
    results, usage, 177
    techniques, 176
E-commerce payments
    consumer perspective, 27–32
    merchant perspective, 32–34
E-commerce sales, growth, 111
Electronic fraudsters, characteristics, 89
E-mail authentication, 157–158
    in-house construction, 158
    process, explanation, 158
    quality, 157–158
    results, usage, 158
    techniques, 157
End-to-end MSP, 116
Escrow services, 177–179
    in-house construction, 179
    process, explanation, 178
    quality, 177–179
    techniques, 178
European Union Privacy Directive on Protection
        of Personal Data, 95
    framework, 96–97

Fair Credit Reporting Act, 96
Financial loss, 112
Fraud
    attacks, organization, 65
    basics, 56
    cross-border transactions, impact, 68
    evolution, 61–65
    expertise, 112
    globalization, impact, 68
    Internet, impact, 60–61
    management terms, 102–103
    merchant cessation, 64
    metrics, understanding, 69–70
    reporting, 94
    rings, 80–82
        cessation, 81–82
    schemes, 71
    screening tool chest, 116
    solutions, merchant considerations, 111–112
    suspicion, action, 94–95
    terminology, 101–106
    tool/solution categories, 117–124
Fraud Practice, solution map (core categories
        usage), 116
Fraud prevention
    data, usage, 66
    techniques, 104, 127
    understanding, 95–96
Fraud-prevention strategy, development, 2
Fraud-related chargebacks, 146–147

Fraud scoring, 183–188
  in-house construction, 188
  process, explanation, 186–187
  quality, 183–186
  results, usage, 187–188
  techniques, 185–186
Fraud-scoring providers, 120
Fraud-screening techniques, 81–82
Fraud-solution providers, 111, 117–118
Fraudsters
  case study, 88–94
  credit card collection, location, 71–72
  identification, 87
  identity creation, 86
  Internet usage, 61–65
  repeat offenders, 77–80
  theft process, 56–59
Fraud strategy
  anatomy, 106–108
  design, risk exposure basis, 109–110
  example, 281–282
  phases, 106, 107e
Fraudulent activities
  observation/cessation, 59
Fraudulent activities, types, 57
Freight forwarders, 158–161
  data collection/identity verification, 160–161
  in-house construction, 160
  process, explanation, 159
  quality, 158–159
  results, usage, 160
  techniques, 159
  usage, 81–82
Front end (core category), 116

Gateway services, 35–36
Geolocation, 249–254
  in-house construction, 253–254
  process, explanation, 252–253
  quality, 250–251
  results, usage, 253
  techniques, 251, 252
Globalization, impact, 68
Guaranteed fraud-solution providers, 117–118
Guaranteed payments, 175, 179–182
  in-house construction, 182
  process, explanation, 181
  quality, 179–181
  results, usage, 181–182
  techniques, 180

Hackers, 88–90
Hactivists, 91–92
Historical analysis, 237

Hot lists, 199–203
  implementation, 75–76
  in-house construction, 202–203
  process, explanation, 201–202
  quality, 200–201
  results, usage, 202
  techniques, 200–201
Hybrid-managed solutions, 115

Identity authentication, 161–163
  process, explanation, 163
  quality, 162–163
  results, usage, 163
  techniques, 162
Identity proofing, 127
Identity providers, 118–119
Identity theft, 57, 84–87
  protection, 277–280
  statistics, 84–85
Identity verification, 160–161
Interchange fees, 7–8
Internal fraud, 57, 82–84
Internal projects, sponsorship (absence), 112
Internal rules, 203–208
  in-house construction, 208
  process, explanation, 205–207
  quality, 203–205
  results, usage, 207–208
  techniques, 204
Internationalization, 24–25
Internet
  fraud, categories, 67–68
  impact, 61–65
Internet Protocol (IP) address
  check, 254
  tracking, 80
Invoice services, 23–24
  providers, examples, 23
Invoicing payment providers, 4
Issuer, 34
  auto enrollment, 150
Issuing bank, 34–35
  consumer contact, credit card dispute, 73

Know Your Customer (KYC) requirements, 162

Law, understanding, 95–96

Managed service provider (MSP), 114–115
Managed services (outsourcing), 113–117
  offloading/outsourcing, description, 114
  understanding/evaluating, importance,
    113–114
Manual reviews, 208–212

basics, cost, 210–211
process, explanation, 211–212
quality, 208–210
results, usage, 212
techniques, 209–210
Mastercard, card association, 37
Master merchants, 13
M-commerce payment providers, market, 22–23
Merchant
consumer selection, 28
threats to, 30
Merchant aggregators, service, 13
Mobile payments, 19–23
providers, 4
examples, 21–22
Mobile phone geolocating, 268–271
process, explanation, 270
quality, 269–270
results, usage, 271
techniques, 269–270
Mod 10 check, 240–242
in-house construction, 242
process, explanation, 242
quality, 241–242
results, usage, 242
techniques, 241
Money flow, 38–43
understanding, 38
Monitoring, 237
Morphing
attack, 78–79
fraud, 77–80
fraudsters
catching, 79–80
Multiple personality, 78

National Finance Center (NFC) transactions/
money transfers, 20
Neural nets, 231–237
in-house construction, 233–237
process, explanation, 232–233
quality, 231–232
results, usage, 233
techniques, 232
usage, 184

Offerpal Media, 18, 19
One-click technology transactions, 147
One hit–multiple merchants fraud scheme, 72–73
One hit–one merchant fraud scheme, 72–73
Online banking
increase, 29
payment rails, leveraging, 11–12
Online fraud, history, 59–60

Online payments
gross value, 6
options, understanding, 1
Operational capabilities (core fraud practice
category), 116
Operational cost, decrease, 113
Operational management (enterprise), 190
Operational providers, 123–124
Order processing, credit cards (usage), 38–39
Out-of-wallet checks, 163–165
in-house construction, 165
process, explanation, 165
quality, 164–165
results, usage, 165
techniques, 164
Outsourcing (managed services), 113–117

Patriot Act, KYC requirements, 162
Payments
aggregators, 3, 13–15
examples, 14
landscape, 3–7
processors, 35–36
solutions, categories, 3–4
PayPal, 156
alternative payment type, 4
PayLater, 15
Phreaks, 91
Point solutions, 115
Positive lists, 199–203
in-house construction, 202–203
process, explanation, 201–202
quality, 200–201
results, usage, 202
techniques, 200–201
Postscreen phase, 108
Privacy policies, third-party organization, 99
Private label credit cards, 34
Proxy detection, 261–264
in-house construction, 264
process, explanation, 263–264
quality, 262–263
results, usage, 264
techniques, 262

Real-time authorization, 190
Red flag rules, FTC/NCUA regulations, 34
Regression analysis, 237
Represent, documentation, 43
Representment, 48–53
Return e-mail, 168–170
in-house construction, 170
process, explanation, 169–170
quality, 168–169

Return e-mail (*Continued*)
  results, usage, 170
  techniques, 169
Return on investment (ROI), 5–6
Reverse lookups (phone/address), 166–168, 183
  in-house construction, 168
  process, explanation, 167–168
  quality, 166–167
  results, usage, 168
  techniques, 167
Risk, levels, 109–110
Risk strategies, real-time control (importance),
    217
Rules engine, 212–218
  process, explanation, 215–216
  quality, 212–214
  results, usage, 217
  techniques, 214
  types, 215–216

Safe Harbor statutes, 97
Sales conversion
  focus, 3
  increase, 112
Script kiddies, 92–93
Secure tokens, 264–266
  process, explanation, 265–266
  quality, 264–265
  results, usage, 266
  techniques, 265
Service connectivity (core category), 116
Settlement, 43, 47–48
Shadowing, 237
Shared negative files, 183
Shared network providers, 121
Shoulder surfing, 85
Silver bullet syndrome, avoidance, 105–106
Slow morph, 78
Smart cards, 266–268
  quality, 267
  results, usage, 268
  technique, 267
Social engineering, 57
  emergence, 65
Solution
  strategy, contrast, 104
  term, usage, 103
Solution map, core categories (usage), 116
Split shipments, 147
Strategy
  design, risk exposure basis, 109–110
  phases, 106, 107e

  solution, contrast, 104
  term, usage, 103

Technical attacks, 62
Technology
  fraud prevention technique, 247
  providers, 121–122
Telephone number identification,
    170–172
  process, explanation, 171–172
  quality, 170–171
  results, usage, 172
  techniques, 171
Telephone verification, 172–174
  in-house construction, 174
  process, explanation, 173–174
  quality, 172–173
  results, usage, 174
  technique, 173
Total Risk Management Methodology (TRMM),
    103
TrialPay, 19

Unfair Trade Practices Act, 97

Velocity of change, 223–229
  in-house construction, 229
  process, explanation, 225–227
  quality, 224–225
  results, usage, 227–229
  techniques, 224–225
Velocity of use, 218–223
  in-house construction, 222–223
  process, explanation, 220–222
  quality, 218–220
  results, usage, 222
  techniques, 219
Vendors, technical attacks, 62
Visa, card association, 37
Vishing, 85

Warm lists, 199–203
  implementation, 75–76
  in-house construction, 202–203
  process, explanation, 201–202
  quality, 200–201
  results, usage, 202
  techniques, 200–201
What-if historical analysis, 237
White-collar criminals, 93–94

Zip code check, 254